STOCK TRADER'S ALMANAC 2004

Yale Hirsch & Jeffrey A. Hirsch

WILEY

John Wiley & Sons, Inc.

 The Hirsch Organization Inc. ♦ 184 Central Avenue ♦ Old Tappan NJ 07675
www.stocktradersalmanac.com

Published by John Wiley & Sons, Inc., Hoboken, New Jersey
Published simultaneously in Canada

Editor in Chief	Jeffrey A. Hirsch
Editor at Large	Yale Hirsch
Holistics	J. Taylor Brown
Associate Editor	Robert Cardwell
Data Advisor	Scott Barrie
Software Development	Gecko Software
Graphic Design	B&W Creative Group

For general information on our other products and services, or technical support, please contact our Customer Care Department within the United States at 800-762-2974, outside the United States at 317-572-3993 or fax 317-572-4002.

Wiley also publishes its books in a variety of electronic formats. Some content that appears in print may not be available in electronic books.

For more information about Wiley products, visit our web site at www.wiley.com.

ISBN: 0-471-47754-0

Printed in the United States of America

10 9 8 7 6 5 4 3 2 1

This Thirty-Seventh Edition is respectfully dedicated to:

William J. O'Neil

A Wall Street pioneer who put investment information at the fingertips of the masses by launching *Investor's Business Daily®* in 1984. His foresight, innovation and disciplined approach to stock market investing will influence investors and traders for generations to come.

The *Stock Trader's Almanac®* is an organizer. Its wealth of information is presented on a calendar basis. The Almanac puts investing in a business framework and makes investing easier because it:

- updates investment knowledge and informs you of new techniques and tools.
- is a monthly reminder and refresher course.
- alerts you to both seasonal opportunities and dangers.
- furnishes an historical viewpoint by providing pertinent statistics on past market performance.
- supplies forms necessary for portfolio planning, record keeping and tax preparation.

We are constantly searching for new insights and nuances about the stock market and welcome any suggestions from our readers.

Have a healthy and prosperous 2004!

 Signifies THIRD FRIDAY OF THE MONTH on calendar pages and alerts you to extraordinary volatility due to expiration of equity and index options and index futures contracts. Triple-witching days appear during March, June, September and December.

 The BULL SYMBOL on calendar pages signifies very favorable trading days based on the S&P 500 rising 60% or more of the time on a particular trading day during the 21-year period January 1982 to December 2002 (see Recent S&P 500 Market Probability Calendar 2004, page 123). Market Probability Calendars for the NASDAQ, Dow and S&P for other time periods appear on pages 120-122. Other seasonalities near the ends, beginnings and middles of months; options expirations; around holidays; and other times are noted for *Almanac* investors' convenience on the weekly planner pages.

INTRODUCTION TO THE THIRTY-SEVENTH EDITION

We are pleased and proud to introduce the Thirty-Seventh Edition of the *Stock Trader's Almanac*. The Almanac provides you with the necessary tools to invest successfully in the twenty-first century.

J.P. Morgan's classic retort "Stocks will fluctuate" is often quoted with a wink-of-the-eye implication that the only prediction one can make about the stock market is that it will go up, down, or sideways. Many investors agree that no one ever really knows which way the market will move. Nothing could be further from the truth. We discovered that while stocks do indeed fluctuate, they do so in well-defined, often predictable patterns. These patterns recur too frequently to be the result of chance or coincidence. How else do we explain that since 1950 practically all the gains in the market were made during November through April compared to almost nothing May through October? (See page 50.)

The Almanac is a practical investment tool. Its wealth of information is organized on a calendar basis. It alerts you to those little-known market patterns and tendencies on which shrewd professionals enhance profit potential.

You will be able to forecast market trends with accuracy and confidence when you use the Almanac to help you understand:

- How our presidential elections affect the economy and the stock market—just as the moon affects the tides. Many investors have made fortunes following the political cycle. You can be sure that money managers who control hundreds of millions of dollars are also political cycle watchers. Astute people do not ignore a pattern that has been working effectively throughout most of our economic history.

- How the passage of the Twentieth Amendment to the Constitution fathered the January Barometer. This barometer has an outstanding record for predicting the general course of the stock market each year with only one error (2001: two January rate cuts and 9/11) in odd-numbered years since 1937.

- Why there is a significant market bias at certain times of the day, week, month and year.

Even if you are an investor who pays scant attention to cycles, indicators and patterns, your investment survival could hinge on your interpretation of one of the recurring patterns found within these pages. One of the most intriguing and important patterns is the symbiotic relationship between Washington and Wall Street. Aside from the potential profitability in seasonal patterns, there's the pure joy of seeing the market very often do just what you expected.

2004 will likely be a dynamic year for investors. Election years tend to be battlegrounds and anytime a president is faced with reelection, obstacles present themselves (pages 10, 78 & 94). Following a successful military campaign in Iraq, the Bush administration will be up against high expectations on the economy and continued unfinished diplomatic business in the Middle East, Asia, Africa and Latin America. Positive market action usually accompanies reelection of a president. But with the current midterm-to-pre-election year rally well underway and likely to continue into the first half of 2004, and pre-election years garnering the lion's share of the gains, year-over-year returns for election-year 2004 are likely to be more tame. —Jeffrey A. Hirsch, July 31, 2003

THE 2004 STOCK TRADER'S ALMANAC

CONTENTS

DIRECTORY OF TRADING PATTERNS & DATABANK

STRATEGY PLANNING & RECORD SECTION

2004 STRATEGY CALENDAR
(Option expiration dates encircled)

	MONDAY	TUESDAY	WEDNESDAY	THURSDAY	FRIDAY	SATURDAY	SUNDAY
JANUARY	29	30	31	1 JANUARY New Year's Day	2	3	4
	5	6	7	8	9	10	11
	12	13	14	15	(16)	17	18
	19 Martin Luther King Day	20	21	22	23	24	25
	26	27	28	29	30	31	1 FEBRUARY
FEBRUARY	2	3	4	5	6	7	8
	9	10	11	12	13	14 ♥	15
	16 Presidents' Day	17	18	19	(20)	21	22
	23	24	25 Ash Wednesday	26	27	28	29
MARCH	1 MARCH	2	3	4	5	6	7
	8	9	10	11	12	13	14
	15	16	17 ♣ St. Patrick's Day	18	(19)	20	21
	22	23	24	25	26	27	28
	29	30	31	1 APRIL	2	3	4 Daylight Savings Time Begins
APRIL	5	6 Passover	7	8	9 Good Friday	10	11 Easter
	12	13	14	15	(16)	17	18
	19	20	21	22	23	24	25
	26	27	28	29	30	1 MAY	2
MAY	3	4	5	6	7	8	9 Mother's Day
	10	11	12	13	14	15	16
	17	18	19	20	(21)	22	23
	24	25	26	27	28	29	30
JUNE	31 Memorial Day	1 JUNE	2	3	4	5	6
	7	8	9	10	11	12	13
	14	15	16	17	(18)	19	20 Father's Day
	21	22	23	24	25	26	27

Market closed on shaded weekdays; closes early when half-shaded.

2004 STRATEGY CALENDAR

(Option expiration dates encircled)

MONDAY	TUESDAY	WEDNESDAY	THURSDAY	FRIDAY	SATURDAY	SUNDAY	
28	29	30	1 JULY	2	3	4 Independence Day	JULY
5	6	7	8	9	10	11	
12	13	14	15	(16)	17	18	
19	20	21	22	23	24	25	
26	27	28	29	30	31	1 AUGUST	
2	3	4	5	6	7	8	AUGUST
9	10	11	12	13	14	15	
16	17	18	19	(20)	21	22	
23	24	25	26	27	28	29	
30	31	1 SEPTEMBER	2	3	4	5	SEPTEMBER
6 Labor Day	7	8	9	10	11	12	
13	14	15	16 Rosh Hashanah	(17)	18	19	
20	21	22	23	24	25 Yom Kippur	26	
27	28	29	30	1 OCTOBER	2	3	OCTOBER
4	5	6	7	8	9	10	
11 Columbus Day	12	13	14	(15)	16	17	
18	19	20	21	22	23	24	
25	26	27	28	29	30	31 Daylight Savings Time Ends	
1 NOVEMBER	2 Election Day	3	4	5	6	7	NOVEMBER
8	9	10	11 Veteran's Day	12	13	14	
15	16	17	18	(19)	20	21	
22	23	24	25 Thanksgiving	26	27	28	
29	30	1 DECEMBER	2	3	4	5	DECEMBER
6	7	8 Chanukah	9	10	11	12	
13	14	15	16	(17)	18	19	
20	21	22	23	24	25 Christmas	26	
27	28	29	30	31			

PROGNOSTICATING TOOLS AND PATTERNS FOR 2004

For 37 years, Almanac readers have profited from being able to predict the timing of the Political Market Cycle. To help you gain perspective in 2004, a presidential election year, a valuable array of tables, charts and pertinent information can be found on the pages noted.

THE FOURTH YEAR OF DECADES
Though "fourth" years have a mixed record, when they contained presidential elections they have fared rather well. Incumbents ran in the last five and they all won (1904, 1924, 1944, 1964 and 1984). *Page 26.*

MARKET CHARTS OF PRESIDENTIAL ELECTION YEARS
Individual charts for each of the last 21 presidential election years, including candidates and winners. *Page 28.*

DO GOVERNMENTS MANIPULATE ECONOMIES TO STAY IN POWER?
Statistical evidence proves that in years divisible by "4" they turn on the money faucets. *Page 34.*

INCUMBENT VICTORIES VS. INCUMBENT DEFEATS
Markets tend to be stronger when the party in power wins. *Page 36.*

ONLY ONE LOSS IN LAST SEVEN MONTHS OF ELECTION YEARS
There were no losses in the last seven months of presidential years in the last half-century, until the contested 2000 election. *Page 42.*

CAN REPUBLICANS BEAT THE ODDS IN 2004?
A president losing the popular vote has never won a second term, and power has changed hands four out of five times after wars were over. *Page 78.*

MARKET ACTS AS A BAROMETER AFTER CONVENTIONS ARE OVER
The market since 1900 rose 14 out of 16 times when the incumbent party retained power. Defeat resulted in losses 7 out 10 times. *Page 80.*

2004 PRESIDENTIAL ELECTION YEAR PERSPECTIVES
Stock prices tend to do far better when elected incumbents win second terms. *Page 94.*

POLITICS AND STOCK MARKETS, THE 170-YEAR SAGA CONTINUES
Stock prices have been impacted by presidential elections for 170 years, gaining 717.5% in second halves of terms vs. 227.6% in first halves. *Page 127.*

MONDAY

22

Prosperity is a great teacher; adversity a greater.
— William Hazlitt (English essayist, 1778-1830)

Watch for Santa Claus Rally (page 116)

TUESDAY

23

On [TV financial news programs], if the stock is near its high, 90%
of the guests like it, if it is near its lows, 90% of the guests hate it.
— Michael L. Burke (*Investors Intelligence*, May 2002)

(Shortened Trading Day)
Day before Christmas Dow up 8 of last 12 (page 86 & 110)

WEDNESDAY

24

Don't worry about people stealing your ideas. If the ideas
are any good, you'll have to ram them down people's throats.
— Howard Aiken (US computer scientist, 1900-1973)

Christmas Day
(Market Closed)

THURSDAY

25

Try to surround yourself with people who can give you a
little happiness, because you can only pass through this
life once, Jack. You don't come back for an encore.
— Elvis Presley (1935-1977)

(Shortened Trading Day)
Day after Christmas Dow up 10 of last 12
New Lows perform better when selected last
settlement day of year (page 112)

FRIDAY

26

I am glad that I paid so little attention to good advice; had I abided
by it I might have been saved from my most valuable mistakes.
— Gene Fowler (Journalist, screenwriter,
film director, biographer, 1890-1960)

SATURDAY

27

January Sector Seasonalities:
Bullish: Banking, Semiconductor;
Bearish: Natural Gas, Utilities (page 118)

SUNDAY

28

JANUARY ALMANAC

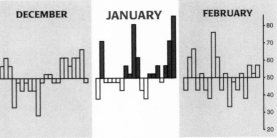

Market Probability Chart above is a graphic representation of the Market Probability Calendar on page 123.

◆ Since 1937 January Barometer had a perfect record in odd-numbered years until 2001 (2 Jan rate cuts and 9/11), 2003 was down ahead of Iraq war but we expect Pre-Election Year forces to override it ◆ Every down January on the S&P since 1950, *without exception*, preceded a new or extended bear market, or a flat market (page 44), six Election Year Januarys followed suit ◆ January's first five days usually decline in a new or continuing bear market ◆ November, December and January constitute the year's best three-month span, a 4.8% Dow gain, 20.2% annualized (page 48) ◆ At this rate, $1000 since 1950 grew to over $20 million ◆ January NASDAQ powerful 4.0% since 1971 (page 54) ◆ "January Effect" starts in mid-December and favors small-cap stocks (pages 106, 114)

JANUARY DAILY POINT CHANGES DOW JONES INDUSTRIALS

Previous Month	1994	1995	1996	1997	1998	1999	2000	2001	2002	2003
Close	3754.09	3834.44	5117.12	6448.27	7908.25	9181.43	11497.12	10786.85	10021.50	8341.63
1	H	H	H	H	H	H	H	H	H	H
2	—	Closed	60.33	− 5.78	56.79	—	—	− 140.70	51.90	265.89
3	2.51	4.04	16.62	101.60	—	—	− 139.61	299.60	98.74	− 5.83
4	27.30	19.17	− 20.23	—	—	2.84	− 359.58	− 33.34	87.60	—
5	14.92	− 6.73	7.59	—	13.95	126.92	124.72	− 250.40	—	—
6	5.06	16.49	—	23.09	− 72.74	233.78	130.61	—	—	171.88
7	16.89	—	—	33.48	− 3.98	− 7.21	269.30	—	− 62.69	− 32.98
8	—	—	16.25	− 51.18	− 99.65	105.56	—	− 40.66	− 46.50	− 145.28
9	—	− 6.06	− 67.55	76.19	− 222.20	—	—	− 48.80	− 56.46	180.87
10	44.74	5.39	− 97.19	78.12	—	—	49.64	31.72	− 26.23	8.71
11	− 15.20	− 4.71	32.16	—	—	− 23.43	− 61.12	5.28	− 80.33	—
12	− 1.68	− 3.03	− 3.98	—	66.76	−145.21	40.02	− 84.17	—	—
13	− 6.20	49.46	—	5.39	84.95	−125.12	31.33	—	—	1.09
14	24.77	—	—	53.11	52.56	−228.63	140.55	—	− 96.11	56.64
15	—	—	− 17.34	− 35.41	− 92.92	219.62	—	H	32.73	− 119.44
16	—	23.88	44.44	38.49	61.78	—	—	127.28	− 211.88	− 25.31
17	3.09	− 1.68	− 21.32	67.73	—	—	H	− 68.32	137.77	− 111.13
18	N/C	− 1.68	57.45	—	—	H	− 162.26	93.94	− 78.19	—
19	14.08	− 46.77	60.33	—	H	14.67	− 71.36	− 90.69	—	—
20	7.59	− 12.78	—	10.77	119.57	− 19.31	− 138.06	—	—	H
21	22.52	—	—	40.03	− 78.72	− 71.83	− 99.59	—	H	− 143.84
22	—	—	34.68	− 33.87	− 63.52	−143.41	—	9.35	− 58.05	− 124.17
23	—	− 2.02	− 27.09	− 94.28	− 30.14	—	—	71.57	17.16	50.74
24	− 1.69	− 4.71	50.57	− 59.27	—	—	− 243.54	2.84	65.11	− 238.46
25	− 17.45	8.75	− 26.01	—	—	82.65	21.72	82.55	44.01	—
26	12.66	− 1.01	54.92	—	12.20	121.26	3.10	− 69.54	—	—
27	18.30	− 12.45	—	− 35.79	102.14	−124.35	− 4.97	—	—	− 141.45
28	19.13	—	—	− 4.61	100.39	81.10	− 289.15	—	25.67	99.28
29	—	—	33.23	84.66	57.55	77.50	—	42.21	− 247.51	21.87
30	—	− 25.91	76.23	83.12	− 66.52	—	—	179.01	144.62	− 165.58
31	32.93	11.78	14.09	− 10.77	—	—	201.66	6.16	157.14	108.68
Close	3978.36	3843.86	5395.30	6813.09	7906.50	9358.83	10940.53	10887.36	9920.00	8053.81
Change	224.27	9.42	278.18	364.82	− 1.75	177.40	− 556.59	100.51	− 101.50	− 287.82

*20th Amendment made "Lame Ducks" disappear
Now, "As January goes, so goes the odd-numbered year"*

DECEMBER/JANUARY 2004

MONDAY

More people and increased income cause resources to become scarcer in the short run. Heightened scarcity causes prices to rise. The higher prices present opportunity and prompt investors to search for solutions. These solutions eventually lead to prices dropping lower than before the scarcity occurred.
— Julian Simon (Businessman, Professor of Business Administration, *The Ultimate Resource*, 1996, 1932-1998)

TUESDAY

There's a lot of talk about self-esteem these days. It seems pretty basic to me. If you want to feel good about yourself, you've got to do things that you can be proud of.
— Osceola McCarty (American author, *Simple Wisdom for Rich Living*, 1908-1999)

Last day of year NASDAQ up 29 of 32, but down 3 in a row
Dow down 7 of last 11

WEDNESDAY

31

Success isn't measured by the position you reach in life; it's measured by the obstacles you overcome.
— Booker T. Washington
(Founder of Tuskegee Institute, 1856-1915)

New Year's Day
(Market Closed)

THURSDAY

1

In the Value Line universe of 1,700 stocks, the 300 lowest-priced stocks as of year-end tend to go up 11% in January.
— Victor Niederhoffer/Laurel Kenner
(Private speculator and financial writer on MSN Money, *The Education of a Speculator*, *Practical Speculation*)

Average January gains last 33 years
NAS 4.0% Dow 2.3% S&P 1.9%
January first trading day Dow up 9 of last 12

FRIDAY

2

While markets often make double bottoms, three pushes to a high is the most common topping pattern.
— John Bollinger (Bollinger Capital Management, created Bollinger Bands, *Capital Growth Letter*, *Bollinger on Bollinger Bands*)

SATURDAY

3

SUNDAY

4

JANUARY'S FIRST FIVE DAYS
AN "EARLY WARNING" SYSTEM

Market action during the first five trading days of January often serves as an excellent "early warning" system for the year as a whole. Thirty-three gains since 1950 were matched by whole-year gains with just five exceptions. 1994 was a flat year. Four were war-related: Vietnam military spending delayed start of 1966 bear market; ceasefire imminence early 1973 raised stocks temporarily; Saddam Hussein turned 1990 into a bear; and the war on terrorism, instability in the near and Middle East and corporate malfeasance shaped 2002 into one of the worst years on record. Twenty Januarys got off to a bad start and ten of those ended on the downside. Investors pushing taxable gains into the New Year cause many bad starts following great bull years. Remember that five days is a brief span and some extraordinary event could sidetrack this indicator as it did on the fifth day of 1986 and 1998.

THE FIRST-FIVE-DAYS-IN-JANUARY INDICATOR

	Chronological Data				Ranked By Performance		
	Previous Year's Close	January 5th Day	5-Day Change	Year Change	Rank		5-Day Change	Year Change
1950	16.76	17.09	2.0%	21.8%	1	1987	6.2%	2.0%
1951	20.41	20.88	2.3	16.5	2	1976	4.9	19.1
1952	23.77	23.91	0.6	11.8	3	1999	3.7	19.5
1953	26.57	26.33	—0.9	— 6.6	4	2003	3.4	??
1954	24.81	24.93	0.5	45.0	5	1983	3.3	17.3
1955	35.98	35.33	—1.8	26.4	6	1967	3.1	20.1
1956	45.48	44.51	—2.1	2.6	7	1979	2.8	12.3
1957	46.67	46.25	—0.9	—14.3	8	1963	2.6	18.9
1958	39.99	40.99	2.5	38.1	9	1958	2.5	38.1
1959	55.21	55.40	0.3	8.5	10	1984	2.4	1.4
1960	59.89	59.50	—0.7	— 3.0	11	1951	2.3	16.5
1961	58.11	58.81	1.2	23.1	12	1975	2.2	31.5
1962	71.55	69.12	—3.4	—11.8	13	1950	2.0	21.8
1963	63.10	64.74	2.6	18.9	14	1973	1.5	—17.4
1964	75.02	76.00	1.3	13.0	15	1972	1.4	15.6
1965	84.75	85.37	0.7	9.1	16	1964	1.3	13.0
1966	92.43	93.14	0.8	—13.1	17	1961	1.2	23.1
1967	80.33	82.81	3.1	20.1	18	1989	1.2	27.3
1968	96.47	96.62	0.2	7.7	19	2002	1.1	—23.4
1969	103.86	100.80	—2.9	—11.4	20	1997	1.0	31.0
1970	92.06	92.68	0.7	0.1	21	1980	0.9	25.8
1971	92.15	92.19	0.04	10.8	22	1966	0.8	—13.1
1972	102.09	103.47	1.4	15.6	23	1994	0.7	— 1.5
1973	118.05	119.85	1.5	—17.4	24	1965	0.7	9.1
1974	97.55	96.12	—1.5	—29.7	25	1970	0.7	0.1
1975	68.56	70.04	2.2	31.5	26	1952	0.6	11.8
1976	90.19	94.58	4.9	19.1	27	1954	0.5	45.0
1977	107.46	105.01	—2.3	—11.5	28	1996	0.4	20.3
1978	95.10	90.64	—4.7	1.1	29	1959	0.3	8.5
1979	96.11	98.80	2.8	12.3	30	1995	0.3	34.1
1980	107.94	108.95	0.9	25.8	31	1992	0.2	4.5
1981	135.76	133.06	—2.0	— 9.7	32	1968	0.2	7.7
1982	122.55	119.55	—2.4	14.8	33	1990	0.1	— 6.6
1983	140.64	145.23	3.3	17.3	34	1971	0.04	10.8
1984	164.93	168.90	2.4	1.4	35	1960	—0.7	— 3.0
1985	167.24	163.99	—1.9	26.3	36	1957	—0.9	—14.3
1986	211.28	207.97	—1.6	14.6	37	1953	—0.9	— 6.6
1987	242.17	257.28	6.2	2.0	38	1974	—1.5	—29.7
1988	247.08	243.40	—1.5	12.4	39	1998	—1.5	26.7
1989	277.72	280.98	1.2	27.3	40	1988	—1.5	12.4
1990	353.40	353.79	0.1	— 6.6	41	1993	—1.5	7.1
1991	330.22	314.90	—4.6	26.3	42	1986	—1.6	14.6
1992	417.09	418.10	0.2	4.5	43	2001	—1.8	—13.0
1993	435.71	429.05	—1.5	7.1	44	1955	—1.8	26.4
1994	466.45	469.90	0.7	— 1.5	45	2000	—1.9	—10.1
1995	459.27	460.83	0.3	34.1	46	1985	—1.9	26.3
1996	615.93	618.46	0.4	20.3	47	1981	—2.0	— 9.7
1997	740.74	748.41	1.0	31.0	48	1956	—2.1	2.6
1998	970.43	956.04	—1.5	26.7	49	1977	—2.3	—11.5
1999	1229.23	1275.09	3.7	19.5	50	1982	—2.4	14.8
2000	1469.25	1441.46	—1.9	—10.1	51	1969	—2.9	—11.4
2001	1320.28	1295.86	—1.8	—13.0	52	1962	—3.4	—11.8
2002	1148.08	1160.71	1.1	—23.4	53	1991	—4.6	26.3
2003	879.82	909.93	3.4	??	54	1978	—4.7	1.1

14

JANUARY

*Second trading day Dow up 9 of last 12
often with larger gains than first trading day*

MONDAY

5

*I have a love affair with America, because there are no
built-in barriers to anyone in America. I come from a
country where there were barriers upon barriers.*
— Michael Caine (Actor, quoted in *Parade Magazine*, February 16, 2003)

TUESDAY

6

*Don't delay! A good plan, violently executed now, is better
than a perfect plan next week. War is a very simple thing,
[like stock trading] and the determining characteristics
are self-confidence, speed, and audacity.*
— General George S. Patton, Jr. (1885-1945)

WEDNESDAY

7

*One only gets to the top rung on the ladder by steadily
climbing up one at a time, and suddenly all sorts of powers,
all sorts of abilities, which you thought never belonged to
you—suddenly become within your own possibility....*
— Margaret Thatcher (British Prime Minister 1979-1990)

*January's First Five Days, an "Early Warning"
System (page 14)*

THURSDAY

8

*The real difference between men is energy. A strong will, a settled
purpose, an invincible determination, can accomplish almost anything;
and in this lies the distinction between great men and little men.*
— Buckminster Fuller (American architect, author, 1895-1983)

FRIDAY

9

*First-rate people hire first-rate people;
second-rate people hire third-rate people.*
— Leo Rosten (American author, 1908-1997)

SATURDAY

10

SUNDAY

11

INCREDIBLE JANUARY BAROMETER (DEVISED 1972) ONLY FOUR SIGNIFICANT ERRORS IN 53 YEARS

Since 1950, January has predicted the annual course of the stock market with amazing precision, registering only four major errors for a 92.5% accuracy ratio. The January Barometer, devised by Yale Hirsch in 1972, is based on whether the S&P 500 is up or down in January. Most years, stocks continue the course set in January. Of the four major errors, two (1966 and 1968) were affected by Vietnam, one (1982) by the start of the powerful bull market that began in August 1982, and in 2001 the Fed's two January rate cuts unnaturally buoyed the market higher. The 9/11 attacks, despite the subsequent rally, still likely held the market down in 2001.

However, there was **only one error in odd years** (2001) when new congresses convened. **Bear markets began or continued when Januarys had a loss** (see page 24). The six flat years switched directions in the year's final months.

AS JANUARY GOES, SO GOES THE YEAR

	Market Performance In January				Ranked By Performance		
	Previous Year's Close	January Close	January Change	Year Change	Rank		January Change	Year Change
1950	16.76	17.05	1.7%	21.8%	1	1987	13.2%	2.0%
1951	20.41	21.66	6.1	16.5	2	1975	12.3	31.5
1952	23.77	24.14	1.6	11.8	3	1976	11.8	19.1
1953	26.57	26.38	− 0.7	− 6.6	4	1967	7.8	20.1
1954	24.81	26.08	5.1	45.0	5	1985	7.4	26.3
1955	35.98	36.63	1.8	26.4	6	1989	7.1	27.3
1956	45.48	43.82	− 3.6	2.6	7	1961	6.3	23.1
1957	46.67	44.72	− 4.2	− 14.3	8	1997	6.1	31.0
1958	39.99	41.70	4.3	38.1	9	1951	6.1	16.5
1959	55.21	55.42	0.4	8.5	10	1980	5.8	25.8
1960	59.89	55.61	− 7.1	− 3.0	11	1954	5.1	45.0
1961	58.11	61.78	6.3	23.1	12	1963	4.9	18.9
1962	71.55	68.84	− 3.8	− 11.8	13	1958	4.3	38.1
1963	63.10	66.20	4.9	18.9	14	1991	4.2	26.3
1964	75.02	77.04	2.7	13.0	15	1999	4.1	19.5
1965	84.75	87.56	3.3	9.1	16	1971	4.0	10.8
1966	92.43	92.88	0.5	− 13.1 X	17	1988	4.0	12.4
1967	80.33	86.61	7.8	20.1	18	1979	4.0	12.3
1968	96.47	92.24	− 4.4	7.7 X	19	2001	3.5	− 13.0 X
1969	103.86	103.01	− 0.8	− 11.4	20	1965	3.3	9.1
1970	92.06	85.02	− 7.6	0.1	21	1983	3.3	17.3
1971	92.15	95.88	4.0	10.8	22	1996	3.3	20.3
1972	102.09	103.94	1.8	15.6	23	1994	3.3	− 1.5 flat
1973	118.05	116.03	− 1.7	− 17.4	24	1964	2.7	13.0
1974	97.55	96.57	− 1.0	− 29.7	25	1995	2.4	34.1
1975	68.56	76.98	12.3	31.5	26	1972	1.8	15.6
1976	90.19	100.86	11.8	19.1	27	1955	1.8	26.4
1977	107.46	102.03	− 5.1	− 11.5	28	1950	1.7	21.8
1978	95.10	89.25	− 6.2	1.1	29	1952	1.6	11.8
1979	96.11	99.93	4.0	12.3	30	1998	1.0	26.7
1980	107.94	114.16	5.8	25.8	31	1993	0.7	7.1
1981	135.76	129.55	− 4.6	− 9.7	32	1966	0.5	− 13.1 X
1982	122.55	120.40	− 1.8	14.8 X	33	1959	0.4	8.5
1983	140.64	145.30	3.3	17.3	34	1986	0.2	14.6
1984	164.93	163.41	− 0.9	1.4	35	1953	− 0.7	− 6.6
1985	167.24	179.63	7.4	26.3	36	1969	− 0.8	− 11.4
1986	211.28	211.78	0.2	14.6	37	1984	− 0.9	1.4 flat
1987	242.17	274.08	13.2	2.0	38	1974	− 1.0	− 29.7
1988	247.08	257.07	4.0	12.4	39	2002	− 1.6	− 23.4
1989	277.72	297.47	7.1	27.3	40	1973	− 1.7	− 17.4
1990	353.40	329.08	− 6.9	− 6.6	41	1982	− 1.8	14.8 X
1991	330.22	343.93	4.2	26.3	42	1992	− 2.0	4.5 flat
1992	417.09	408.79	− 2.0	4.5	43	2003	− 2.7	??
1993	435.71	438.78	0.7	7.1	44	1956	− 3.6	2.6 flat
1994	466.45	481.61	3.3	− 1.5	45	1962	− 3.8	− 11.8
1995	459.27	470.42	2.4	34.1	46	1957	− 4.2	− 14.3
1996	615.93	636.02	3.3	20.3	47	1968	− 4.4	7.7 X
1997	740.74	786.16	6.1	31.0	48	1981	− 4.6	− 9.7
1998	970.43	980.28	1.0	26.7	49	1977	− 5.1	− 11.5
1999	1229.23	1279.64	4.1	19.5	50	2000	− 5.1	− 10.1
2001	1320.28	1366.01	3.5	− 13.0 X	52	1990	− 6.9	− 6.6
2002	1148.08	1130.20	− 1.6	− 23.4	53	1960	− 7.1	− 3.0
2003	879.82	855.70	− 2.7	??	54	1970	− 7.6	0.1 flat

X = 4 major errors   *Based on S&P 500*

JANUARY

MONDAY
12

*All free governments are managed by the combined
wisdom and folly of the people.*
— James A. Garfield (20th US President, 1831-1881)

TUESDAY
13

*When you loved me I gave you the whole sun and stars to play with. I gave
you eternity in a single moment, strength of the mountains in one clasp of
your arms, and the volume of all the seas in one impulse of your soul.*
— George Bernard Shaw (Irish dramatist,
Getting Married, 1856-1950)

WEDNESDAY
14

Make it idiot-proof and someone will make a better idiot.
— Bumper sticker

THURSDAY
 ## 15

*I want the whole of Europe to have one currency;
it will make trading much easier.*
— Napoleon Bonaparte
(Emperor of France 1804-1815, 1769-1821)

FRIDAY

*I am sorry to say that there is too much point to the
wisecrack that life is extinct on other planets because
their scientists were more advanced than ours.*
— John F. Kennedy (35th US President, 1917-1963)

SATURDAY
17

SUNDAY
18

JANUARY BAROMETER IN GRAPHIC FORM SINCE 1950

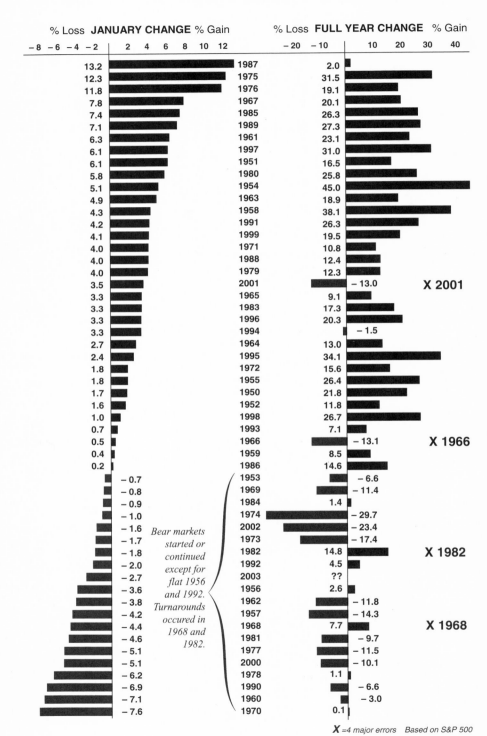

% Loss	JANUARY CHANGE	% Gain		% Loss	FULL YEAR CHANGE	% Gain
−8 −6 −4 −2		2 4 6 8 10 12		−20 −10		10 20 30 40

January	Year	Full Year
13.2	1987	2.0
12.3	1975	31.5
11.8	1976	19.1
7.8	1967	20.1
7.4	1985	26.3
7.1	1989	27.3
6.3	1961	23.1
6.1	1997	31.0
6.1	1951	16.5
5.8	1980	25.8
5.1	1954	45.0
4.9	1963	18.9
4.3	1958	38.1
4.2	1991	26.3
4.1	1999	19.5
4.0	1971	10.8
4.0	1988	12.4
4.0	1979	12.3
3.5	2001	− 13.0 X 2001
3.3	1965	9.1
3.3	1983	17.3
3.3	1996	20.3
3.3	1994	− 1.5
2.7	1964	13.0
2.4	1995	34.1
1.8	1972	15.6
1.8	1955	26.4
1.7	1950	21.8
1.6	1952	11.8
1.0	1998	26.7
0.7	1993	7.1
0.5	1966	− 13.1 X 1966
0.4	1959	8.5
0.2	1986	14.6
− 0.7	1953	− 6.6
− 0.8	1969	− 11.4
− 0.9	1984	1.4
− 1.0	1974	− 29.7
− 1.6	2002	− 23.4
− 1.7	1973	− 17.4
− 1.8	1982	14.8 X 1982
− 2.0	1992	4.5
− 2.7	2003	??
− 3.6	1956	2.6
− 3.8	1962	− 11.8
− 4.2	1957	− 14.3
− 4.4	1968	7.7 X 1968
− 4.6	1981	− 9.7
− 5.1	1977	− 11.5
− 5.1	2000	− 10.1
− 6.2	1978	1.1
− 6.9	1990	− 6.6
− 7.1	1960	− 3.0
− 7.6	1970	0.1

Bear markets started or continued except for flat 1956 and 1992. Turnarounds occured in 1968 and 1982.

X =4 major errors   *Based on S&P 500*

JANUARY

Martin Luther King Jr. Day
(Market Closed)

MONDAY

19

*The difference between genius and stupidity
is that genius has its limits.*
— Anonymous

TUESDAY

20

*The essence of the liberal outlook lies not in what opinions are
held but in how they are held: Instead of being held dogmatically
they are held tentatively, and with a consciousness that new
evidence may at any moment lead to their abandonment.*
— Bertrand Russell
(British mathematician and philosopher, 1872-1970)

WEDNESDAY

21

Amongst democratic nations, each generation is a new people.
— Alexis de Tocqueville
(Author, *Democracy in America*, 1840, 1805-1859)

THURSDAY

22

*Bull markets are born on pessimism,
grow on skepticism, mature on optimism,
and die on euphoria.*
— Sir John Templeton
(Founder Templeton Funds, philanthropist, 1994)

FRIDAY

23

*Our philosophy here is identifying change, anticipating change.
Change is what drives earnings growth, and if you identify
the underlying change, you recognize the growth
before the market, and the deceleration of that growth.*
— Peter Vermilye (Baring America Asset management, 1987)

SATURDAY

24

SUNDAY

25

FEBRUARY ALMANAC

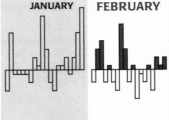

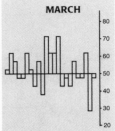

Market Probability Chart above is a graphic representation of the Market Probability Calendar on page 123.

◆ Sharp January moves usually correct or consolidate in February ◆ Compare January and February performance on page 140 ◆ Tends to follow current market trend ◆ RECORD: S&P 28 up, 26 down ◆ Average S&P change –0.1% for 54 years, recent 15 years –0.2% ◆ Best NASDAQ month in Election Years (page 150) average 4.1% gain, up 6, down 2 ◆ Eleven dogs in a row day before Presidents' Day weekend, off 295.05 Dow points in 2000, 91.20 in 2001, 98.95 in 2002, gained 158.93 in 2003 after prior eight-day 360-point drop; days after no prize either lately (see below and page 86) ◆ Many technicians modify market predictions based on January's market

FEBRUARY DAILY POINT CHANGES DOW JONES INDUSTRIALS

	1994	1995	1996	1997	1998	1999	2000	2001	2002	2003
Previous Month Close	3978.36	3843.86	5395.30	6813.09	7906.50	9358.83	10940.53	10887.36	9920.00	8053.81
1	– 14.35	3.70	9.76	—	—	– 13.13	100.52	96.27	– 12.74	—
2	11.53	23.21	– 31.07	—	201.28	– 71.58	– 37.85	– 119.53	—	—
3	– 7.88	57.87	—	– 6.93	52.57	92.69	10.24	—	—	56.01
4	– 96.24	—	—	27.32	– 30.64	– 62.31	– 49.64	—	– 220.17	– 96.53
5	—	—	33.60	– 86.58	– 12.46	– 0.26	—	101.75	– 1.66	– 28.11
6	—	9.09	52.02	26.16	72.24	—	—	– 8.43	– 32.04	– 55.88
7	34.90	– 0.34	32.51	82.74	—	—	– 58.01	– 10.70	– 27.95	65.07
8	– 0.29	– 2.02	47.33	—	—	– 13.13	51.81	– 66.17	118.80	—
9	25.89	– 2.69	2.17	—	– 8.97	– 158.08	– 258.44	– 99.10	—	—
10	– 36.58	6.39	—	– 49.26	115.09	44.28	– 55.53	—	—	55.88
11	0.56	—	—	51.57	18.94	186.15	– 218.42	—	140.54	– 77.00
12	—	—	58.53	103.52	55.05	– 88.57	—	165.32	– 21.04	– 84.94
13	—	15.14	1.08	60.81	0.50	—	—	– 43.45	125.93	– 8.30
14	9.28	4.04	– 21.68	– 33.48	—	—	94.63	– 107.91	12.32	158.93
15	24.21	27.92	– 28.18	—	H	H	198.25	95.61	– 98.95	—
16	9.00	1.35	– 48.05	—	H	22.14	– 156.68	– 91.20	—	—
17	– 14.63	– 33.98	—	H	28.40	– 101.56	– 46.84	—	—	H
18	– 35.18	—	—	78.50	52.56	103.16	– 295.05	—	H	132.35
19	—	—	H	– 47.33	– 75.84	41.32	—	H	– 157.90	– 40.55
20	—	H	– 44.79	– 92.75	38.36	—	—	– 68.94	196.03	– 85.64
21	H	10.43	57.44	4.24	—	—	H	– 204.30	– 106.49	103.15
22	24.20	9.08	92.49	—	—	212.73	85.32	0.23	133.47	—
23	– 19.98	30.28	22.03	—	– 3.74	– 8.26	– 79.11	– 84.91	—	—
24	– 51.78	8.41	—	76.58	– 40.10	– 144.75	– 133.10	—	—	– 159.87
25	– 1.12	—	—	30.01	87.68	– 33.33	– 230.51	—	177.56	51.26
26	—	—	– 65.39	– 55.03	32.89	– 59.76	—	200.63	– 30.45	– 102.52
27	—	– 23.17	– 15.89	– 58.11	55.05	—	—	– 5.65	12.32	78.01
28	– 6.76	22.48	– 43.00	– 47.33	—	—	176.53	– 141.60	– 21.45	6.09
29			– 20.59				89.66			
Close	3832.02	4011.05	5485.62	6877.74	8545.72	9306.58	10128.31	10495.28	10106.13	7891.08
Change	–146.34	167.19	90.32	64.65	639.22	– 52.25	– 812.22	– 392.08	186.13	– 162.73

Either go short, or stay away
The day before Presidents' Day

JANUARY/FEBRUARY

MONDAY
26

*There is nothing like a ticker tape except a woman—
nothing that promises, hour after hour, day after day,
such sudden developments; nothing that disappoints so often or
occasionally fulfills with such unbelievable, passionate magnificence.*
— Walter K. Gutman (Financial analyst, described as the "Proust of Wall Street" by
New Yorker, You Only Have to Get Rich Once, 1961, *The Gutman Letter*, 1903-1986)

FOMC Meeting (2 days)

TUESDAY
27

*Mankind is divided into three classes:
Those that are immovable,
those that are movable, and those that move.*
— Arabian proverb (also attributed to Benjamin Franklin)

WEDNESDAY
28

A small debt produces a debtor; a large one, an enemy.
— Publilius Syrus (Syrian-born Roman mime
and former slave, 83-43 B.C.)

THURSDAY
 # 29

*Liberal institutions straightaway cease from being liberal
the moment they are firmly established.*
— Friedrich Nietzsche (German philosopher, 1844-1900)

*"January Barometer" 92.5% accurate (page 16)
For official final results go to stocktradersalmanac.com*

FRIDAY
 # 30

*The job of central banks: To take away the
punch bowl just as the party is getting going.*
— William McChesney Martin
(Federal Reserve Chairman 1951-1970, 1906-1998)

SATURDAY
31

*February Sector Seasonalities:
Bullish: Natural Gas; Bearish: Internet (page 118)*

SUNDAY
1

HOT JANUARY INDUSTRIES
BEAT S&P NEXT 11 MONTHS

Just as January tends to be a barometer of the market's direction for the whole year, stocks moving quickly out of the starting gate in January outperform the market the rest of the year.

Sam Stovall, Chief Investment Strategist of US Equity Research at Standard & Poor's, massaged the data and proved this premise for the Almanac. Since 1970, January's 10 best performing industries within the S&P 500's 114 Sub-Industries (Sam calls it the January Barometer Portfolio or JBP) went on to outperform the S&P 500 during the remaining 11 months of the year 73% of the time, 15.7% to 7.1%, on average.

Investing in a top 10 industries portfolio only when the January S&P is up increases the average portfolio gain to 22.0% for the last 11 months of the year vs. 13.0% for the S&P. The best gain after a down January was 37.2% in turnaround year 1982, in the middle of the second year of a bear market. More information about the S&P 500 industries can be found in the investing area of *www.businessweek.com*.

AS JANUARY GOES, SO GOES THE YEAR
FOR TOP PERFORMING INDUSTRIES
January's Top 10 Industries vs. S&P 500 Next 11 Months

	11 Month % Change		S&P Jan	After S&P Up in January		After S&P Down in January	
	Portfolio	S&P	%	Portfolio	S&P	Portfolio	S&P
1970	− 4.7	− 0.3	− 7.6			− 4.7	− 0.3
1971	23.5	6.1	4.0	23.5	6.1		
1972	19.7	13.7	1.8	19.7	13.7		
1973	5.2	− 20.0	− 1.7			5.2	− 20.0
1974	− 29.2	− 30.2	− 1.0			− 29.2	− 30.2
1975	57.3	22.2	12.3	57.3	22.2		
1976	16.3	8.1	11.8	16.3	8.1		
1977	− 9.1	− 9.6	− 5.1			− 9.1	− 9.6
1978	7.3	6.5	− 6.2			7.3	6.5
1979	21.7	8.1	4.0	21.7	8.1		
1980	38.3	20.4	5.8	38.3	20.4		
1981	5.0	− 6.9	− 4.6			5.0	− 6.9
1982	37.2	18.8	− 1.8			37.2	18.8
1983	17.2	13.9	3.3	17.2	13.9		
1984	− 5.0	− 1.1	− 0.9			− 5.0	− 1.1
1985	28.2	20.8	7.4	28.2	20.8		
1986	18.1	19.4	0.2	18.1	19.4		
1987	− 1.5	− 8.9	13.2	− 1.5	− 8.9		
1988	18.4	10.4	4.0	18.4	10.4		
1989	16.1	22.1	7.1	16.1	22.1		
1990	− 4.4	− 3.3	− 6.9			− 4.4	− 3.3
1991	35.7	19.4	4.2	35.7	19.4		
1992	14.6	4.7	− 2.0			14.6	4.7
1993	23.7	7.2	0.7	23.7	7.2		
1994	− 7.1	− 4.6	3.3	− 7.1	− 4.6		
1995	25.6	30.9	2.4	25.6	30.9		
1996	5.4	16.5	3.3	5.4	16.5		
1997	4.7	23.4	6.1	4.7	23.4		
1998	45.2	25.4	1.0	45.2	25.4		
1999	67.9	14.8	4.1	67.9	14.8		
2000	23.6	− 5.3	− 5.1			23.6	− 5.3
2001	− 13.1	− 16.0	3.5	− 13.1	− 16.0		
2002	− 16.2	− 22.2	− 1.6			− 16.2	− 22.2
2003			− 2.7				
Averages	14.7%	6.2%		22.0%	13.0%	2.0%	-5.7%

FEBRUARY

*"Best Three-Month Span" normally ends here
(pages 48, 54, 138 and 139)*

MONDAY

2

*Why is it right-wing [conservatives] always stand
shoulder to shoulder in solidarity,
while liberals always fall out among themselves?*
— Yevgeny Yevtushenko (Russian poet, *Babi Yar*,
quoted in London *Observer* December 15, 1991, b. 1933)

*Average February gains last 33 years
NAS 0.7% Dow 0.4% S&P 0.1%*

TUESDAY

3

*What is conservatism? Is it not adherence to
the old and tried, against the new and untried?*
— Abraham Lincoln (16th US President, 1809-1865)

WEDNESDAY

4

Bankruptcy was designed to forgive stupidity, not reward criminality.
— William P. Barr (Verizon executive VP and General Counsel,
after calling for government liquidation of
MCI-WorldCom in Chap. 7, April 14, 2003)

THURSDAY

5

*What's going on...is the end of Silicon Valley as we know it.
The next big thing ain't computers...it's bio-technology.*
— Larry Ellison (Oracle CEO
quoted in *The Wall Street Journal*, April 8, 2003)

FRIDAY

6

Technology has no respect for tradition.
— Peter C. Lee (Merchants' Exchange CEO, quoted in
Stocks, Futures & Options Magazine, May 2003)

SATURDAY

7

SUNDAY

8

1933 "LAME DUCK" AMENDMENT REASON JANUARY BAROMETER WORKS

Between 1901 and 1933 the market's direction in January was similar to that of the whole year 19 times and different 14 times. Comparing January to the 11 subsequent months, 16 were similar and 17 dissimilar.

A dramatic change occurred in 1934—the Twentieth Amendment to the Constitution! Since then it has essentially been "As January goes, so goes the year." January's direction has correctly forecasted the major trend for the market in most of the subsequent years.

JANUARY BAROMETER (ODD YEARS)

January % Change	12 Month % Change	Same	Opposite
– 4.2%	41.2%		1935
3.8	– 38.6		1937
– 6.9	– 5.4	1939	
– 4.8	– 17.9	1941	
7.2	19.4	1943	
1.4	30.7	1945	
2.4	N/C	1947	
0.1	10.3	1949	
6.1	16.5	1951	
– 0.7	– 6.6	1953	
1.8	26.4	1955	
– 4.2	– 14.3	1957	
0.4	8.5	1959	
6.3	23.1	1961	
4.9	18.9	1963	
3.3	9.1	1965	
7.8	20.1	1967	
– 0.8	– 11.4	1969	
4.0	10.8	1971	
– 1.7	– 17.4	1973	
12.3	31.5	1975	
– 5.1	– 11.5	1977	
4.0	12.3	1979	
– 4.6	– 9.7	1981	
3.3	17.3	1983	
7.4	26.3	1985	
13.2	2.0	1987	
7.1	27.0	1989	
4.1	26.3	1991	
0.7	7.1	1993	
2.4	34.1	1995	
6.1	31.0	1997	
4.1	19.5	1999	
3.5	– 13.0		2001
–2.7	??	2003?	2003?

12 month's % change includes January's % change
Based on S&P 500

Prior to 1934, newly elected Senators and Representatives did not take office until December of the following year, 13 months later (except when new Presidents were inaugurated). Defeated Congressmen stayed in Congress for all of the following session. They were known as "lame ducks."

Since the Twentieth (Lame Duck) Amendment was ratified in 1933, Congress convenes January 3 and includes those members newly elected the previous November. Inauguration Day was also moved up from March 4 to January 20. As a result several events have been squeezed into January which affect our economy and our stock market and quite possibly those of many nations of the world. During January, Congress convenes, the President gives the State of the Union message, presents the annual budget and sets national goals and priorities. Switch these events to any other month and chances are the January Barometer would become a memory.

The table shows the January Barometer in odd years. In 1935 and 1937, the Democrats already had the most lopsided congressional margins in history, so when these two Congresses convened it was anticlimactic. **The January Barometer in all subsequent odd-numbered years had compiled a perfect record until 2001. Two January interest rate cuts pushed stocks higher for the month while the 9/11 attack and war on terror pushed the market down for the year.**

FEBRUARY

MONDAY
9

A national debt, if it is not excessive, will be to us a national blessing.
— Alexander Hamilton (US Treasury Secretary 1789-1795,
The Federalist 1788, in April 30, 1781 letter to Robert Morris)

TUESDAY
10

*Never overpay for a stock. More money is lost
than in any other way by projecting above-average
growth and paying an extra multiple for it.*
— Charles Neuhauser (Bear Stearns)

WEDNESDAY
  11

*There is no tool to change human nature...
people are prone to recurring bouts of optimism and
pessimism that manifest themselves from time to time
in the buildup or cessation of speculative excesses.*
— Alan Greenspan (Fed Chairman, July 18, 2001
monetary policy report to the Congress)

THURSDAY
  12

*Of 120 companies from 1987 to 1992 that relied primarily
on cost cutting to improve the bottom line, 68 percent failed
to achieve profitable growth during the next five years.*
— Mercer Management Consulting
(*Smart Money Magazine*, August 2001)

*2003 broke run of 11 Dow dogs in a row, day
before Presidents' Day weekend (page 20)*

FRIDAY
13

*Mate selection is usually a far greater determinant of
individual well-being than stock selection.*
— Ross Miller (President, Miller Risk Advisors,
*Paving Wall Street: Experimental Economics and
the Quest for the Perfect Market*, December 2001)

Valentine's Day

SATURDAY
14

SUNDAY
15

THE FOURTH YEAR OF DECADES

Four out of the last nine decades had "four" years that occurred in election years. Except for 1984 all were strong years. A solid 2004 will bode well for President Bush's reelection bid.

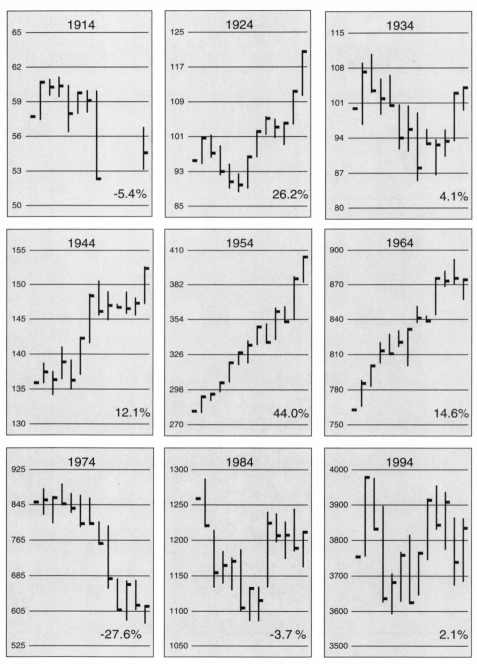

Based on Dow Jones Industrial Average monthly ranges and closing

FEBRUARY

Presidents' Day
(Market Closed)

MONDAY

Companies that announce mass layoffs or a series of firings underperform
the stock market over a three-year period.
— Bain & Company (*Smart Money Magazine*, August 2001)

First trading day of Expiration Week Dow up 10 straight
Day after Presidents' Day Dow up 7 of last 10

TUESDAY
17

Life does not consist mainly of facts and happenings.
It consists mainly of the storm of thoughts
that are forever blowing through one's mind.
— Mark Twain (1835-1910, pen name of
Samuel Longhorne Clemens, American novelist and satirist)

WEDNESDAY
18

640K ought to be enough for anybody.
— William H. Gates (Microsoft founder, 1981,
try running Microsoft XP on less than 256 megs)

THURSDAY
19

Whom the gods would destroy,
they first put on the cover of Business Week.
— Paul Krugman (Economist, referring to CEO of Enron,
New York Times Op-Ed August 17, 2001, on cover February 12,
gets pie in the face June 23, and quits August 16)

FRIDAY

Whenever you see a successful business,
someone once made a courageous decision.
— Peter Drucker (Management consultant, "The man who
invented the corporate society," born in Austria 1909)

SATURDAY
21

SUNDAY
22

MARKET CHARTS OF PRESIDENTIAL ELECTION YEARS

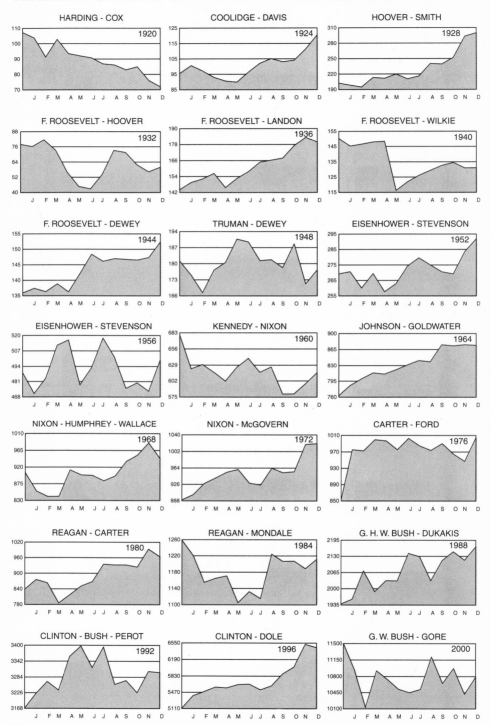

Based on Dow Jones Industial Average monthly closing prices

FEBRUARY

*Brilliant men are often strikingly ineffectual;
they fail to realize that the brilliant insight is not by itself
achievement. They never have learned that insights become
effectiveness only through hard systematic work.*
— Peter Drucker

*When teachers held high expectations of their students, that alone was
enough to cause an increase of 25 points in the students' IQ scores.*
— Warren Bennis (Author, *The Unconscious Conspiracy:
Why Leaders Can't Lead*, 1976)

Ash Wednesday

*Everyone wants to make the same three things:
money, a name, and a difference. What creates diversity
in the human race is how we prioritize the three.*
— Roy H. Williams (Author, *Secret Formulas of the Wizard of Ads*)

*So at last I was going to America! Really, really going,
at last! The boundaries burst. The arch of heaven soared!
A million suns shone out for every star. The winds rushed in from
outer space, roaring in my ears, "America! America!"*
— Mary Antin (1881-1949, Immigrant writer,
The Promised Land, 1912)

The time to buy is when blood is running in the streets.
— Baron Nathan Rothschild (London financier, 1777-1836)

*March Sector Seasonalities:
Bullish: Airlines, Broker/Dealers
Bearish: Biotech (page 118)*

MARCH ALMANAC

MARCH						
S	M	T	W	T	F	S
	1	2	3	4	5	6
7	8	9	10	11	12	13
14	15	16	17	18	19	20
21	22	23	24	25	26	27
28	29	30	31			

APRIL						
S	M	T	W	T	F	S
				1	2	3
4	5	6	7	8	9	10
11	12	13	14	15	16	17
18	19	20	21	22	23	24
25	26	27	28	29	30	

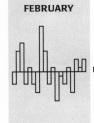

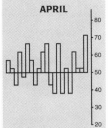

Market Probability Chart above is a graphic representation of the Market Probability Calendar on page 123.

◆ Mid-month strength and end-of month weakness are most evident above ◆ Three record Dow point gains in a row, a big loss in 2001, then strong in 2002 ◆ RECORD: S&P 36 up, 18 down ◆ Average S&P gain 1.1%, fifth best ◆ March has been taking some mean end-of-quarter hits—revealed below, down 1469 Dow points first three weeks March 2001 ◆ Last three or four days a net loser ten out of last eleven years ◆ NASDAQ hard hit in 2001, down 14.5% after 22.4% drop in February ◆ Market much luckier the day before St. Patrick's Day ◆ Worst NASDAQ month during Election Years average drop –2.5%, up 4, down 4

MARCH DAILY POINT CHANGES DOW JONES INDUSTRIALS

	1994	1995	1996	1997	1998	1999	2000	2001	2002	2003
Previous Month Close	3832.02	4011.05	5485.62	6877.74	8545.72	9306.58	10128.31	10495.28	10106.13	7891.08
1	– 22.79	– 16.25	50.94	—	—	18.20	9.62	– 45.14	262.73	—
2	22.51	– 14.87	—	—	4.73	– 27.17	26.99	16.17	—	—
3	– 7.32	9.68	—	41.18	34.38	– 21.73	202.28	—	—	– 53.22
4	7.88	—	63.59	– 66.20	– 45.59	191.52	—	—	217.96	– 132.99
5	—	—	42.27	93.13	– 94.91	268.68	—	95.99	– 153.41	70.73
6	—	7.95	– 12.65	– 1.15	125.06	—	– 196.70	28.92	140.88	– 101.61
7	23.92	– 34.93	11.92	56.19	—	—	– 374.47	138.38	– 48.92	66.04
8	– 4.50	16.60	–171.24	—	—	– 8.47	60.50	128.65	47.12	—
9	1.69	4.16	—	—	– 2.25	– 33.85	154.20	– 213.63	—	—
10	– 22.79	52.22	—	78.50	75.98	79.08	– 81.91	—	—	– 171.85
11	32.08	—	110.55	5.77	32.63	124.60	—	—	38.75	– 44.12
12	—	—	2.89	– 45.79	– 16.19	– 21.09	—	– 436.37	21.11	28.01
13	—	– 10.38	– 15.17	–160.48	– 57.04	—	18.31	82.54	– 130.50	269.68
14	0.28	23.52	17.34	56.57	—	—	– 135.89	– 317.34	15.29	37.96
15	– 13.39	– 10.38	– 1.09	—	—	82.42	320.17	57.83	90.09	—
16	– 1.44	30.78	—	—	116.33	– 28.30	499.19	– 207.87	—	—
17	16.99	4.50	—	20.02	31.14	– 51.06	– 35.37	—	—	282.21
18	30.51	—	98.63	– 58.92	25.41	118.21	—	—	– 29.48	52.31
19	—	—	– 14.09	– 18.88	27.65	– 94.07	—	135.70	57.50	71.22
20	—	10.03	– 14.09	– 57.40	103.38	—	85.01	– 238.35	– 133.68	21.15
21	– 30.80	– 11.07	– 28.54	– 15.49	—	—	227.10	– 233.76	– 21.73	235.37
22	– 2.30	10.38	9.76	—	—	– 13.04	– 40.64	– 97.52	– 52.17	—
23	6.91	4.84	—	—	– 90.18	–218.68	253.16	115.30	—	—
24	– 48.37	50.84	—	100.46	88.19	– 4.99	– 7.14	—	—	– 307.29
25	– 46.36	—	7.22	– 29.08	– 31.64	169.55	—	—	– 146.00	65.55
26	—	—	26.74	4.53	– 25.91	– 14.15	—	182.75	71.69	– 50.35
27	—	18.67	– 43.72	–140.11	– 50.81	—	– 86.87	260.01	73.55	– 28.43
28	– 12.38	– 5.53	3.97	H	—	—	– 89.74	– 162.19	– 22.97	– 55.68
29	– 63.33	8.99	– 43.71	—	—	184.54	82.61	13.71	H	—
30	– 72.27	11.76	—	—	– 13.96	– 93.52	– 38.47	79.72	—	—
31	9.21	– 14.87	—	–157.11	17.69	–127.10	– 58.33	—	—	– 153.64
Close	3635.96	4157.69	5587.14	6583.48	8799.81	9786.16	10921.92	9878.78	10403.94	7992.13
Change	–196.06	146.64	101.52	– 294.26	254.09	479.58	793.61	– 616.50	297.81	101.05

March has Ides and St. Patrick's Day
Begins bullishly, then fades away

MARCH

MONDAY

1

Successful innovation is not a feat of intellect, but of will.
— Joseph A. Schumpeter (Austrian-American economist,
Theory of Economic Development, 1883-1950)

Average March gains last 33 years
NAS 0.4% Dow 1.0% S&P 1.0%

TUESDAY

2

You can't grow long-term if you can't eat short-term.
Anybody can manage short. Anybody can manage long.
Balancing those two things is what management is.
— Jack Welch (CEO of General Electric,
Business Week, June 8, 1998)

WEDNESDAY

3

A fanatic is one who can't change his mind
and won't change the subject.
— Winston Churchill (British statesman, 1874-1965)

THURSDAY

4

An appeaser is one who feeds a crocodile—
hoping it will eat him last.
— Winston Churchill

FRIDAY

5

The world has changed! You can't be an 800-pound
gorilla; you need to be an economic gazelle.
You've got to be able to change directions quickly.
— Mark Breier (*The 10-Second Internet Manager*)

SATURDAY

6

SUNDAY

7

PROFIT ON DAY BEFORE ST. PATRICK'S DAY

Days before major legal holidays tend to be bullish. We also track the seasonality around St. Patrick's Day. Results appear below.

Note the stellar performance of the market on the day before St. Patrick's Day. It outperforms the days before many legal holidays. The average gain of 0.33% on the S&P is equivalent to more than 30 Dow points (at current levels for the Dow). That's equal to an annualized rate of return of over 100%. Irish luck, or coincidence?

During the past 50 years, St. Patrick's Day itself has posted just a wee gain of 0.12%. In 2003 St. Pat's was the Monday before Triple-Witching Day and the whole week was up (thanks to decisive action in Iraq). In 2004 St. Patrick's Day falls on Wednesday, making Tuesday, March 16th, a likely up day. Also, Monday, March 15th, is a Monday before Triple-Witching Day, which has been up 9 of the last 10 times on the Dow. With mid-March exhibiting strength of late, it could be your lucky week in 2004.

ST. PATRICK'S DAY TRADING RECORD (DAYS BEFORE AND AFTER)

Year	St. Pat's Day	% Change 2 Days Prior	% Change 1 Day Prior	S&P 500 St. Pat's Day or Next *	% Change St. Pat's Day *	% Change Day After
1953	Tue	0.19%	0.15%	26.33	0.42%	− 0.34%
1954	Wed	− 0.45	− 0.04	26.62	0.23	0.41
1955	Thu	2.15	0.76	36.12	0.39	0.17
1956	Sat	0.97	0.31	48.59	0.93	0.58
1957	Sun	0.07	− 0.05	43.85	− 0.45	0.43
1958	Mon	0.12	− 0.31	42.04	− 0.69	− 0.36
1959	Tue	0.12	− 1.08	56.52	0.82	− 0.23
1960	Thu	0.77	0.55	54.96	− 0.15	0.09
1961	Fri	0.30	1.01	64.60	0.61	0.40
1962	Sat	0.21	− 0.17	70.85	− 0.13	− 0.27
1963	Sun	− 0.47	0.50	65.61	− 0.49	− 0.21
1964	Tue	0.08	0.00	79.32	0.23	0.08
1965	Wed	0.03	− 0.13	87.02	− 0.13	− 0.24
1966	Thu	− 0.57	0.58	88.17	0.35	0.41
1967	Fri	0.95	1.01	90.25	0.18	− 0.06
1968	Sun	− 1.90	0.88	89.59	0.55	− 0.67
1969	Mon	− 0.67	− 0.40	98.25	0.26	0.24
1970	Tue	− 0.53	− 1.08	87.29	0.44	0.29
1971	Wed	1.14	0.50	101.12	− 0.09	0.07
1972	Fri	0.13	− 0.23	107.92	0.39	− 0.31
1973	Sat	− 0.75	− 0.51	112.17	− 1.21	− 0.20
1974	Sun	− 0.09	− 0.37	98.05	− 1.24	− 0.84
1975	Mon	0.18	1.22	86.01	1.47	− 1.02
1976	Wed	− 1.05	1.12	100.86	− 0.06	− 0.41
1977	Thu	0.55	0.19	102.08	− 0.09	− 0.22
1978	Fri	− 0.26	0.44	90.20	0.77	0.69
1979	Sat	0.15	0.83	101.06	0.37	− 0.55
1980	Mon	− 1.17	− 0.18	102.26	− 3.01	1.80
1981	Tue	− 0.06	1.18	133.92	− 0.56	0.22
1982	Wed	0.77	− 0.16	109.08	− 0.18	1.12
1983	Thu	0.35	− 1.03	149.59	− 0.14	0.21
1984	Sat	0.41	1.18	157.78	− 0.94	0.68
1985	Sun	− 0.20	− 0.74	176.88	0.20	1.50
1986	Mon	0.28	1.44	234.67	− 0.79	0.47
1987	Tue	− 0.46	− 0.57	292.47	1.47	0.11
1988	Thu	− 0.09	0.95	271.22	0.96	− 0.04
1989	Fri	0.52	0.93	292.69	− 2.25	− 0.95
1990	Sat	0.36	1.14	343.53	0.47	− 0.57
1991	Sun	− 0.29	0.02	372.11	− 0.40	− 1.48
1992	Tue	0.48	0.14	409.58	0.78	− 0.10
1993	Wed	0.36	− 0.01	448.31	− 0.68	0.80
1994	Thu	− 0.08	0.52	470.89	0.31	0.04
1995	Fri	− 0.20	0.72	495.52	0.02	0.13
1996	Sun	0.37	0.09	652.65	1.75	− 0.15
1997	Mon	− 1.83	0.46	795.71	0.32	− 0.76
1998	Tue	− 0.13	1.00	1080.45	0.11	0.47
1999	Wed	0.98	− 0.07	1297.82	− 0.65	1.44
2000	Fri	2.43	4.76	1464.47	0.41	− 0.54
2001	Sat	0.59	− 1.96	1170.81	1.76	− 2.41
2002	Sun	− 0.09	1.14	1165.55	− 0.05	− 0.41
2003	Mon	3.45	0.16	862.79	3.54	0.42
Average		**0.16%**	**0.33%**		**0.12%**	**0.01%**

When St. Patrick's Day falls on Saturday or Sunday, the following trading day is used. Based on S&P 500

MARCH

MONDAY

8

People with a sense of fulfillment think the world is good,
while the frustrated blame the world for their failure.
— Eric Hoffer (*The True Believer*, 1951)

TUESDAY

9

Of a stock's move, 31% can be attributed to the
general stock market, 12% to the industry influence,
37% to the influence of other groupings, and the
remaining 20% is peculiar to the one stock.
— Benjamin F. King (*Market and Industry Factors in*
Stock Price Behavior, Journal of Business, January 1966)

WEDNESDAY

10

You don't learn to hold your own in the world by standing on
guard, but by attacking and getting well hammered yourself.
— George Bernard Shaw

THURSDAY

11

The CROWD is always wrong at market turning points but often
times right once a trend sets in. The reason many market fighters
go broke is they believe the CROWD is always wrong. There is nothing
further from the truth. Unless volatility is extremely low or
very high one should think twice before betting against the CROWD.
— Shawn Andrew (Trader, Ricercar Fund /SA, December 21, 2001)

FRIDAY

12

Life is what happens, while you're
busy making other plans.
— John Lennon (Beatle)

SATURDAY

13

SUNDAY
14

HOW THE GOVERNMENT MANIPULATES THE ECONOMY TO STAY IN POWER

Bull markets tend to occur in the third and fourth years of presidential terms while markets tend to decline in the first and second years. The "making of presidents" is accompanied by an unsubtle manipulation of the economy. Incumbent administrations are duty-bound to retain the reins of power. Subsequently, the "piper must be paid," producing what we have coined the "Post-Presidential Year Syndrome." Most big, bad bear markets began in such years—1929, 1937, 1957, 1969, 1973, 1977 and 1981. Our major wars also began in years following elections—Civil War (1861), WWI (1917), WWII (1941) and Vietnam (1965). Post-election 2001 combined with 2002 for the worst back-to-back years since 1973-74 (also first and second years). Plus we had 9/11, the war on terror and the build-up to confrontation with Iraq.

Some cold, hard facts to prove economic manipulation appeared in a book by Edward R. Tufte, *Political Control of the Economy* (Princeton University Press). Stimulative fiscal measures designed to increase per capita disposable income, providing a sense of well-being to the voting public, included: increases in federal budget deficits, government spending and social security benefits; interest rate reductions on government loans; and speed-ups of projected funding.

Federal Spending: During 1962-1973, the average increase was 29% higher in election years than in non-election years.

Social Security: There were nine increases during the 1952-1974 period. Half of the six election-year increases became effective in September eight weeks before Election Day. The average increase was 100% higher in presidential than in midterm election years.

Real Disposable Income: Accelerated in all but one election year between 1947 and 1973 (excluding the Eisenhower years). Only one of the remaining odd-numbered years (1973) showed a marked acceleration.

These moves were obviously not coincidences and explain why we tend to have a political (four-year) stock market cycle.

Under Reagan we paid the piper in 1981 and 1982 followed by eight straight years of expansion. However, we ran up a larger deficit than the total deficit of the previous 200 years of our national existence.

Alan Greenspan took over the Fed from Paul Volker August 11, 1987, and was able to keep the economy rolling until an exogenous event in the Persian Gulf pushed us into a real recession in August 1990 which lasted long enough to choke off the Bush re-election effort in 1992. Three other incumbents in this century failed to retain power: Taft in 1912 when the Republican Party split in two; Hoover in 1932 in the depths of the Great Depression; and Carter in 1980 during the Iran Hostage Crisis.

Bill Clinton, warts and all, presided for two terms over the incredible economic expansion and market gains of the nineties. Mr. Clinton was keen to have former Goldman Sachs chief, Robert Rubin, run the treasury for a stretch, helping his administration create a smooth and beneficial relationship with Wall Street, Main Street and the Fed.

As we go to press, George W. Bush is fresh off success in Iraq and focused intently on stimulating the economy and the stock market. Major tax cuts have already passed, including a bone to Wall Street in a dividend tax cut. Pre-election year 2003 is delivering as promised with strong market gains after a recession and war plagued 2001-2002. Though no strong Democrat has come forward yet, Mr. Bush will have to do all he can to avert economic setbacks and market declines as the election approaches.

MARCH

 MONDAY

15

Those who cannot remember the past are condemned to repeat it.
— George Santayana (American philosopher, poet)

FOMC Meeting
Market much luckier day before St. Patrick's Day (page 32)

 TUESDAY
16

Individualism, private property, the law of accumulation of wealth and
the law of competition...are the highest result of human experience,
the soil in which, so far, has produced the best fruit.
— Andrew Carnegie (Scottish-born US industrialist, philanthropist,
The Gospel Of Wealth, 1835-1919)

St. Patrick's Day **WEDNESDAY**

17

It is not how right or how wrong you are that
matters, but how much money you make when right
and how much you do not lose when wrong.
— George Soros

THURSDAY

18

The monuments of wit survive the monuments of power.
— Francis Bacon (English philosopher,
essayist, statesman, 1561-1626)

Triple-Witching Day   **FRIDAY**
Dow up 7 of last 12
19

Keep me away from the wisdom which does not cry,
the philosophy which does not laugh and the
greatness which does not bow before children.
— Kahlil Gibran (Lebanese-born
American mystic, poet and artist, 1883-1931)

SATURDAY
20

SUNDAY
21

INCUMBENT VICTORIES VS. INCUMBENT DEFEATS

Since 1944 stocks tend to move up earlier when White House occupants are popular but do even better in November and December when unpopular administrations are ousted.

TREND OF S&P 500 INDEX IN ELECTION YEARS 1944-2000

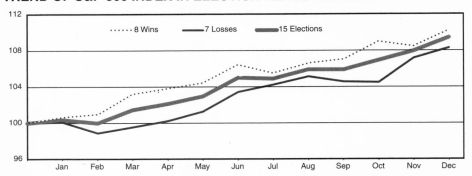

Actual percent changes reveal that March, June, October and December are best when incumbents stay in power and February, July and September are the worst when they are removed. Ironically, November is best when incumbents are ousted and second worst when they win.

Other interesting tidbits: there were no major losses in October (1984 off fractionally) and only one in March, June and December when incumbent parties retained the White House; Republican wins in November resulted in total gains of 19.7% (excluding no-decision 2000); Democratic victories produced total gains of 2.7%; however, Democrats "gained" 15.6% in December, the Republicans 4.7%.

MONTHLY % CHANGES DURING ELECTION YEARS

Incumbents Win

Year	Jan	Feb	Mar	Apr	May	Jun	Jul	Aug	Sep	Oct	Nov	Dec
1944	1.5	− 0.3	1.7	− 1.3	4.0	5.1	− 2.1	0.9	− 0.3	N/C	0.4	3.5
1948	− 4.0	− 4.7	7.7	2.7	7.8	0.3	− 5.3	0.8	− 3.0	6.8	−10.8	3.1
1956	− 3.6	3.5	6.9	− 0.2	− 6.6	3.9	5.2	− 3.8	− 4.5	0.5	− 1.1	3.5
1964	2.7	1.0	1.5	0.6	1.1	1.6	1.8	− 1.6	2.9	0.8	− 0.5	0.4
1972	1.8	2.5	0.6	0.4	1.7	− 2.2	0.2	3.4	− 0.5	0.9	4.6	1.2
1984	− 0.9	− 3.9	1.3	0.5	− 5.9	1.7	− 1.6	10.6	− 0.3	− 0.01	1.5	2.2
1988	4.0	4.2	− 3.3	0.9	0.3	4.3	− 0.5	− 3.9	4.0	2.6	− 1.9	1.5
1996	3.3	0.7	0.8	1.3	2.3	0.2	− 4.6	1.9	5.4	2.6	7.3	− 2.2
Totals	**4.8**	**3.0**	**17.2**	**4.9**	**4.7**	**14.9**	**− 6.9**	**8.3**	**3.7**	**14.2**	**− 3.5**	**13.2**
Average	**0.6**	**0.4**	**2.2**	**0.6**	**0.6**	**1.9**	**− 0.9**	**1.0**	**0.5**	**1.8**	**− 0.4**	**1.7**

Incumbents Lose

Year	Jan	Feb	Mar	Apr	May	Jun	Jul	Aug	Sep	Oct	Nov	Dec
1952	1.6	− 3.6	4.8	− 4.3	2.3	4.6	1.8	− 1.5	− 2.0	− 0.1	4.6	3.5
1960	− 7.1	0.9	− 1.4	− 1.8	2.7	2.0	− 2.5	2.6	− 6.0	− 0.2	4.0	4.6
1968	− 4.4	− 3.1	0.9	8.2	1.1	0.9	− 1.8	1.1	3.9	0.7	4.8	− 4.2
1976	11.8	− 1.1	3.1	− 1.1	− 1.4	4.1	− 0.8	− 0.5	2.3	− 2.2	− 0.8	5.2
1980	5.8	− 0.4	−10.2	4.1	4.7	2.7	6.5	0.6	2.5	1.6	10.2	− 3.4
1992	− 2.0	1.0	− 2.2	2.8	0.1	− 1.7	3.9	− 2.4	0.9	0.2	3.0	1.0
2000	− 5.1	− 2.0	9.7	− 3.1	− 2.2	2.4	− 1.6	6.1	− 5.3	− 0.5	− 8.0*	0.4
Totals	**0.6**	**− 8.3**	**4.7**	**4.8**	**7.3**	**15.0**	**5.5**	**6.0**	**− 3.7**	**− 0.5**	**17.8**	**7.1**
Average	**0.1**	**− 1.2**	**0.7**	**0.7**	**1.0**	**2.1**	**0.8**	**0.9**	**− 0.5**	**− 0.1**	**2.5**	**1.0**

	Jan	Feb	Mar	Apr	May	Jun	Jul	Aug	Sep	Oct	Nov	Dec
15 Elections	**5.4**	**− 5.3**	**21.9**	**9.7**	**12.0**	**29.9**	**− 1.4**	**14.3**	**N/C**	**13.7**	**14.3**	**20.3**
Average	**0.4**	**− 0.4**	**1.5**	**0.6**	**0.8**	**2.0**	**− 0.1**	**1.0**	**N/C**	**1.0**	**1.0**	**1.4**

*Undecided election

MONDAY
22

You're perhaps the most accomplished confidence man since Charles Ponzi. I'd say you were a carnival barker, except that wouldn't be fair to carnival barkers. A carnie will at least tell you up front that he's running a shell game.
—Senator Peter G. Fitzgerald (In comments to Kenneth L. Lay, former chairman of Enron, February 13, 2002)

TUESDAY
23

Bill Gates' One-Minus Staffing*: For every project, figure out the bare minimum of people needed to staff it. Cut to the absolute muscle and bones, then take out one more. When you understaff, people jump on the loose ball. You find out who the real performers are. Not so when you're overstaffed. People sit around waiting for somebody else to do it.*
— Quoted by Rich Karlgaard (Publisher, *Forbes,* December 25, 2000)

WEDNESDAY
24

The whole secret to our success is being able to con ourselves into believing that we're going to change the world [even though] we are unlikely to do it.
— Tom Peters (*Fortune*, November 13, 2000)

THURSDAY
25

You get stepped on, passed over, knocked down, but you have to come back.
— 90-year old Walter Watson (MD, *Fortune*, November 13, 2000)

FRIDAY
26

Fight until death over taxes? Oh, no. Women, country, God, things like that. Taxes? No.
— Daniel Patrick Moynihan (US Senator New York 1976-2001, in response to Tim Russert on "Meet The Press" May 23, 1993, 1927-March 26, 2003)

SATURDAY
27

Bullish April Sector Seasonalities: Biotech, Forest/Paper, Semiconductor, Utilities (page 118)

SUNDAY
28

APRIL ALMANAC

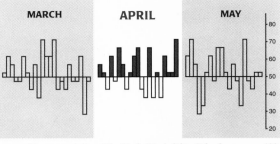

Market Probability Chart above is a graphic representation of the Market Probability Calendar on page 123.

◆ April has been the best Dow month (average 1.9%) since 1950 (page 48) ◆ April 1999 first month ever to gain 1000 Dow points, 856 in 2001, knocked off its high horse in 2002 down 458, 2003 up 489 ◆ First half of month no longer does better than second half ◆ Stocks anticipate great first quarter earnings by rising sharply before earnings are reported, rather than after ◆ Rarely a dangerous month except in big bear markets (like 2002) ◆ "Best six months" of the year end with April (page 50) ◆ Election Year Aprils are mediocre, net down on NASDAQ, up fractionally on S&P

APRIL DAILY POINT CHANGES DOW JONES INDUSTRIALS

Previous Month	1994	1995	1996	1997	1998	1999	2000	2001	2002	2003
Close	3635.96	4157.69	5587.14	6583.48	8799.81	9786.16	10921.92	9878.78	10403.94	7992.13
1	H	—	50.58	27.57	68.51	46.35	—	—	− 41.24	77.73
2	—	—	33.96	− 94.04	118.32	H	—	− 100.85	− 48.99	215.20
3	—	10.72	18.06	− 39.66	− 3.23	—	300.01	− 292.22	− 115.42	− 44.68
4	− 42.61	33.20	− 6.86	48.72	—	—	− 57.09	29.71	36.88	36.77
5	82.06	− 1.04	H	—	—	174.82	− 130.92	402.63	36.47	—
6	4.32	4.84	—	—	49.82	− 43.84	80.35	− 126.96	—	—
7	13.53	− 12.79	—	29.84	− 76.73	121.82	− 2.79	—	—	23.26
8	− 19.00	—	− 88.51	53.25	− 65.02	112.39	—	—	− 22.56	− 1.49
9	—	—	− 33.96	− 45.32	103.38	− 23.86	—	54.06	− 40.41	− 100.98
10	—	5.53	− 74.43	− 23.79	H	—	75.08	257.59	173.06	23.39
11	14.57	− 11.07	1.09	−148.36	—	—	100.52	− 89.27	− 205.65	− 17.92
12	− 7.14	10.73	45.52	—	—	165.67	− 161.95	113.47	14.74	—
13	− 20.22	10.37	—	60.21	17.44	55.50	− 201.58	H	—	—
14	1.78	H	—	135.26	97.90	16.65	− 617.78	—	—	147.69
15	− 1.78	—	60.33	135.26	52.07	51.06	—	—	− 97.15	51.26
16	—	—	27.10	92.71	− 85.70	31.17	—	31.62	207.65	− 144.75
17	—	− 12.80	− 70.09	− 21.27	90.93	—	276.74	58.17	− 80.54	80.04
18	− 41.05	− 16.25	1.81	44.95	—	—	184.91	399.10	− 15.50	H
19	− 0.60	28.36	− 16.26	—	—	− 53.36	− 92.46	77.88	51.83	—
20	− 21.11	23.17	—	—	− 25.66	8.02	169.09	− 113.86	—	—
21	53.83	39.43	—	− 43.34	43.10	132.87	H	—	—	− 8.75
22	− 3.86	—	29.26	173.38	− 8.22	145.76	—	—	− 120.68	156.09
23	—	—	23.85	− 20.87	− 33.39	− 37.51	—	− 47.62	− 47.19	30.67
24	—	33.89	− 34.69	− 20.47	− 78.71	—	62.05	− 77.89	− 58.81	− 75.62
25	57.10	− 3.81	13.01	− 53.38	—	—	218.72	170.86	4.63	− 133.69
26	− 6.24	− 0.34	1.08	—	—	28.92	− 179.32	67.15	− 124.34	—
27	H*	14.87	—	—	− 146.98	113.12	− 57.40	117.70	—	—
28	− 31.23	6.57	—	44.15	− 18.68	13.74	− 154.19	—	—	165.26
29	13.38	—	5.42	179.01	52.56	32.93	—	—	− 90.85	31.38
30	—	—	− 4.33	46.96	111.85	− 89.34	—	− 75.08	126.35	− 22.90
Close	3681.69	4321.27	5569.08	7008.99	9063.37	10789.04	10733.91	10734.97	9946.22	8480.09
Change	45.73	163.58	− 18.06	425.51	263.56	1002.88	− 188.01	856.19	− 457.72	487.96

* Nixon Memorial

April "Best Month" for Dow since 1950
Day-before-Good Friday gains are nifty

MARCH/APRIL

End of March terrible lately

MONDAY

29

*Vietnam, the original domino in the Cold War, now
faces the prospect of becoming, in the words of political
scientist Sunai Phasuk of Chulalongkorn University
in Bangkok, one of the new "dominos of democracy."*
— Quoted by Seth Mydans (*New York Times*, January 6, 2001)

TUESDAY

30

An autobiography must be such that one can sue oneself for libel.
— Thomas Hoving (Museum director)

WEDNESDAY

31

*Always grab the reader by the throat in the first paragraph, sink
your thumbs into his windpipe in the second,
and hold him against the wall until the tag line.*
— Paul O'Neil (Marketer, *Writing Changes Everything*)

April first trading day Dow up 9 of last 12

THURSDAY

1

*Liberal democracies do not fight wars with one another
because they see the same human nature and the same rights
applicable everywhere and to everyone. Cultures fight wars
with one another. Cultures have different perceptions, which
determine what the world is. They cannot come to terms.*
— Allan Bloom (*The Closing of the American Mind,* 1987)

*Average April gains last 33 years
NAS 1.3% Dow 2.2% S&P 1.4%*

FRIDAY

2

*If you want to raise a crop for one year, plant corn.
If you want to raise a crop for decades, plant trees.
If you want to raise a crop for centuries, raise men.
If you want to plant a crop for eternities, raise democracies.*
— Carl A. Schenk

SATURDAY

3

Daylight Saving Time Begins

SUNDAY

4

ADD THE DECEMBER LOW INDICATOR TO YOUR PROGNOSTICATING ARSENAL

Jeffrey Saut, chief equity strategist at Raymond James, brought a forgotten but very interesting indicator to our attention. The original analysis is credited to Lucien Hooper, a *Forbes* columnist and Wall Street analyst back in the 70s. Hooper dismissed the importance of January and January's first week as reliable indicators. He noted that the trend could be random or even manipulated during a holiday-shortened week. Instead, said Hooper, "pay much more attention to the December low. If that low is violated during the first quarter of the New Year, watch out!"

The December Low Indicator is compared here to the January Barometer in years when the Dow closed below its previous December's closing low in the first quarter. Since 1950, though Hooper's indicator was wrong 11 of the 25 times on a full-year basis, he was absolutely correct in his "Watch Out" warning, as the Dow fell an additional 10.7% on average when December's low was breached in Q1. Only three significant drops occurred (not shown) when December's low was not breached in Q1 (1974, 1981 and 1987) and both indicators were wrong only four times. If we do not cross the December low, turn to our January Barometer for guidance. It has been virtually perfect, right nearly 100% of these times. (Email *service@hirschorg.com* for a copy of the complete results.)

YEARS DOW FELL BELOW DECEMBER LOW IN FIRST QUARTER

Year	Previous Dec Low	Date Crossed	Crossing Price	Subseq. Low	% Change Cross-Low	Rest of Year % Change	Full Year % Change	Jan Bar
1952	262.29	2/19/52	261.37	256.35	— 1.9%	11.7%	8.4%	1.6%[2]
1953	281.63	2/11/53	281.57	255.49	— 9.3	— 0.2	— 3.8	— 0.7
1956	480.72	1/9/56	479.74	462.35	— 3.6	4.1	2.3	— 3.6 [1][2]
1957	480.61	1/18/57	477.46	419.79	— 12.1	— 8.7	— 12.8	— 4.2
1960	661.29	1/12/60	660.43	566.05	— 14.3	— 6.7	— 9.3	— 7.1
1962	720.10	1/5/62	714.84	535.76	— 25.1	— 8.8	— 10.8	— 3.8
1966	939.53	3/1/66	938.19	744.32	— 20.7	— 16.3	— 18.9	0.5 [1]
1968	879.16	1/22/68	871.71	825.13	— 5.3	8.3	4.3	— 4.4 [1][2]
1969	943.75	1/6/69	936.66	769.93	— 17.8	— 14.6	— 15.2	— 0.8
1970	769.93	1/26/70	768.88	631.16	— 17.9	9.1	4.8	— 7.6 [1][2]
1973	1000.00	1/29/73	996.46	788.31	— 20.9	— 14.6	— 16.6	— 1.7
1977	946.64	2/7/77	946.31	800.85	— 15.4	— 12.2	— 17.3	— 5.1
1978	806.22	1/5/78	804.92	742.12	— 7.8	0.0	— 3.1	— 6.2
1980	819.62	3/10/80	818.94	759.13	— 7.3	17.7	14.9	5.8 [2]
1982	868.25	1/5/82	865.30	776.92	— 10.2	20.9	19.6	— 1.8 [1][2]
1984	1236.79	1/25/84	1231.89	1086.57	— 11.8	— 1.6	— 3.7	— 0.9
1990	2687.93	1/15/90	2669.37	2365.10	— 11.4	— 1.3	— 4.3	— 6.9
1991	2565.59	1/7/91	2522.77	2470.30	— 2.1	25.6	20.3	4.2 [2]
1993	3255.18	1/8/93	3251.67	3241.95	— 0.3	15.5	13.7	0.7 [2]
1994	3697.08	3/30/94	3626.75	3593.35	— 0.9	5.7	2.1	3.3 [2]
1996	5059.32	1/10/96	5032.94	5032.94	0.0	28.1	26.0	3.3 [2]
1998	7660.13	1/9/98	7580.42	7539.07	— 0.5	21.1	16.1	1.0 [2]
2000	10998.39	1/4/00	10997.93	9796.03	— 10.9	— 1.9	— 6.2	— 5.1
2001	10318.93	3/12/01	10208.25	8235.81	— 19.3	— 1.8	— 7.1	3.5 [1]
2002	9763.96	1/16/02	9712.27	7286.27	— 25.0	— 14.1	— 16.8	— 1.6
2003	8303.78	1/24/03	8131.01	7524.06	— 7.5	*At Press-time*		— 2.7
			Average Drop		**— 10.7%**			

[1] *January Barometer wrong*   [2] *December Low Indicator wrong*

APRIL

Start looking for Dow and S&P MACD seasonal SELL Signal (page 52)
Almanac Investor subscribers will be emailed the alert when it triggers
Details at stocktradersalmanac.com

MONDAY

5

If you create an act, you create a habit.
If you create a habit, you create a character.
If you create a character, you create a destiny.
— André Maurois (Novelist, biographer, essayist, 1885-1967)

Passover

TUESDAY

6

No horse gets anywhere until he is harnessed.
No steam or gas ever drives anything until it is confined.
No Niagara is ever turned into light and power until it is tunneled.
No life ever grows great until it is focused, dedicated, disciplined.
— Harry Emerson Fosdick (Protestant minister, author, 1878-1969)

WEDNESDAY

7

With globalization, the big [countries]
don't eat the small, the fast eat the slow.
— Thomas L. Friedman (Op-ed columnist,
referring to the Arab nations, *New York Times*)

Day before April Good Fridays Dow up 5 in a row (page 38)   **THURSDAY**

8

The advice of the elders to young men is very
apt to be as unreal as a list of the best books.
— Oliver Wendell Holmes Jr.
(*The Mind and Faith of Justice Holmes,*
edited by Max Lerner)

Good Friday
(Market Closed)

FRIDAY

9

What is it that attracts me to the young? When I am with
mature people I feel their rigidities, their tight crystallizations.
They have become...like the statues of the famous. Achieved. Final.
— Anaïs Nin (*The Diaries of Anaïs Nin, Vol. IV*)

SATURDAY

10

Easter Sunday

SUNDAY

11

ONLY ONE LOSS LAST 7 MONTHS OF ELECTION YEARS

Election years are traditionally up years. Incumbent administrations shamelessly attempt to massage the economy so voters will keep them in power. But, sometimes overpowering events occur and the market crumbles, usually resulting in a change of political control. The Republicans won in 1920 as the post-war economy contracted and President Wilson ailed. The Democrats came back during the 1932 Depression when the Dow hit its lowest level of the 20th century. A world at war and the fall of France jolted the market in 1940 but Roosevelt won an unprecedented third term. Cold War confrontations and Truman's historic upset of Dewey held markets down through the end of 1948.

Since 1948, investors have barely been bruised during election years, except for a brief span early in the year—until 2000. An undecided election plagued the country with uncertainty, hammering stock prices in November and keeping them down until December 12 when the US Supreme Court prevented the Democrats' controversial bid for a manual recount of the challenged Florida vote and cleared the way for George W. Bush to be elected President.

The table below presents a very positive picture for the last seven or eight months of election years.

- Since 1952, January through April losses occurred in six of thirteen election years. Incumbent parties were ousted on five of these six losses. Ironically, bear markets began the year following four of seven gainers in 1957, 1969, 1973 and 1977.

- Comparing month-end June with month-end April reveals losses in 1956, 1972, 1984 and 1992 for the sixty-day period, when Republicans ran for reelection.

- Of the twelve Julys since 1952, seven were losers (1960, 1968, 1976, 1984, 1988, 1996 and 2000). Four were years when, at convention time, no strong incumbent was running for re-election. Note that April through July periods had only four losers: 1972 by a small margin, 1984 as the market was turning around, 1996, and 2000 as the bubble began to work off its excesses.

- For a longer perspective, we extended the table to December. Just two losing eight-month periods in an election year are revealed and only one loss in the last seven months of all these years.

S&P 500 DURING ELECTION YEARS

Election Year	% Change First 4 Months	April	May	June	July	Dec	% Change Last 8 Months	Last 7 Months
1952*	− 1.9%	**23.32**	23.86	24.96	25.40	26.57	13.9%	11.4%
1956	6.4	**48.38**	**45.20**	46.97	49.39	46.67	− 3.5	3.3
1960*	− 9.2	**54.37**	55.83	56.92	**55.51**	58.11	6.9	4.1
1964	5.9	79.46	80.37	81.69	83.18	84.75	6.7	5.4
1968*	1.2	97.59	98.68	99.58	**97.74**	**103.86**	6.4	5.2
1972	5.5	107.67	109.53	**107.14**	107.39	118.05	9.6	7.8
1976*	12.7	**101.64**	**100.18**	104.28	**103.44**	107.46	5.7	7.3
1980*	− 1.5	106.29	111.24	114.24	121.67	**135.76**	27.7	22.0
1984	− 3.0	160.05	**150.55**	153.18	**150.66**	167.24	4.5	11.1
1988	5.8	261.33	262.16	273.50	**272.02**	277.72	6.3	5.9
1992*	− 0.5	414.95	415.35	**408.14**	424.21	435.71	5.0	4.9
1996	6.2	654.17	669.12	670.63	**639.95**	**740.74**	13.2	10.7
2000**	− 1.1	**1452.43**	**1420.60**	1454.60	**1430.83**	1320.28	− 9.1	− 7.1
Totals	26.5%						93.3%	92.0%
Average	2.0%						7.2%	7.1%

*Incumbents ousted ** Incumbent ousted & undecided election*

Down months are bold

APRIL

Monday before expiration Dow up 7 of last 8

MONDAY

12

> *Every age has a blind eye and sees nothing wrong in practices and institutions, which its successors view with just horror.*
> — Sir Richard Livingston (*On Education*)

TUESDAY

13

> *The only way to even begin to manage this new world is by focusing on…nation building—helping others restructure their economies and put in place decent non-corrupt government.*
> — Thomas L. Friedman (*New York Times*)

WEDNESDAY

14

> *To an imagination of any scope the most far-reaching form of power is not money, it is the command of ideas.*
> — Oliver Wendell Holmes Jr.
> (*The Mind and Faith of Justice Holmes,* edited by Max Lerner)

Income Tax Deadline

THURSDAY

 15

> *The common denominator: Something that matters! Something that counts! Something that defines! Something that is imbued with soul. And with life!*
> — Tom Peters (referring to projects, *Reinventing Work,* 1999)

Expiration day Dow up 7 of last 9

FRIDAY

 **16**

> *One of the more prolonged and extreme periods favoring large-cap stocks was 1994-1999. The tide turned in 2000. A cycle has begun of investors favoring small-cap stocks, which is likely to continue through the next several years.*
> — Jim Oberweis (*The Oberweis Report,* February 2001)

SATURDAY

17

SUNDAY

18

DOWN JANUARYS: A REMARKABLE RECORD

In the first third of the 20th century there was no correlation between January markets and the year as a whole (page 24). Then in 1972 we discovered that the 1933 "Lame Duck" Amendment to the Constitution changed the political calendar and the January Barometer was born. And its record has been magnificent. But to those who would like bull and bear markets to begin on January First and end on the last day of December, sorry, we can't oblige. Critics look at the record of down Januarys and see a mixed bag. We look at it and always see the "pony."

Down Januarys are harbingers of trouble ahead, in the economic, political, or military arenas. Eisenhower's heart attack in 1955 cast doubt on whether he could run in 1956, a flat year. Two other election years were also flat. Eleven bear markets began with poor Januarys and four of them continued into second years. 1968 started down as we were mired in Vietnam, but Johnson's "bombing halt" changed the climate. Affected by uncertainty regarding pending military action in Iraq, January 2003 closed down and the market apparently triple-bottomed in March just before US-led forces began their blitz to Baghdad. With three years of the bear behind us and a pre-election year on hand, 2003 should finish on the upside.

Excluding 1956, down Januarys were followed by substantial declines averaging minus 13.0%, providing excellent buying opportunities later in most years.

DOWN JANUARY S&P CLOSES TO LOW AND NEXT 11 MONTHS

Year	January Close	% Change	11-Month Low	Date of Low	Jan Close to low %	% Feb to Dec	Year % Change	
1953	26.38	− 0.7	22.71	14-Sep	− 13.9%	− 6.0%	− 6.6	bear
1956	43.82	− 3.6	44.10	28-May	0.9	6.5	2.6	FLAT
1957	44.72	− 4.2	38.98	22-Oct	− 12.8	− 10.6	− 14.3	bear
1960	55.61	− 7.1	52.30	25-Oct	− 6.0	4.5	− 3.0	bear
1962	68.84	− 3.8	52.32	26-Jun	− 24.0	− 8.3	− 11.8	bear
1968	92.24	− 4.4	87.72	5-Mar	− 4.9	12.6	7.7	Cont. bear
1969	103.01	− 0.8	89.20	17-Dec	− 13.4	− 10.6	− 11.4	bear
1970	85.02	− 7.6	69.20	26-May	− 18.6	8.4	0.1	Cont. bear
1973	116.03	− 1.7	92.16	5-Dec	− 20.6	− 15.9	− 17.4	bear
1974	96.57	− 1.0	62.28	3-Oct	− 35.5	− 29.0	− 29.7	bear
1977	102.03	− 5.1	90.71	2-Nov	− 11.1	− 6.8	− 11.5	bear
1978	89.25	− 6.2	86.90	6-Mar	− 2.6	7.7	1.1	Cont. bear
1981	129.55	− 4.6	112.77	25-Sep	− 13.0	− 5.4	− 9.7	bear
1982	120.40	− 1.8	102.42	12-Aug	− 14.9	16.8	14.8	Cont. bear
1984	163.42	− 0.9	147.82	24-Jul	− 9.5	2.3	1.4	FLAT
1990	329.07	− 6.9	295.46	11-Oct	− 10.2	0.4	− 6.6	bear
1992	408.79	− 2.0	394.50	8-Apr	− 3.5	6.6	4.5	FLAT
2000	1394.46	− 5.1	1264.74	20-Dec	− 9.3	− 5.3	− 10.1	bear
2002	1130.20	− 1.6	776.76	9-Oct	− 31.3	− 22.2	− 23.4	Cont. bear
2003	855.70	− 2.7	800.73	11-Mar	− 6.4	*At Press-time*		
Totals					**− 260.6%**	**− 54.3%**	**− 123.4%**	
Average					**− 13.0%**	**− 2.9%**	**− 6.5%**	

APRIL

MONDAY

19

Life is like riding a bicycle.
You don't fall off unless you stop pedaling.
— Claude D. Pepper

TUESDAY

20

We are handicapped by policies based
on old myths rather than current realities.
— James William Fulbright
(1905-1995, US Senator 1944-1974)

WEDNESDAY

21

Every great advance in natural knowledge has
involved the absolute rejection of authority.
— Thomas H. Huxley (British scientist and humanist,
defender of Darwinism, 1825-1895)

THURSDAY
22

The difference between life and the movies is
that a script has to make sense, and life doesn't.
— Joseph L. Mankiewicz (Film director,
writer, producer, 1909-1993)

FRIDAY
23

Innovation can't depend on trying to please
the customer or the client. It is an elitist act
by the inventor who acts alone and breaks rules.
— Dean Kamen (Inventor, president of DEKA R&D,
Business Week, February 12, 2001)

SATURDAY

24

SUNDAY
25

MAY ALMANAC

MAY							JUNE					
S	M	T	W	T	F	S	S	M	T	W	T	F	S

MAY
S M T W T F S
                1
2 3 4 5 6 7 8
9 10 11 12 13 14 15
16 17 18 19 20 21 22
23 24 25 26 27 28 29
30 31

JUNE
S M T W T F S
      1 2 3 4 5
6 7 8 9 10 11 12
13 14 15 16 17 18 19
20 21 22 23 24 25 26
27 28 29 30

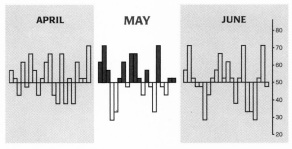

Market Probability Chart above is a graphic representation of the Market Probability Calendar on page 123.

◆ "May/June disaster area" between 1964 and 1984 with 15 out of 20 down Mays ◆ Between 1985 and 1997 May was the best month, gaining 3.3% per year on average ◆ Recent record four of last six Mays down after 13 straight gains in S&P ◆ Still sports a 2.0% average in last 15 years ◆ Worst six months of the year begin with May (page 50) ◆ A $10,000 investment compounded to $471,774 for November-April in 53 years compared to $1,625 loss for May-October ◆ Memorial Day week record: up 12 years in a row (1984-1995), down five of the last eight years; up 240 Dow points in 1999, 495 points in 2000 and 249 in 2003 ◆ Election Year Mays rank near the bottom, net down on NASDAQ, up fractionally on S&P

MAY DAILY POINT CHANGES DOW JONES INDUSTRIALS

Previous Month	1994	1995	1996	1997	1998	1999	2000	2001	2002	2003
Close	3681.69	4321.27	5569.08	7008.99	9063.37	10789.04	10733.91	10734.97	9946.22	8480.09
1	—	– 5.19	6.14	– 32.51	83.70	—	77.87	163.37	113.41	– 25.84
2	19.33	12.80	– 76.95	94.72	—	—	– 80.66	– 21.66	32.24	128.43
3	13.39	44.27	– 20.24	—	—	225.65	– 250.99	– 80.03	– 85.24	—
4	– 16.66	– 13.49	—	—	45.59	– 128.58	– 67.64	154.59	—	—
5	– 1.78	– 16.26	—	143.29	– 45.09	69.30	165.37	—	—	– 51.11
6	– 26.47	—	– 13.72	10.83	– 92.92	– 8.59	—	—	– 198.59	56.79
7	—	—	– 43.36	– 139.67	– 77.97	84.77	—	16.07	28.51	– 27.73
8	– 40.46	40.47	53.11	50.97	78.47	—	25.77	– 51.66	305.28	– 69.41
9	– 40.46	6.91	1.08	32.91	—	—	– 66.88	– 16.53	– 104.41	113.38
10	27.37	13.84	43.00	—	—	– 24.34	– 168.97	43.46	97.50	—
11	– 27.37	6.57	—	—	36.37	18.90	178.19	– 89.13	—	—
12	23.80	19.37	—	123.22	70.25	– 25.78	63.40	—	—	122.13
13	6.84	—	64.46	– 18.54	50.07	106.82	—	—	169.74	– 47.48
14	—	—	42.11	11.95	– 39.61	– 193.87	—	56.02	188.48	– 31.43
15	—	6.91	0.73	47.39	– 76.23	—	198.41	– 4.36	– 54.46	65.32
16	11.82	– 2.42	9.61	– 138.88	—	—	126.79	342.95	45.53	– 34.17
17	49.11	– 12.45	52.45	—	—	– 59.85	– 164.83	32.66	63.87	—
18	12.28	– 81.96	—	—	– 45.09	– 16.52	7.54	53.16	—	—
19	26.09	0.69	—	34.21	3.74	50.44	– 150.43	—	—	– 185.58
20	7.37	—	61.32	74.58	116.83	– 20.65	—	—	– 123.58	– 2.03
21	—	—	– 12.56	– 12.77	– 39.11	– 37.46	—	36.18	– 123.79	25.07
22	—	54.30	41.74	– 32.56	– 17.93	—	– 84.30	– 80.68	52.17	77.59
23	– 23.94	40.81	– 15.88	87.78	—	—	– 120.28	– 151.73	58.20	7.36
24	2.76	1.72	0.74	—	—	– 174.61	113.08	16.91	– 111.82	—
25	10.13	– 25.93	—	—	H	– 123.58	– 211.43	– 117.05	—	—
26	– 1.84	– 43.23	—	H	– 150.71	171.07	– 24.68	—	—	H
27	3.68	—	H	37.50	– 27.16	– 235.23	—	—	H	179.97
28	—	—	– 53.19	26.18	33.63	92.81	—	H	– 122.68	11.77
29	—	H	– 35.84	27.05	– 70.25	—	H	33.77	– 58.54	– 81.94
30	H	9.68	19.58	0.86	—	—	227.89	– 166.50	– 11.35	139.08
31	1.23	86.46	– 50.23	—	—	H	– 4.80	39.30	13.56	—
Close	3758.37	4465.14	5643.18	7331.04	8899.95	10559.74	10522.33	10911.94	9925.25	8850.26
Change	76.68	143.87	74.10	322.05	– 163.42	– 229.30	– 211.58	176.97	– 20.97	370.17

Was Number One month for nine straight years
But four of the last six have caused May tears

MONDAY

26

There is nothing as invigorating as the ego boost that comes from having others sign on when your company is just a dream. What they are saying when they agree to service customers, suppliers, employers or distributors is that they believe in you.
— Joshua Hyatt (*Inc. Magazine, Mapping the Entrepreneurial Mind,* August 1991)

TUESDAY

 27

You have powers you never dreamed of. You can do things you never thought you could do. There are no limitations in what you can do except the limitations in your own mind.
— Darwin P. Kingsley (President New York Life, 1857-1932)

WEDNESDAY

28

We are like tenant farmers chopping down the fence around our house for fuel when we should be using Nature's inexhaustible sources of energy—sun, wind and tide. I'd put my money on the sun and solar energy. What a source of power! I hope we don't have to wait until oil and coal run out before we tackle that.
— Thomas Alva Edison (1847-1931)

THURSDAY

29

Awareness of competition and ability to react to it is a fundamental competence every business must have if it is to be long lived.
— Paul Allen (Microsoft founder)

End of "Best Six Months" of the year (page 50) ### FRIDAY

 30

If you are not willing to study, if you are not sufficiently interested to investigate and analyze the stock market yourself, then I beg of you to become an outright long-pull investor, to buy good stocks, and hold on to them; for otherwise your chances of success as a trader will be nil.
— Humphrey B. Neill (*Tape Reading and Market Tactics,* 1931)

SATURDAY

1

Bearish May Sector Seasonalities: Forest/Paper (page 118) ### SUNDAY

2

TOP PERFORMING MONTHS PAST 53½ YEARS
STANDARD & POOR'S 500 & DOW JONES INDUSTRIALS

Monthly performance of the S&P and the Dow are ranked over the past 53½ years. NASDAQ monthly performance is shown on page 54.

January, April, November and December still hold the top four positions in both the Dow and S&P. This led to our discovery in 1986 of the market's best-kept secret. You can divide the year into two sections and have practically all the gains in one six-month section and very little in the other. September has been the worst month on both lists. (See "Best Six Months" on page 50.)

MONTHLY % CHANGES (JANUARY 1950 – JUNE 2003)

Standard & Poor's 500

Month	Total % Change	Avg.% Change	# Up	# Down
Jan	78.3%	1.4%	34	20
Feb	– 4.1	– 0.1	28	26
Mar	58.9	1.1	36	18
Apr	75.5	1.4	37	17
May	13.0	0.2	30	24
Jun	11.7	0.2	29	25
Jul	47.5	0.9	28	25
Aug	– 1.0	– 0.02	28	25
Sep*	– 38.0	– 0.7	21	31
Oct	43.9	0.8	31	22
Nov	90.8	1.7	35	18
Dec	87.4	1.6	40	13

% Rank				
Nov	90.8%	1.7%	35	18
Dec	87.4	1.6	40	13
Jan	78.3	1.4	34	20
Apr	75.5	1.4	37	17
Mar	58.9	1.1	36	18
Jul	47.5	0.9	28	25
Oct	43.9	0.8	31	22
May	13.0	0.2	30	24
Jun	11.7	0.2	29	25
Aug	– 1.0	– 0.02	28	25
Feb	– 4.1	– 0.1	28	26
Sep*	– 38.0	– 0.7	21	31
Total	**463.9%**	**8.5%**		
Average		**0.71%**		

*No change 1979

Dow Jones Industrials

Month	Total % Change	Avg. % Change	# Up	# Down
Jan	77.2%	1.4%	36	18
Feb	7.8	0.1	30	24
Mar	54.8	1.0	35	19
Apr	103.4	1.9	34	20
May	3.2	0.1	28	26
Jun	– 5.9	– 0.1	27	27
Jul	56.0	1.1	32	21
Aug	– 5.0	– 0.1	29	24
Sep	– 56.0	– 1.1	19	34
Oct	26.3	0.5	31	22
Nov	87.9	1.7	36	17
Dec	88.6	1.7	38	15

% Rank				
Apr	103.4%	1.9%	34	20
Dec	88.6	1.7	38	15
Nov	87.9	1.7	36	17
Jan	77.2	1.4	36	18
Jul	56.0	1.1	32	21
Mar	54.8	1.0	35	19
Oct	26.3	0.5	31	22
Feb	7.8	0.1	30	24
May	3.2	0.1	28	26
Aug	– 5.0	– 0.1	29	24
Jun	– 5.9	– 0.1	27	27
Sep	– 56.0	– 1.1	19	34
Total	**438.3%**	**8.2%**		
Average		**0.68%**		

The greatest bull cycle in history has altered the normal seasonality. Here is how the months ranked over the past 15 years (180 months) using total percentage gains on the Dow: April 39.5%, November 35.0%, May 30.9%, October 30.1%, December 27.3%, July 20.2%, January 18.9%, March 17.1%, February 6.0%, June –10.1%, September –24.8%, August –29.0%.

During the last 15 years, notice how May and October have edged out December while July jumped ahead of January and March. The October 1987 crash month that was down 23.2% is no longer in the most recent 15 years. Big losses in the period were August 1990 (Kuwait), off 10.0%; August 1998 (SE Asia crisis), off 15.1%; September 2001 (9/11 attack), off 11.1%; September 2002 (Iraq war drums), off 12.4%.

MAY

May first trading day Dow up 5 of last 6

MONDAY

3

*One determined person can make a
significant difference;
a small group of determined people
can change the course of history.*
— Sonia Johnson (Author, lecturer)

FOMC Meeting

TUESDAY

4

Genius is the ability to put into effect what is in your mind.
— F. Scott Fitzgerald (Author, 1896-1940)

*Average May gains last 33 years
NAS 0.9% Dow 0.5% S&P 0.8%*

WEDNESDAY

5

*The years teach much
which the days never know.*
— Ralph Waldo Emerson

THURSDAY

6

*To know values is to know
the meaning of the market.*
— Charles Dow

Day before Mother's Day Dow up 7 of last 9

FRIDAY

7

*I keep hearing "Should I buy? Should I buy?"
When I start hearing "Should I sell?" that's the bottom.*
— Nick Moore (Portfolio manager, Jurika & Voyles,
TheStreet.com March 12, 2001)

SATURDAY

8

Mother's Day

SUNDAY

9

OUR "BEST SIX MONTHS" DISCOVERY (IN 1986) CONTINUES TO RACK UP PHENOMENAL GAINS

Since 1950 an excellent strategy has been to invest in the market between November 1st and April 30th each year and then switch into fixed income securities for the other six months. A glance at the chart on page 138 shows that November, December, January, March and April have been outstanding months since 1950. Add February, and voilà, an eye-opening strategy! These six consecutive months gained 10175.23 Dow points in 53 years, while the remaining May through October months *lost* 1909.47 points. The S&P gained 970.55 points in the same best six months and lost 71.70 points in the worst six.

Percentage changes for the Dow during each six-month period since 1950 are shown along with a compounding $10,000 investment.

The November-April $461,774 gain overshadows the May-October $1,625 loss. (S&P results were $330,764 to $4,923.) Just two November-April losses were double-digit and were due to our April 1970 Cambodian invasion and the fall 1973 OPEC oil embargo.

When we discovered this strategy in 1986, November-April outperformed May-October by $88,163 to minus $1,522. Results improved substantially these past 17 years, $373,611 to minus $103.

As sensational as these results are, they are nearly tripled with a simple timing indicator; see page 52.

SIX-MONTH SWITCHING STRATEGY

	DJIA % Change May 1-Oct 31	Investing $10,000	DJIA % Change Nov 1-Apr 30	Investing $10,000
1950	5.0%	$10,500	15.2%	$11,520
1951	1.2	10,626	− 1.8	11,313
1952	4.5	11,104	2.1	11,551
1953	0.4	11,148	15.8	13,376
1954	10.3	12,296	20.9	16,172
1955	6.9	13,144	13.5	18,355
1956	− 7.0	12,224	3.0	18,906
1957	− 10.8	10,904	3.4	19,549
1958	19.2	12,998	14.8	22,442
1959	3.7	13,479	− 6.9	20,894
1960	− 3.5	13,007	16.9	24,425
1961	3.7	13,488	− 5.5	23,082
1962	− 11.4	11,950	21.7	28,091
1963	5.2	12,571	7.4	30,170
1964	7.7	13,539	5.6	31,860
1965	4.2	14,108	− 2.8	30,968
1966	− 13.6	12,189	11.1	34,405
1967	− 1.9	11,957	3.7	35,678
1968	4.4	12,483	− 0.2	35,607
1969	− 9.9	11,247	− 14.0	30,622
1970	2.7	11,551	24.6	38,155
1971	− 10.9	10,292	13.7	43,382
1972	0.1	10,302	− 3.6	41,820
1973	3.8	10,693	− 12.5	36,593
1974	− 20.5	8,501	23.4	45,156
1975	1.8	8,654	19.2	53,826
1976	− 3.2	8,377	− 3.9	51,727
1977	− 11.7	7,397	2.3	52,917
1978	− 5.4	6,998	7.9	57,097
1979	− 4.6	6,676	0.2	57,211
1980	13.1	7,551	7.9	61,731
1981	− 14.6	6,449	− 0.5	61,422
1982	16.9	7,539	23.6	75,918
1983	− 0.1	7,531	− 4.4	72,578
1984	3.1	7,764	4.2	75,626
1985	9.2	8,478	29.8	98,163
1986	5.3	8,927	21.8	119,563
1987	− 12.8	7,784	1.9	121,835
1988	5.7	8,228	12.6	137,186
1989	9.4	9,001	0.4	137,735
1990	− 8.1	8,272	18.2	162,803
1991	6.3	8,793	9.4	178,106
1992	− 4.0	8,441	6.2	189,149
1993	7.4	9,066	0.03	189,206
1994	6.2	9,628	10.6	209,262
1995	10.0	10,591	17.1	245,046
1996	8.3	11,470	16.2	284,743
1997	6.2	12,181	21.8	346,817
1998	− 5.2	11,548	25.6	435,602
1999	− 0.5	11,490	0.04	435,776
2000	2.2	11,743	− 2.2	426,189
2001	− 15.5	9,923	9.6	467,103
2002	− 15.6	8,375	1.0	471,774
53-Year Gain (Loss)		**($1,625)**		**$461,774**

50

MAY

MONDAY

10

If you can ever buy with a P/E equivalent to growth,
that's a good starting point.
— Alan Lowenstein (Co-portfolio manager,
John Hancock Technology Fund, *TheStreet.com*, Mach. 12, 2001)

TUESDAY

 11

What technology does is make people
more productive. It doesn't replace them.
— Michael Bloomberg

WEDNESDAY

12

Corporate guidance has become something of an art. The CFO
has refined and perfected his, gracefully leading on the bulls
with the calculating grace and cunning of a great matador.
— Joe Kalinowski (I/B/E/S)

THURSDAY

 13

If a man has no talents, he is unhappy enough;
but if he has, envy pursues him in proportion to his ability.
— Leopold Mozart (To his son Wolfgang Amadeus, 1768)

FRIDAY

 14

Industrial capitalism has generated the greatest
productive power in human history. To date, no
other socioeconomic system has been able to
generate comparable productive power.
— Peter L. Berger (*The Capitalist Revolution*)

SATURDAY

15

SUNDAY

16

"BEST SIX MONTHS" RECORD SKYROCKETS WITH A SIMPLE MARKET-TIMING INDICATOR

Three years ago *Street Smart Report* writer Sy Harding, in his book *Riding The Bear*, took our November-through-April strategy (page 50), enhanced it, and termed it the "best mechanical system ever."

He simply used the MACD (Moving Average Convergence Divergence) indicator developed by our friend Gerald Appel to enter the Best Six Months period up to a month earlier, if the market was in an uptrend. Conversely, Harding would exit up to a month later as long as the market kept moving up. But, if the market was trending down, you could delay a month getting in and even exit a month earlier. Thus, our "Best Six Months" could be lengthened or shortened a month or so.

The results are astounding applying the simple MACD signals. Instead of $10,000 gaining $461,774 over the 53 recent years when invested only during the best six months (page 50), the gain nearly tripled to $1,308,314. Ironically, the $1,625 loss during the worst six months deepened dramatically and that $10,000 investment lost $7,077 for the 53 years.

Impressive results for being invested during only 6½ months of the year on average! For the rest of the year you could park in a money market fund, or if a long-term holder, you could write options on your stocks (sell call options).

Updated signals are emailed to our monthly newsletter subscribers as soon as they are triggered. For further information on how the MACD indicator is calculated, the dates when signals were given or for a FREE newsletter sample, please email your name and address to *service@hirschorg.com*, call 201-767-4100 or visit our website *www.stocktradersalmanac.com*.

Correction: Previous editions had the spring 1958 sell incorrect. It has been corrected, improving the results a few percent.

SIX-MONTH SWITCHING STRATEGY+TIMING

	DJIA % Change May 1-Oct 31*	Investing $10,000	DJIA % Change Nov 1-Apr 30*	Investing $10,000
1950	7.3%	$10,730	13.3%	$11,330
1951	0.1	10,741	1.9	11,545
1952	1.4	10,891	2.1	11,787
1953	0.2	10,913	17.1	13,803
1954	13.5	12,386	16.3	16,053
1955	7.7	13,340	13.1	18,156
1956	– 6.8	12,433	2.8	18,664
1957	– 12.3	10,904	4.9	19,579
1958	17.3	12,790	16.7	22,849
1959	1.6	12,995	– 3.1	22,141
1960	– 4.9	12,358	16.9	25,883
1961	2.9	12,716	– 1.5	25,495
1962	– 15.3	10,770	22.4	31,206
1963	4.3	11,233	9.6	34,202
1964	6.7	11,986	6.2	36,323
1965	2.6	12,298	– 2.5	35,415
1966	– 16.4	10,281	14.3	40,479
1967	– 2.1	10,065	5.5	42,705
1968	3.4	10,407	0.2	42,790
1969	– 11.9	9,169	– 6.7	39,923
1970	– 1.4	9,041	20.8	48,227
1971	– 11.0	8,046	15.4	55,654
1972	– 0.6	7,998	– 1.4	54,875
1973	– 11.0	7,118	0.1	54,930
1974	– 22.4	5,524	28.2	70,420
1975	0.1	5,530	18.5	83,448
1976	– 3.4	5,342	– 3.0	80,945
1977	– 11.4	4,733	0.5	81,350
1978	– 4.5	4,520	9.3	88,916
1979	– 5.3	4,280	7.0	95,140
1980	9.3	4,678	4.7	99,612
1981	– 14.6	3,995	0.4	100,010
1982	15.5	4,614	23.5	123,512
1983	2.5	4,729	– 7.3	114,496
1984	3.3	4,885	3.9	118,961
1985	7.0	5,227	38.1	164,285
1986	– 2.8	5,081	28.2	210,613
1987	– 14.9	4,324	3.0	216,931
1988	6.1	4,588	11.8	242,529
1989	9.8	5,038	3.3	250,532
1990	– 6.7	4,700	15.8	290,116
1991	4.8	4,926	11.3	322,899
1992	– 6.2	4,621	6.6	344,210
1993	5.5	4,875	5.6	363,486
1994	3.7	5,055	13.1	411,103
1995	7.2	5,419	16.7	479,757
1996	9.2	5,918	21.9	584,824
1997	3.6	6,131	18.5	693,016
1998	– 12.4	5,371	39.9	969,529
1999	– 6.4	5,027	5.1	1,018,975
2000	– 6.0	4,725	5.4	1,074,000
2001	– 17.3	3,908	15.8	1,243,692
2002	– 25.2	2,923	6.0	1,318,314
53-Year Gain (Loss)	**(7,077)**		**$1,308,314**	

*MACD generated entry and exit points (earlier or later) can lengthen or shorten six-month periods

MAY

Monday before expiration Dow up 15 of last 16

Of the S&P 500 companies in 1957, only 74 were still on the list in 1998 and only 12 outperformed the index itself over that period. By 2020, more than 375 companies in the S&P 500 will consist of companies we don't know today.
— Richard Foster and Sarah Kaplan (*Creative Destruction*)

Buy when you are scared to death; sell when you are tickled to death.
— Market Maxim (*The Cabot Market Letter*, April 12, 2001)

A leader has the ability to create infectious enthusiasm.
— Ted Turner (Billionaire, *New Yorker Magazine*, April 23, 2001)

The average man desires to be told specifically which particular stock to buy or sell. He wants to get something for nothing. He does not wish to work.
— William Lefevre (*Reminiscences of a Stock Operator*)

Expiration Day Dow down 5 of last 7

The most dangerous thing that takes place [in companies] is that success breeds arrogance, and arrogance seems to make people stop listening to their customers and to their employees. And that is the beginning of the end. The challenge is not to be a great company; the challenge is to remain a great company.
— George Fisher (Motorola)

TOP PERFORMING NASDAQ MONTHS PAST 32½ YEARS

Prior to the recent 77.9% drop, the worst bear market in its history, NASDAQ stocks ran away during four consecutive months, November, December, January and February, with an average gain of 11.1%. This was equal to a compounded annual rate of 37.2%. These months were also the best months to own high-tech stocks. Then came the slaughter of November 2000, down 22.9%; the massacre of February 2001, down 22.4%; December 2001, up only 1.0%; January 2002, – 0.8%; February 2002, –10.5%; and December 2002, –9.7%.

You can see the months graphically on page 139. January by itself is awesome, up 4.0% on average. What appears as a Death Valley abyss occurs during NASDAQ's bleakest four months: July, August, September and October.

MONTHLY CHANGES (JANUARY 1971 – JUNE 2003)

NASDAQ Composite*					Dow Jones Industrials				
Month	Total % Change	Avg.% Change	# Up	# Down	Month	Total % Change	Avg. % Change	# Up	# Down
Jan	130.8%	4.0%	23	10	Jan	67.3%	2.0%	22	11
Feb	23.4	0.7	19	14	Feb	13.4	0.4	18	15
Mar	13.6	0.4	21	12	Mar	33.7	1.0	22	11
Apr	44.5	1.3	22	11	Apr	72.4	2.2	19	14
May	31.3	0.9	19	14	May	16.7	0.5	18	15
Jun	40.7	1.2	21	12	Jun	11.2	0.3	19	14
Jul	– 14.1	– 0.4	15	17	Jul	12.6	0.4	16	16
Aug	5.7	0.2	17	15	Aug	– 7.6	– 0.2	17	15
Sep	– 36.6	– 1.1	17	15	Sep	– 52.1	– 1.6	9	23
Oct	7.6	0.2	16	16	Oct	15.1	0.5	19	13
Nov	62.3	1.9	21	11	Nov	43.8	1.4	22	10
Dec	65.9	2.1	19	13	Dec	52.2	1.6	23	9
% Rank			% Rank		% Rank			% Rank	
Jan	130.8%	4.0%	23	10	Apr	72.4%	2.2%	19	14
Dec	65.9	2.1	19	13	Jan	67.3	2.0	22	11
Nov	62.3	1.9	21	11	Dec	52.2	1.6	23	9
Apr	44.5	1.3	22	11	Nov	43.8	1.4	22	10
Jun	40.7	1.2	21	12	Mar	33.7	1.0	22	11
May	31.3	0.9	19	14	May	16.7	0.5	18	15
Feb	23.4	0.7	19	14	Oct	15.1	0.5	19	13
Mar	13.6	0.4	21	12	Feb	13.4	0.4	18	15
Oct	7.6	0.2	16	16	Jul	12.6	0.4	16	16
Aug	5.7	0.2	17	15	Jun	11.2	0.3	19	14
Jul	– 14.1	– 0.4	15	17	Aug	– 7.6	– 0.2	17	15
Sep	– 36.6	– 1.1	17	15	Sep	– 52.1	– 1.6	9	23
Totals	375.1%	11.4%			Totals	278.7%	8.5%		
Average		0.95%			Average		0.71%		

For comparison, Dow figures are shown. During the period NASDAQ averaged a 0.95% gain per month, nearly 34 percent more than the Dow's 0.71% per month. Between January 1971 and January 1982, NASDAQ's composite index doubled in the twelve years, while the Dow stayed flat. NASDAQ's Best 8 Months seasonal strategy using MACD timing is displayed on page 58.

*Based on NASDAQ composite, prior to February 5, 1971, based on National Quotation Bureau indices

MAY

MONDAY

24

*People who can take a risk, who believe in
themselves enough to walk away [from a company],
are generally people who bring about change.*
— Cynthia Danaher (Exiting GM of Hewlett-Packard's
Medical Products Group, *Newsweek*)

TUESDAY
25

*Around the world, red tape is being cut. Whether it's
telecom in Europe, water in South America, or power in
Illinois, governments are stepping back, and competition
is thriving where regulated monopolies once dominated.*
— (*Fortune,* December 20, 1999)

WEDNESDAY
26

*By the law of nature the father continues master of his child
no longer than the child stands in need of his assistance;
after that term they become equal, and then the son, entirely
independent of the father, owes him no obedience, but only respect.*
— Jean-Jacques Rousseau (*The Social Contract*)

THURSDAY
27

*When someone told me "We're going with you guys
because no one ever got fired for buying Cisco (products)."
That's what they used to say in IBM's golden age.*
— Mark Dickey (Formerly of Cisco, now at Smart Pipes, *Fortune*)

Friday before Memorial Day Dow down 6 of last 12 ## FRIDAY
28

*In the stock market those who expect history
to repeat itself exactly are doomed to failure.*
— Yale Hirsch

SATURDAY
29

Bearish June Sector Seasonalities: Natural Gas (page 118) ## SUNDAY
30

JUNE ALMANAC

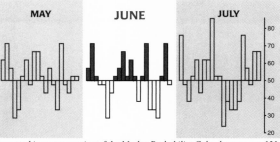

JUNE						
S	M	T	W	T	F	S
		1	2	3	4	5
6	7	8	9	10	11	12
13	14	15	16	17	18	19
20	21	22	23	24	25	26
27	28	29	30			

JULY						
S	M	T	W	T	F	S
				1	2	3
4	5	6	7	8	9	10
11	12	13	14	15	16	17
18	19	20	21	22	23	24
25	26	27	28	29	30	31

Market Probability Chart above is a graphic representation of the Market Probability Calendar on page 123.

◆ The "summer rally" in most years is the weakest rally of all four seasons (page 70) ◆ Week after June triple-witching day in last 13 years was up in 1995 and 1998 and down all other eleven times (page 76) ◆ RECORD: S&P up 29, down 24; Dow 27/26; NAS 21/12 ◆ Average gain a mere 0.2% on the S&P, –0.1% on the Dow but a surprisingly strong 1.2% for NASDAQ ◆ June ranks near the bottom on the Dow along with August and September since 1950 (see page 48) ◆ Watch out for end-of-quarter "portfolio pumping" on last day of June, Dow down 9 of last 12, S&P down 8 of last 12, but surprise NASDAQ up 11 of last 12 ◆ Election Year Junes average +2.9%, up 5, down 3

JUNE DAILY POINT CHANGES DOW JONES INDUSTRIALS

Previous Month	1994	1995	1996	1997	1998	1999	2000	2001	2002	2003
Close	3758.37	4465.14	5643.18	7331.04	8899.95	10559.74	10522.33	10911.94	9925.25	8850.26
1	2.46	7.61	—	—	22.42	36.52	129.87	78.47	—	—
2	– 1.84	– 28.36	—	– 41.64	– 31.13	– 18.37	142.56	—	—	47.55
3	13.23	—	– 18.47	22.75	– 87.44	85.80	—	—	– 215.46	25.14
4	—	—	41.00	– 42.49	66.76	136.15	—	71.11	– 21.95	116.03
5	—	32.16	31.77	35.63	167.15	—	20.54	114.32	108.96	2.32
6	– 3.70	8.65	– 30.29	130.49	—	—	– 79.73	– 105.60	– 172.16	21.49
7	– 12.61	– 23.17	29.92	—	—	109.54	77.29	20.50	– 34.97	—
8	– 6.46	– 3.46	—	—	31.89	– 143.74	– 144.14	– 113.74	—	—
9	3.69	– 34.58	—	42.72	– 19.68	– 75.35	– 54.66	—	—	– 82.79
10	20.31	—	– 9.24	60.77	– 78.22	69.02	—	—	55.73	74.89
11	—	—	– 19.21	36.56	– 159.93	– 130.76	—	– 54.91	– 128.14	128.33
12	—	22.47	– 0.37	135.64	23.17	—	– 49.85	26.29	100.45	13.33
13	9.67	38.05	– 10.34	70.57	—	72.82	57.63	– 76.76	– 114.91	– 79.43
14	31.71	6.57	– 8.50	—	—	72.82	66.11	– 181.49	– 28.59	—
15	– 24.42	5.19	—	—	– 207.01	31.66	26.87	– 66.49	—	—
16	20.93	14.52	—	– 9.95	37.36	189.96	– 265.52	—	—	201.84
17	– 34.56	—	3.33	– 11.31	164.17	56.68	—	—	213.21	4.06
18	—	—	– 24.75	– 42.07	– 16.45	13.93	—	21.74	18.70	– 29.22
19	—	42.89	20.32	58.35	– 100.14	—	108.54	– 48.71	– 144.55	– 114.27
20	– 34.88	– 3.12	11.08	19.45	—	—	– 122.68	50.66	– 129.80	21.22
21	– 33.93	– 3.46	45.80	—	—	– 39.58	62.58	68.10	– 177.98	—
22	16.80	42.54	—	—	– 1.74	– 94.35	– 121.62	– 110.84	—	—
23	– 25.68	– 3.80	—	– 192.25	117.33	– 54.77	28.63	—	—	– 127.80
24	– 62.15	—	12.56	153.80	95.41	– 132.03	—	—	28.03	36.90
25	—	—	1.48	– 68.08	11.71	17.73	—	– 100.37	– 155.00	– 98.32
26	—	– 34.59	– 36.57	– 35.73	8.96	—	138.24	– 31.74	– 6.71	67.51
27	48.56	– 8.64	– 5.17	33.47	—	—	– 38.53	– 37.64	149.81	– 89.99
28	– 15.86	14.18	– 22.90	—	—	102.59	23.33	131.37	– 26.66	—
29	– 2.59	– 6.23	—	—	52.82	160.20	– 129.75	– 63.81	—	—
30	– 42.09	5.54	—	– 14.93	– 45.34	155.45	49.85	—	—	– 3.61
Close	3624.96	4556.10	5654.63	7672.79	8952.02	10970.80	10447.89	10502.40	9243.26	8985.44
Change	–133.41	90.96	11.45	341.75	52.07	411.06	– 74.44	– 409.54	– 681.99	135.18

Last Day of June not hot for the Dow
But for stocks on NASDAQ, WOW!

MONDAY

31

Memorial Day
(Market Closed)

*Resentment is like taking poison and
waiting for the other person to die.*
— Malachy McCourt
(*A Monk Swimming: A Memoir*)

June first trading day Dow up 9 of last 12

TUESDAY

1

*If we hire people bigger than ourselves,
we will become a company of giants—
smaller than ourselves, a company of midgets.*
— David Oglivy (*Forbes ASAP*)

---

*Average June gains last 33 years
NAS 1.2% Dow 0.3% S&P 0.8%*

WEDNESDAY

2

*The single best predictor of overall excellence is a company's
ability to attract, motivate, and retain talented people.*
— Bruce Pfau (*Fortune*)

---

*Start looking for NASDAQ MACD seasonal SELL Signal (page 58)
Almanac Investor subscribers will be emailed
Visit stocktradersalmanac.com for details*

THURSDAY

3

*Show me a good phone receptionist
and I'll show you a good company.*
— Harvey Mackay (*Pushing the Envelope*, 1999)

FRIDAY

4

*It's not the strongest of the species [think
"traders"] that survive, nor the most intelligent,
but the one most responsive to change.*
— Charles Darwin

SATURDAY

5

SUNDAY

6

NASDAQ'S "BEST EIGHT MONTHS" SHOOT THE MOON WITH A SIMPLE MACD TIMING INDICATOR

We never thought we could find a system that could top the "Best Six Months" with MACD timing (page 52) but we did. Look at NASDAQ's monthly performance (pages 54 and 139) and you'll see NASDAQ's amazing eight-month run from November through June. A $10,000 investment in these eight months since 1971 gained $292,016 versus a loss of $5,016 during the void that is the four-month period July-October.

Using the same MACD timing indicators on the NASDAQ as is done for the Dow (page 52) sends NASDAQ's results to the moon. Over the 32 years since NASDAQ began, the same $10,000 increases 60-fold to $606,247 and the loss during the four-month void increases to -$7,566. Only four sizeable losses occur during the favorable period and the bulk of NASDAQ's bear markets were avoided, including the worst of the 2000-2002 bear.

BEST EIGHT MONTHS STRATEGY + TIMING

MACD Signal Date	Worst 4 Months July 1-Oct 31* NASDAQ	% Change	Investing 10,000	MACD Signal Date	Best 8 Months Nov 1-June 30* NASDAQ	% Change	Investing 10,000
22-Jul-71	109.54	− 3.6%	9,640	4-Nov-71	105.56	24.1%	12,410
7-Jun-72	131.00	− 1.8	9,466	23-Oct-72	128.66	− 22.7	9,593
25-Jun-73	99.43	− 7.2	8,784	7-Dec-73	92.32	− 20.2	7,655
3-Jul-74	73.66	− 23.2	6,746	7-Oct-74	56.57	47.8	11,314
11-Jun-75	83.60	− 9.2	6,125	7-Oct-75	75.88	20.8	13,667
22-Jul-76	91.66	− 2.4	5,978	19-Oct-76	89.45	13.2	15,471
27-Jul-77	101.25	− 4.0	5,739	4-Nov-77	97.21	26.6	19,586
7-Jun-78	123.10	− 6.5	5,366	6-Nov-78	115.08	19.1	23,327
3-Jul-79	137.03	− 1.1	5,307	30-Oct-79	135.48	15.5	26,943
20-Jun-80	156.51	26.2	6,697	9-Oct-80	197.53	11.2	29,961
4-Jun-81	219.68	− 17.6	5,518	1-Oct-81	181.09	− 4.0	28,763
7-Jun-82	173.84	12.5	6,208	7-Oct-82	195.59	57.4	45,273
1-Jun-83	307.95	− 10.7	5,544	3-Nov-83	274.86	− 14.2	38,844
1-Jun-84	235.90	5.0	5,821	15-Oct-84	247.67	17.3	45,564
3-Jun-85	290.59	− 3.0	5,646	1-Oct-85	281.77	39.4	63,516
10-Jun-86	392.83	− 10.3	5,064	1-Oct-86	352.34	20.5	76,537
30-Jun-87	424.67	− 22.7	3,914	2-Nov-87	328.33	20.1	91,921
8-Jul-88	394.33	− 6.6	3,656	29-Nov-88	368.15	22.4	112,511
13-Jun-89	450.73	0.7	3,682	9-Nov-89	454.07	1.9	114,649
11-Jun-90	462.79	− 23.0	2,835	2-Oct-90	356.39	39.3	159,706
11-Jun-91	496.62	6.4	3,016	1-Oct-91	528.51	7.4	171,524
11-Jun-92	567.68	1.5	3,061	14-Oct-92	576.22	20.5	206,686
7-Jun-93	694.61	9.9	3,364	1-Oct-93	763.23	− 4.4	197,592
17-Jun-94	729.35	5.0	3,532	11-Oct-94	765.57	13.5	224,267
1-Jun-95	868.82	17.2	4,140	13-Oct-95	1018.38	21.6	272,709
3-Jun-96	1238.73	1.0	4,181	7-Oct-96	1250.87	10.3	300,798
4-Jun-97	1379.67	24.4	5,201	3-Oct-97	1715.87	1.8	306,212
1-Jun-98	1746.82	− 7.8	4,795	15-Oct-98	1611.01	49.7	458,399
1-Jun-99	2412.03	18.5	5,682	6-Oct-99	2857.21	35.7	622,047
29-Jun-00	3877.23	− 18.2	4,648	18-Oct-00	3171.56	− 32.2	421,748
1-Jun-01	2149.44	− 31.1	3,202	1-Oct-01	1480.46	5.5	444,944
3-Jun-02	1562.56	− 24.0	2,434	2-Oct-02	1187.30	38.5	616,247
20-Jun-03	1644.72						
	32-Year Loss	**($7,566)**			**32-Year Gain**	**$606,247**	

* MACD generated entry and exit points (earlier or later) can lengthen or shorten eight-month periods

JUNE

MONDAY

7

*There are no secrets to success. Don't waste your time looking
for them. Success is the result of perfection, hard work, learning
from failure, loyalty to those for whom you work, and persistence.*
— General Colin Powell

TUESDAY

8

*Investors operate with limited funds and limited intelligence,
they don't need to know everything. As long as they
understand something better than others, they have an edge.*
— George Soros (Quoted in *Beating the Dow*)

WEDNESDAY

9

*From very early on, I understood that you can touch a
piece of paper once…if you touch it twice, you're dead.
Therefore, paper only touches my hand once. After that, it's
either thrown away, acted on or given to somebody else.*
— Manuel Fernandez (Businessman, *Investor's Business Daily*)

THURSDAY

10

Fortune favors the brave.
— Virgil (Roman poet, *Aeneid*, 70-19 B.C.)

FRIDAY
11

*The thing always happens that you really believe in.
The belief in a thing makes it happen.*
— Frank Lloyd Wright (American architect)

SATURDAY
12

SUNDAY
13

DON'T-SELL-STOCKS-ON-MONDAY MANTRA MAY BE BACK

Mondays were on a dazzling eleven-year winning streak. From 1990 through 2000 Mondays gained 6067.37 Dow points, while all four other days gained a total of 1966.28 points. In 2001, 2002 and the first half of 2003, Mondays lost 1263.95 Dow points versus −533.85 on the other days. In past flat years and bear market cycles, Monday was the worst day of the week. See pages 66, 132-135.

ANNUAL DOW POINT CHANGES FOR DAYS OF THE WEEK SINCE 1953

Year	Monday	Tuesday	Wednesday	Thursday	Friday	Year's Closing DJIA	Year's Point Change
1953	— 37.39	— 6.70	19.63	7.25	6.21	280.90	— 11.00
1954	9.80	9.15	24.31	36.05	44.18	404.39	123.49
1955	— 56.09	34.31	45.83	0.78	59.18	488.40	84.01
1956	— 30.15	— 16.36	— 15.30	9.86	63.02	499.47	11.07
1957	—111.28	— 5.93	64.12	4.26	— 14.95	435.69	— 63.78
1958	14.36	26.73	29.10	24.25	53.52	583.65	147.96
1959	— 35.69	20.25	4.11	20.49	86.55	679.36	95.71
1960	—104.89	— 9.90	— 5.62	10.35	46.59	615.89	— 63.47
1961	— 17.66	4.29	87.51	— 5.74	46.85	731.14	115.25
1962	— 88.44	13.03	9.97	— 4.46	— 9.14	652.10	— 79.04
1963	— 43.61	81.85	16.23	26.07	30.31	762.95	110.85
1964	— 3.89	— 14.34	39.84	21.96	67.61	874.13	111.18
1965	— 70.23	36.65	57.03	2.75	68.93	969.26	95.13
1966	—126.73	— 54.24	56.13	— 45.69	13.04	785.69	— 183.57
1967	— 73.17	35.94	25.50	98.37	32.78	905.11	119.42
1968*	3.28	37.97	25.16	— 59.00	31.23	943.75	38.64
1969	—152.05	— 48.82	18.33	17.79	21.36	800.36	— 143.39
1970	— 99.00	— 47.14	116.07	1.81	66.82	838.92	38.56
1971	— 15.89	22.44	13.70	6.23	24.80	890.20	51.28
1972	— 85.08	— 3.55	65.24	6.14	147.07	1020.02	129.82
1973	—192.68	29.09	— 5.94	41.56	— 41.19	850.86	— 169.16
1974	—130.99	29.13	— 20.31	— 12.60	— 99.85	616.24	— 234.62
1975	59.80	— 129.96	56.93	129.48	119.92	852.41	236.17
1976	81.16	61.32	50.88	— 26.79	— 14.33	1004.65	152.24
1977	— 66.38	— 43.66	— 79.61	8.53	7.64	831.17	— 173.48
1978	— 31.79	— 70.34	71.33	— 65.71	70.35	805.01	— 26.16
1979	— 27.72	4.72	— 18.84	73.97	1.60	838.74	33.73
1980	— 89.40	137.92	137.77	— 112.78	51.74	963.99	125.25
1981	— 55.47	— 39.72	— 13.95	— 13.66	33.81	875.00	— 88.99
1982	21.69	70.22	28.37	14.65	36.61	1046.54	171.54
1983	39.34	— 39.75	149.28	48.30	14.93	1258.64	212.10
1984	— 40.48	44.70	— 129.24	84.36	— 6.41	1211.57	— 47.07
1985	86.96	43.97	56.19	49.45	98.53	1546.67	335.10
1986	— 56.03	113.72	178.65	32.17	80.77	1895.95	349.28
1987	—651.77	338.45	382.03	142.47	— 168.30	1938.83	42.88
1988	139.28	295.28	— 60.48	— 220.90	76.56	2168.57	229.74
1989	— 3.23	93.25	233.25	70.08	191.28	2753.20	584.63
Subtotal	*—2041.51*	*1053.97*	*1713.20*	*422.10*	*1313.54*		*2461.30*
1990	153.11	41.57	47.96	— 330.48	— 31.70	2633.66	— 119.54
1991	174.58	64.52	174.53	251.08	— 129.54	3168.83	535.17
1992	302.94	— 114.81	3.12	90.38	— 149.35	3301.11	132.28
1993	441.72	— 155.93	243.87	— 0.04	— 76.64	3754.09	452.98
1994	133.77	— 22.69	29.98	— 159.66	98.95	3834.44	80.35
1995	203.99	269.04	357.02	150.44	302.19	5117.12	1282.68
1996	631.88	150.08	— 34.24	261.66	321.77	6448.27	1331.15
1997	761.96	2362.53	— 590.17	— 989.48	— 85.58	7908.25	1459.98
1998	271.31	1057.74	591.63	—1576.91	929.21	9181.43	1273.18
1999	955.60	—1562.34	826.68	984.45	1111.30	11497.12	2315.69
2000	2035.79	536.13	—1978.34	407.30	—1711.15	10786.85	— 710.27
2001	—388.48	336.01	— 396.53	1089.88	—1406.23	10021.50	— 765.35
2002	—710.86	—1317.84	1243.69	— 451.09	— 443.77	8341.63	—1679.87
2003**	—164.61	589.19	— 451.84	313.33	361.35	8989.05	647.42
Subtotal	*4803.42*	*2233.20*	*67.36*	*41.06*	*— 909.19*		*6235.85*
Totals	**2761.91**	**3287.17**	**1780.56**	**463.16**	**404.35**		**8697.15**

*Most Wednesdays closed last 7 months of 1968   **Partial year through June 27, 2003

Monday before Triple-Witching Dow up 8 of last 12

14

> *If there's anything duller than being on a board*
> *in Corporate America, I haven't found it.*
> — Ross Perot (*New York Times*, October 10, 1992)

TUESDAY

15

> *Never doubt that a small group of thoughtful,*
> *committed citizens can change the world:*
> *indeed it's the only thing that ever has.*
> — Margaret Mead (American anthropologist)

WEDNESDAY

16

> *I had an unshakable faith. I had it in my head that if I had to,*
> *I'd crawl over broken glass. I'd live in a tent—*
> *it was gonna happen. And I think when you have that kind*
> *of steely determination...people get out of the way.*
> — Rick Newcombe (Syndicator, *Investor's Business Daily*)

THURSDAY

17

> *The secret to business is to know something*
> *that nobody else knows.*
> — Aristotle Onassis (Greek shipping billionaire)

June Triple-Witching Dow up 8 of last 14

FRIDAY

18

> *Excellent firms don't believe in excellence—*
> *only in constant improvement and constant change.*
> — Tom Peters (*In Search Of Excellence*)

SATURDAY

19

Father's Day

SUNDAY

20

FIRST-TRADING-DAY-OF-THE-MONTH PHENOMENON

For 38 months the sun shined regularly on first trading days of the month, except for seven occasions. But between October 2000, when the major bear trend really started to bare its teeth, and September 2002, frightened investors switched from pouring money into the market on that day to pulling it out, fourteen months out of twenty-three. Even so, first trading days retain an eye-popping history.

The Dow gained 1418.53 points in the last 71 months between September 2, 1997 (7622.42) and July 2003 (9040.95). It is incredible that 3082.34 points were gained on 71 first trading days of the month. The remaining 1395 trading days combined saw the Dow lose 1663.81 points during the period.

This averages out to gains of 43.41 points on first days, in contrast to a small point loss on all others. Converting to annual rates of return, at today's Dow levels, gives you about 216% versus a negative rate of return.

There doesn't seem to be any plausible explanation for the fact that first days of August have performed miserably, falling four times out of five. In rising market trends first days perform much better, so now that 2001 and 2002 are behind us, perhaps first days of the month will again lead the market much higher, though its current performance is surely nothing to complain about.

DOW POINTS GAINED ON FIRST DAY OF MONTH
FROM SEPTEMBER 1997 TO JULY 1, 2003

	1997	1998	1999	2000	2001	2002	2003	Totals
Jan		56.79	2.84	−139.61	− 140.70	51.90	265.89	97.11
Feb		201.28	− 13.13	100.52	96.27	− 12.74	56.01	428.21
Mar		4.73	18.20	9.62	− 45.14	262.73	− 53.22	196.92
Apr		68.51	46.35	300.01	− 100.85	− 41.24	77.73	350.51
May		83.70	225.65	77.87	163.37	113.41	− 25.84	638.16
Jun		22.42	36.52	129.87	78.47	− 215.46	47.55	99.37
Jul		96.65	95.62	112.78	91.32	− 133.47	55.51	318.41
Aug		− 96.55	− 9.19	84.97	− 12.80	− 229.97		− 263.54
Sep	257.36	288.36	108.60	23.68	47.74	− 355.45		370.29
Oct	70.24	− 210.09	− 63.95	49.21	− 11.49	346.86		180.78
Nov	232.31	114.05	− 81.35	− 71.67	188.76	120.61		502.71
Dec	189.98	16.99	120.58	− 40.95	− 89.67	− 33.52		163.41
Totals	749.89	646.84	486.74	636.30	265.28	− 126.34		3082.34

FIRST DAYS VS. OTHER DAYS OF MONTH

	# of Days	Total Points Gained	Average Daily Point Gain	Annual Return
First days	71	3082.34	43.41	216%
Other days	1395	− 1663.81	− 1.19	− 3.1%

JUNE

MONDAY

21

A good manager is a man who isn't worried about his own career but rather the careers of those who work for him... Don't worry about yourself! Take care of those who work for you and you'll float to greatness on their achievements.
— H.S.M. Burns

TUESDAY

22

Setting a goal is not the main thing. It is deciding how you will go about achieving it and staying with that plan.
— Tom Landry (Head Coach Dallas Cowboys 1960-1988)

WEDNESDAY

23

Technology will gradually strengthen democracies in every country and at every level.
— Bill Gates

THURSDAY

24

The way a young man spends his evenings is a part of that thin area between success and failure.
— Robert R. Young

FRIDAY
25

I sold enough papers last year of high school to pay cash for a BMW.
— Michael Dell (Founder Dell Computer, *Forbes*)

SATURDAY
26

Bearish July Sector Seasonalities: Airline, Internet, Russell 2000 (page 118)

SUNDAY
27

JULY ALMANAC

JULY							AUGUST						
S	M	T	W	T	F	S	S	M	T	W	T	F	S
				1	2	3							
4	5	6	7	8	9	10	1	2	3	4	5	6	7
11	12	13	14	15	16	17	8	9	10	11	12	13	14
18	19	20	21	22	23	24	15	16	17	18	19	20	21
25	26	27	28	29	30	31	22	23	24	25	26	27	28
							29	30	31				

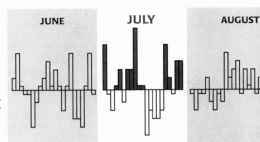

Market Probability Chart above is a graphic representation of the Market Probability Calendar on page 123.

◆ July is the best month of the third quarter (page 74) ◆ Start of second half brings an inflow of retirement funds ◆ First trading day up thirteen out of fifteen times 1989-2003 ◆ S&P and NASDAQ down five in a row till 2003 ◆ Graph above shows strength through most of July except after middle ◆ July closes well except if bear market in progress ◆ Average move of 0.9% on S&P, 1.1% on Dow, –0.4% on NASDAQ ◆ RECORD: S&P up 28, down 25 ◆ Huge gain in July usually provides better buying opportunity over next four months ◆ Start of NASDAQ's worst four months of the year (page 54) ◆ Election Year Julys second worse on NASDAQ average drop –1.1%, up 3, down 5

JULY DAILY POINT CHANGES DOW JONES INDUSTRIALS

Previous Month Close	1993	1994	1995	1996	1997	1998	1999	2000	2001	2002
	3516.08	3624.96	4556.10	5654.63	7672.79	8952.02	10970.80	10447.89	10502.40	9243.26
1	– 5.54	21.69	—	75.35	49.54	96.65	95.62	—	—	– 133.47
2	– 26.57	—	—	– 9.60	73.05	– 23.41	72.82	—	91.32	– 102.04
3	—	—	29.05	– 17.36	100.43	Closed	—	112.78*	– 22.61*	47.22*
4	H	H	H	H	H	H	H	H	H	H
5	Closed	5.83	30.08	– 114.88	—	—	Closed	– 77.07	– 91.25	324.53
6	– 34.04	22.02	48.77	—	—	66.51	– 4.12	2.13	– 227.18	—
7	25.74	13.92	38.73	—	– 37.32	– 6.73	52.24	154.51	—	—
8	38.75	20.72	—	– 37.31	103.82	89.93	– 60.47	—	—	– 104.60
9	6.64	—	—	31.03	– 119.88	– 85.19	66.81	—	46.72	– 178.81
10	—	—	– 0.34	21.79	44.33	15.96	—	10.60	– 123.76	– 282.59
11	—	– 6.15	– 21.79	– 83.11	35.06	—	—	80.61	65.38	– 11.97
12	3.32	– 0.33	46.69	– 9.98	—	—	7.28	56.22	237.97	– 117.00
13	– 8.94	1.62	0.19	—	—	– 9.53	– 25.96	5.30	60.07	—
14	27.11	34.97	– 18.66	—	1.16	149.33	– 26.92	24.04	—	—
15	8.38	14.56	—	– 161.05	52.73	– 11.07	38.31	—	—	– 45.34
16	– 22.64	—	—	9.25	63.17	93.72	23.43	—	– 66.94	– 166.08
17	—	—	27.47	18.12	– 18.11	9.78	—	– 8.48	134.27	69.37
18	—	1.62	– 50.01	87.30	– 130.31	—	—	– 64.35	– 36.56	– 132.99
19	6.99	– 7.12	– 57.41	– 37.36	—	—	– 22.16	– 43.84	40.17	– 390.23
20	9.50	– 21.04	12.68	—	—	– 42.22	– 191.55	147.79	– 33.35	—
21	10.62	5.18	N/C	—	16.26	– 105.56	6.65	– 110.31	—	—
22	– 30.18	2.59	—	– 35.88	154.93	– 61.28	– 33.56	—	—	– 234.68
23	21.52	—	—	– 44.39	26.71	– 195.93	– 58.26	—	– 152.23	– 82.24
24	—	—	27.12	8.14	28.57	4.38	—	– 48.44	– 183.30	488.95
25	—	6.80	45.78	67.32	– 3.49	—	—	14.85	164.55	– 4.98
26	20.96	– 6.16	– 7.39	51.05	—	—	– 47.80	– 183.49	49.96	78.08
27	– 2.24	– 15.21	25.71	—	—	90.88	115.88	69.65	– 38.96	—
28	– 12.01	10.36	– 17.26	—	7.67	– 93.46	6.97	– 74.96	—	—
29	13.97	33.67	—	– 38.47	53.42	– 19.82	– 180.78	—	—	447.49
30	– 27.95	—	—	47.34	80.36	111.99	– 136.14	—	– 14.95	– 31.85
31	—	—	– 7.04	46.98	– 32.28	– 143.66	—	10.81	121.09	56.56
Close	3539.47	3764.50	4708.47	5528.91	8222.61	8883.29	10655.15	10521.98	10522.81	8736.59
Change	23.39	139.54	152.37	– 125.72	549.82	– 68.73	– 315.65	74.09	20.41	– 506.67

*Shortened trading day

When Dow and S&P in July are inferior
NASDAQ days tend to be even drearier

Introducing The Almanac Investor Platform
Almanac Investor Newsletter and New Online Research Tool

Now you can update *Almanac* strategies, learn whether seasonal patterns are on course and be informed about upcoming favorable market periods.

Almanac Investor Platform includes:

Almanac Investor Newsletter: monthly issue provides market timing, seasonal strategies, unusual investing opportunities, exciting small-cap growth stocks and seasoned, undervalued equities, special situations hedging to preserve capital, safe, high-yield situations and investment strategies focusing on Exchange Traded Funds. Emailed to subscribers immediately on completion.

Online Almanac Research Tool: this new product is designed to allow Almanac Investors to do their own historical research, update Almanac market indicators and strategies as well as create their own.

Almanac Investor Alerts: Subscribers receive important *Alerts* via email such as the January Barometer, MACD Seasonal Buy and Sell Signals, stock and strategy updates, the year-end FREE-LUNCH Menu, and more!

See page 104 for more information about getting inside the market with this new tool. Then use the coupon below to try *Almanac Investor Newsletter* and the Research Tool risk free at 50% off…Or order from our website for an additional 10% discount off the prices below by using promotion code STA4.

Jeff Hirsch

Jeff Hirsch

PS: You can try the entire **Almanac Investor Platform** which includes *Almanac Investor Newsletter* and the **Online Research Tool** FREE for one month. Just go to our website *stocktradersalmanac.com*.

Order online today or by calling Toll-Free 800-477-3400, Ext. 20, mailing the card below or faxing it to 201-767-7337.

Keep Your Almanac Updated

Now you can find out what seasonal trends are on schedule
and which are not...how to take advantage of them...
what market-moving events are coming up...
what the indicators say about the next move.
All of the important *Almanac Investor Alerts* via email
such as the MACD Seasonal Buy and Sell Signals, important
updates, the year-end FREE-LUNCH Menu, and much more!

PLUS...Stock research focused on high-potential issues
Wall Street hasn't yet discovered...
Special situations with hidden value...
Yield-enhancing strategies and more.

The Hirsch Organization
P.O. Box 2069
River Vale NJ 07675

JUNE/JULY

June ends NASDAQ's "Best Eight Months" (page 54)

MONDAY

28

*Every time everyone's talking about
something, that's the time to sell.*
— George Lindemann (Billionaire, *Forbes*)

FOMC Meeting (2 days)

TUESDAY

29

*A day will come when all nations on our continent will
form a European brotherhood…A day will come when we shall see…
the United States of Europe…reaching out for each other across the seas.*
— Victor Hugo (French novelist, playwright,
Hunchback of Notre Dame and *Les Misérables*, 1802-1885)

---

*Last day of second quarter Dow down 9 of last 12,
but NASDAQ up 11 of last 12*

WEDNESDAY

30

*Let me tell you the secret that has led me to
my goal. My strength lies solely in my tenacity.*
— Louis Pasteur (French chemist,
founder of microbiology, 1822-1895)

---

*July begins NASDAQ's Worst 4 months of the year
July first trading day Dow up 12 of last 14*

THURSDAY

1

Success is going from failure to failure without loss of enthusiasm.
— Winston Churchill (British statesman, 1874-1965)

---

*Average July change last 32 years
NAS –0.4% Dow 0.4% S&P –0.1%*

FRIDAY

2

Ideas are easy; it's execution that's hard.
— Jeff Bezos (Amazon.com)

SATURDAY

3

Independence Day

SUNDAY

4

2002 DAILY DOW POINT CHANGES (DOW JONES INDUSTRIAL AVERAGE)

Week #		Monday**	Tuesday	Wednesday	Thursday	Friday**	Weekly Dow Close	Net Point Change
						2001 Close	10021.50	
1	J		H	51.90	98.74	87.60	10259.74	238.24
2	A	− 62.69	− 46.50	− 56.46	− 26.23	− 80.33	9987.53	−272.21
3	N	− 96.11	32.73	−211.88	137.77	− 78.19	9771.85	−215.68
4		H	− 58.05	17.16	65.11	44.01	9840.08	68.23
5	F	25.67	−247.51	144.62	157.14	− 12.74	9907.26	67.18
6	E	−220.17	− 1.66	− 32.04	− 27.95	118.80	9744.24	−163.02
7	B	140.54	− 21.04	125.93	12.32	− 98.95	9903.04	158.80
8		H	−157.90	196.03	−106.49	133.47	9968.15	65.11
9		177.56	− 30.45	12.32	− 21.45	262.73	10368.86	400.71
10	M	217.96	−153.41	140.88	− 48.92	47.12	10572.49	203.63
11	A	38.75	21.11	−130.50	15.29	90.09	10607.23	34.74
12	R	− 29.48	57.50	−133.68	− 21.73	− 52.17	10427.67	−179.56
13		−146.00	71.69	73.55	− 22.97	H	10403.94	− 23.73
14	A	− 41.24	− 48.99	−115.42	36.88	36.47	10271.64	−132.30
15	P	− 22.56	− 40.41	173.06	−205.65	14.74	10190.82	− 80.82
16	R	− 97.15	207.65	− 80.54	− 15.50	51.83	10257.11	66.29
17		−120.68	− 47.19	− 58.81	4.63	−124.34	9910.72	−346.39
18		− 90.85	126.35	113.41	32.24	− 85.24	10006.63	95.91
19	M	−198.59	28.51	305.28	−104.41	− 97.50	9939.92	− 66.71
20	A	169.74	188.48	− 54.46	45.53	63.87	10353.08	413.16
21	Y	−123.58	−123.79	52.17	58.20	−111.82	10104.26	−248.82
22		H	−122.68	− 58.54	− 11.35	13.56	9925.25	−179.01
23	J	−215.46	− 21.95	108.96	−172.16	− 34.97	9589.67	−335.58
24	U	55.73	−128.14	100.45	−114.91	− 28.59	9474.21	−115.46
25	N	213.21	18.70	−144.55	−129.80	−177.98	9253.79	−220.42
26		28.03	−155.00	− 6.71	149.81	− 26.66	9243.26	− 10.53
27		−133.47	−102.04	47.22	H	324.53*	9379.50	136.24
28	J	−104.60	−178.81	−282.59	− 11.97	−117.00	8684.53	−694.97
29	U	− 45.34	−166.08	69.37	−132.99	−390.23	8019.26	−665.27
30	L	−234.68	− 82.24	488.95	− 4.98	78.08	8264.39	245.13
31		447.49	− 31.85	56.56	−229.97	−193.49	8313.13	48.74
32	A	−269.50	230.46	182.06	255.87	33.43	8745.45	432.32
33	U	− 56.56	−206.50	260.92	74.83	− 40.08	8778.06	32.61
34	G	212.73	−118.72	85.16	96.41	−180.68	8872.96	94.90
35		46.05	− 94.60	−130.32	− 23.10	− 7.49	8663.50	−209.46
36	S	H	−355.45	117.07	−141.42	143.50	8427.20	−236.30
37	E	92.18	83.23	− 21.44	−201.76	− 66.72	8312.69	−114.51
38	P	67.49	−172.63	− 35.10	−230.06	43.63	7986.02	−326.67
39		−113.87	−189.02	158.69	155.30	−295.67	7701.45	−284.57
40		−109.52	346.86	−183.18	− 38.42	−188.79	7528.40	−173.05
41	O	−105.56	78.65	−215.22	247.68	316.34	7850.29	321.89
42	C	27.11	378.28	−219.65	239.01	47.36	8322.40	472.11
43	T	215.84	− 88.08	44.11	−176.93	126.65	8443.99	121.59
44		− 75.95	0.90	58.47	− 30.38	120.61	8517.64	73.65
45		53.96	106.67	92.74	−184.77	− 49.11	8537.13	19.49
46	N	−178.18	27.05	12.49	143.64	36.96	8579.09	41.96
47	O	− 92.52	− 11.79	148.23	222.14	− 40.31	8804.84	225.75
48	V	44.56	−172.98	255.26	H	− 35.59*	8896.09	91.25
49		− 33.52	−119.64	− 5.08	−114.57	22.49	8645.77	−250.32
50	D	−172.36	100.85	14.88	− 50.74	−104.69	8433.71	−212.06
51	E	193.69	− 92.01	− 88.04	− 82.55	146.52	8511.32	77.61
52	C	− 18.03	− 45.18*	H	− 15.50	−128.83	8303.78	−207.54
53		29.07	8.78			Year's Close	8341.63	37.85†
TOTALS		**−1404.94****	**−823.76**	**1443.69**	**−428.12**	**−466.74****		**−1679.87**

Bold Color: Down Friday, Down Monday   *Shortened trading days: Jul 5, Nov 29, Dec 24   †Partial week*

Market closed for four days following 9/11 attack
** On Monday holidays, the following Tuesday is included in the Monday total
** On Friday holidays, the preceding Thursday is included in the Friday total

JULY

MONDAY 5

(Market Closed)

*Buy when others are despondently selling
and sell when others are greedily buying.*
— Mark Mobius (On investing in foreign countries)

TUESDAY 6

*The finest thought runs the risk of being
irrevocably forgotten if we do not write it down.*
— Arthur Schopenhauer (German philosopher)

WEDNESDAY 7

*Nothing gives one person so much advantage over another as
to remain always cool and unruffled under all circumstances.*
— Thomas Jefferson

THURSDAY 8

All you need to succeed is a yellow pad and a pencil.
— Andre Meyer (Top deal maker at Lazard Freres)

FRIDAY 9

*Give me a stock clerk with a goal and I will give
you a man who will make history. Give me a man without a goal, and
I will give you a stock clerk.*
— James Cash Penney (J.C. Penney founder)

SATURDAY 10

SUNDAY 11

TAKE ADVANTAGE OF DOWN FRIDAY/ DOWN MONDAY WARNING

For market professionals and serious traders, Fridays and Mondays are the most important days of the week. Friday is the day for squaring positions—trimming longs or covering shorts before taking off for the weekend. Pros want to limit their exposure (particularly to stocks that are not acting well) since there could be unfavorable developments before trading resumes two or more days later.

Monday is important because the market then has the chance to reflect any weekend news, plus what traders think after digesting the previous week's action and the many Monday morning research and strategy comments.

We've been watching Friday-Monday market behavior for over 30 years. It has varied in that time, with Monday going from being a bad day to a good day on balance and back to a bad day again.

But one consistent pattern is the negative implication when a down Monday (or first trading day of the week) follows a down Friday (or last trading day of the week):

1. Two out of three times, stocks extend Monday's drop within two days.
2. An overwhelming six out of seven times, stocks are lower within five days including two Monday selling climaxes (down 554.26 Dow points October 27, 1997; off 512.61 August 31, 1998).
3. In the last six and a half years, the Dow failed to drop quickly just ten times after a DF/DM combination. In each of these cases, the market was only two to three weeks from a mostly good-sized drop.
4. More DFs/DMs occur in bear years.

Another fascinating phenomenon involves clusters of DFs/DMs, which are important danger signals. The second table shows seventeen such clusters over the recent six-and-a-half-year period and the subsequent market action. Usually a significant market drop soon follows a DF/DM cluster.

Observe 2002 Daily Dow Point Changes on page 66. Notice the market topped just before the cluster around Good Friday on March 19 at 10635.25 and bottomed on October 9 at 7286.27 following a cluster of two consecutive DF/DMs the week before.

DOWN FRIDAYS/DOWN MONDAYS

Year	Total	Day Dow Closed Lower Than Monday					Mon. 500 pt.	
		Day 1	Day 2	Day 3	Day 4	Day 5	Sell Climax	Errors
1997	6	2	3				1	0
1998	9	3	1			1	1	3
1999	9	7		1				1
2000	12	4	4	1	2	1		0
2001	12	7	3			1		1
2002	18	7	3		1	2		5
2003**	5	2		1				2
Totals	71	32	14	3	3	5	2	12

DF/DM CLUSTERS*		Ending	Top	Approx.	Weeks
Year	# of Weeks	Wk #	Wk #	Point Lost	it took
1997	2 Consecutive	6	10	600	5
1998	2 Consecutive	22	29	1800	6
1999	2 Consecutive	22	24	400	1
	3 Consecutive	33	35	1200	5
2000	2 out of 3	6	6	1100	3
	2 Consecutive	38	38	800	3
	2 Consecutive	47	47	200	2
2001	2 out of 3	4	5	1600	7
	2 out of 3	26	26	300	2
	3 Consecutive	32	32	2400	6
2002**	2 Consecutive	3	5	200	1
	2 out of 3	8	11	800	6
	2 Consecutive	14	14	400	5
	2 Consecutive	19	20	2600	10
	3 out of 4	32	30	1400	5
	2 Consecutive	41	41	200	1
2003**	2 Consecutive	5	5	400	6

*Excluding those ending with Selling Climax   ** Partial year through July 26, 2002*

JULY

MONDAY

12

Monday before expiration day Dow up 6 of last 12

It is tact that is golden, not silence.
— Samuel Butler (English writer, 1600-1680)

TUESDAY

13

*There has never been a commercial technology like this (Internet)
in the history of the world, whereby the minute you adopt it, it
forces you to think and act globally.*
— Robert Hormats (Goldman, Sachs)

WEDNESDAY

14

*The difference between great people and others
is largely a habit —a controlled habit of
doing every task better, faster and more efficiently.*
— William Danforth (Ralston Purina founder)

THURSDAY

15

The man who can master his time can master nearly anything.
— Winston Churchill

Expiration day Dow down 5 of last 8

FRIDAY

16

Eighty percent of success is showing up.
— Woody Allen

SATURDAY

17

SUNDAY

18

A RALLY FOR ALL SEASONS

In any year when the market is a disappointment, you hear talk of a summer rally. Parameters for this "rally" were defined by the late Ralph Rotnem as the lowest close in the Dow industrial average in May or June to the highest close in July, August, or September. Such a big deal is made of the "summer rally" that one might get the impression the market puts on its best razzle-dazzle performance in the summertime. Nothing could be further from the truth! Not only does the market "rally" in every season of the year, but it does so with more gusto in the winter, spring, and fall than in the summer.

Winters in 40 years averaged a 13.5% gain as measured from the low in November or December to the first quarter closing high. Spring was up 11.1% followed by fall with 10.8%. Last and least was the average 9.2% "summer rally." Nevertheless, no matter how thick the gloom or grim the outlook, don't despair! There's always a rally for all seasons, statistically.

SEASONAL GAINS IN DOW JONES INDUSTRIALS

	WINTER RALLY Nov/Dec Low to 1 Q. High	SPRING RALLY Feb/Mar Low to 2 Q. High	SUMMER RALLY May/Jun Low to 3 Q. High	FALL RALLY Aug/Sep Low to 4 Q. High
1964	15.3%	6.2%	9.4%	8.3%
1965	5.7	6.6	11.6	10.3
1966	5.9	4.8	3.5	7.0
1967	11.6	8.7	11.2	4.4
1968	7.0	11.5	5.2	13.3
1969	0.9	7.7	1.9	6.7
1970	5.4	6.2	22.5	19.0
1971	21.6	9.4	5.5	7.4
1972	19.1	7.7	5.2	11.4
1973	8.6	4.8	9.7	15.9
1974	13.1	8.2	1.4	11.0
1975	36.2	24.2	8.2	8.7
1976	23.3	6.4	5.9	4.6
1977	8.2	3.1	2.8	2.1
1978	2.1	16.8	11.8	5.2
1979	11.0	8.9	8.9	6.1
1980	13.5	16.8	21.0	8.5
1981	11.8	9.9	0.4	8.3
1982	4.6	9.3	18.5	37.8
1983	15.7	17.8	6.3	10.7
1984	5.9	4.6	14.1	9.7
1985	11.7	7.1	9.5	19.7
1986	31.1	18.8	9.2	11.4
1987	30.6	13.6	22.9	5.9
1988	18.1	13.5	11.2	9.8
1989	15.1	12.9	16.1	5.7
1990	8.8	14.5	12.4	8.6
1991	21.8	11.2	6.6	9.3
1992	14.9	6.4	3.7	3.3
1993	8.9	7.7	6.3	7.3
1994	9.7	5.2	9.1	5.0
1995	13.6	19.3	11.3	13.9
1996	19.2	7.5	8.7	17.3
1997	17.6	6.5	18.4	7.3
1998	20.3	13.6	7.2	23.1
1999	15.1	21.6	8.2	12.6
2000	10.8	14.4	9.8	3.4
2001	5.9	20.8	1.7	23.1
2002	14.8	7.9	2.8	17.6
2003	6.5	23.9		
Totals	**541.0%**	**445.7%**	**360.1%**	**420.7%**
Average	**13.5%**	**11.1%**	**9.2%**	**10.8%**

JULY

Historically one of the two (October 11) worst trading days of the year (page 123)

MONDAY

19

At the age of 24, I began setting clear, written goals for each area of my life. I accomplished more in the following year than I had in the previous 24.
— Brian Tracy (Motivational speaker)

TUESDAY

20

Anyone who has achieved excellence knows that it comes as a result of ceaseless concentration.
— Louise Brooks (Writer)

WEDNESDAY

21

People become attached to their burdens sometimes more than the burdens are attached to them.
— George Bernard Shaw

THURSDAY

22

Don't fritter away your time. Create, act, take a place wherever you are and be somebody.
— Theodore Roosevelt

FRIDAY

23

Some people are so boring they make you waste an entire day in five minutes.
— Jules Renard (French author, 1864-1910)

SATURDAY

24

SUNDAY

25

AUGUST ALMANAC

AUGUST						
S	M	T	W	T	F	S
1	2	3	4	5	6	7
8	9	10	11	12	13	14
15	16	17	18	19	20	21
22	23	24	25	26	27	28
29	30	31				

SEPTEMBER						
S	M	T	W	T	F	S
				1	2	3	4
5	6	7	8	9	10	11
12	13	14	15	16	17	18
19	20	21	22	23	24	25
26	27	28	29	30		

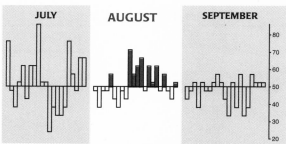

Market Probability Chart above is a graphic representation of the Market Probability Calendar on page 123.

◆ Harvesting made August the best stock market month 1901-1936 ◆ Now that little more than 2% farm, August has become the worst month in the past 15 years on Dow and S&P, second worst on NASDAQ (though up 11.7% in 2000 but down 10.9 in 2001) ◆ Shortest bear in history (45 days) caused by turmoil in Russia ended here in 1998, with a record 1344.22 point drop in the Dow, off 15.1% ◆ Saddam Hussein triggered a 10.0% slide in 1990 ◆ Best Dow gains: 1982 (11.5%) and 1984 (9.8%) as bear markets ended ◆ Election Year Augusts do much better: ranked #2 on NASDAQ, average gain 3.5%, up 5, down 3; #4 on S&P, average gain 1.0%, up 7, down 6 ◆ Fares better when incumbents are running ◆ End of August murderous 6 of the last 7 years average loss last 5 days Dow –4.0%, S&P –3.8%, Naz –3.5%

AUGUST DAILY POINT CHANGES DOW JONES INDUSTRIALS

Previous Month Close	1993 3539.47	1994 3764.50	1995 4708.47	1996 5528.91	1997 8222.61	1998 8883.29	1999 10655.15	2000 10521.98	2001 10522.81	2002 8736.59
1	—	33.67	– 8.10	65.84	– 28.57	—	—	84.97	– 12.80	– 229.97
2	21.52	– 1.95	– 10.22	85.08	—	—	9.19	80.58	41.17	– 193.49
3	0.28	– 3.56	11.27	—	—	– 96.55	31.35	19.05	– 38.40	—
4	– 9.22	– 26.87	– 17.96	—	4.41	– 299.43	– 2.54	61.17	—	—
5	– 3.08	– 18.77	—	– 5.55	– 10.91	59.47	119.05	—	—	– 269.50
6	11.46	—	—	21.83	71.77	30.90	– 79.79	—	– 111.47	230.46
7	—	—	9.86	22.56	– 71.31	20.34	—	99.26	57.43	182.06
8	—	6.79	N/C	– 5.18	– 156.78	—	—	109.88	– 165.24	255.87
9	15.65	1.95	– 21.83	– 32.18	—	—	– 6.33	– 71.06	5.06	33.43
10	– 3.35	11.00	– 27.83	—	—	– 23.17	– 52.55	2.93	117.69	—
11	10.62	– 15.86	– 25.36	—	30.89	– 112.00	132.65	119.04	—	—
12	– 14.26	17.81	—	23.67	– 101.27	90.11	1.59	—	—	– 56.56
13	0.56	—	—	– 57.70	– 32.52	– 93.46	184.26	—	– 0.34	– 206.50
14	—	—	41.56	19.60	13.71	– 34.50	—	148.34	– 3.74	260.92
15	—	– 8.42	– 19.02	– 1.10	– 247.37	—	—	– 109.14	– 66.22	74.83
16	9.50	24.28	– 1.76	23.67	—	—	73.14	– 58.61	46.57	– 40.08
17	7.83	– 8.09	– 8.45	—	—	149.85	70.29	47.25	– 151.74	—
18	17.88	– 21.05	– 13.03	—	108.70	139.80	– 125.70	9.16	—	—
19	7.27	– 0.32	—	9.99	114.74	– 21.37	– 27.54	—	—	212.73
20	3.35	—	—	21.82	103.13	– 81.87	136.77	—	79.29	– 118.72
21	—	—	– 2.82	– 31.44	– 127.28	– 77.76	—	33.33	– 145.93	85.16
22	—	– 3.89	5.64	43.65	– 6.04	—	—	59.34	102.76	96.41
23	– 9.50	24.61	– 35.57	– 10.73	—	—	199.15	5.50	– 47.75	– 180.68
24	32.98	70.90	– 4.23	—	—	32.96	– 16.46	38.09	194.02	—
25	13.13	– 16.84	20.78	—	– 28.34	36.04	42.74	9.89	—	—
26	– 3.91	51.16	—	– 28.85	– 77.35	– 79.30	– 127.59	—	—	46.05
27	– 7.55	—	—	17.38	5.11	– 357.36	– 108.28	—	40.82	– 94.60
28	—	—	– 7.40	1.11	– 92.90	– 114.31	—	60.21	– 160.32	– 130.32
29	—	17.80	14.44	– 64.73	– 72.01	—	—	– 37.74	– 131.13	– 23.10
30	3.36	18.45	– 3.87	– 31.44	—	—	– 176.04	– 112.09	– 171.32	– 7.49
31	7.26	– 3.88	5.99	—	—	– 512.61	– 84.85	112.09	30.17	—
Close	**3651.25**	**3913.42**	**4610.56**	**5616.21**	**7622.42**	**7539.07**	**10829.28**	**11215.10**	**9949.75**	**8663.50**
Change	**111.78**	**148.92**	**– 97.91**	**87.30**	**– 600.19**	**– 1344.22**	**174.13**	**693.12**	**– 573.06**	**– 73.09**

August's a good month to go on vacation
Trading stocks will likely lead to frustration

Democratic Convention begins

MONDAY

26

*Great spirits have always encountered violent
opposition from mediocre minds.*
— Albert Einstein

End of July closes well, EXCEPT if bear market in progress

TUESDAY

27

*Most people can stay excited for two
or three months. A few people can stay
excited for two or three years. But a
winner will stay excited for 20 to 30
years—or as long as it takes to win.*
— A.L. Williams (Motivational speaker)

WEDNESDAY

28

*I have learned as a composer chiefly through my
mistakes and pursuits of false assumptions, not by
my exposure to founts of wisdom and knowledge.*
— Igor Stravinsky (Russian composer)

Democratic Convention ends

THURSDAY

29

*It's not that I am so smart; it's just
that I stay with problems longer.*
— Albert Einstein

FRIDAY

30

*What counts more than luck, is determination and perseverance.
If the talent is there, it will come through. Don't be too impatient.*
— Fred Astaire (The report from his first screen test stated,
"Can't act. Can't sing. Balding. Can dance a little.")

SATURDAY
31

*August Sector Seasonalities:
Bullish: Biotech; Bearish: Cyclical (page 118)*

SUNDAY
1

FIRST MONTH OF FIRST THREE QUARTERS IS THE MOST BULLISH

Looking at monthly percent changes over the years, one can't help noticing that the market is the strongest in the opening month of the first three quarters. The investment calendar reflects the annual, semi-annual and quarterly operations of institutions during January, April and July. The fourth quarter behaves differently since it is affected by year-end portfolio adjustments and presidential and congressional elections in even-numbered years.

The average month-to-month change between 1950 and 1990 shows the S&P 500 gaining 1.3% on average in first months of the first three quarters. Second months barely eked out any gain, while third months, thanks to March, moved up 0.3% on average.

After experiencing the most powerful bull market of all time during the 1990s, followed by the down cycle of a generation (perhaps two), we separated all the figures for the Dow Industrial average beginning with 1991. First months' average gain dropped to 1.50% due to big hits in January and April 2002 related to Middle East violence and corporate malfeasance. Second months gained only 0.22% and third months lost 0.38%. The first month of the first three quarters still outgains the other months manyfold.

We tallied figures for NAS-DAQ (page 150) and results in the same period for first months were 1.64%. Second months averaged 0.45% and third months, 0.27%.

AVERAGE S&P 500 % CHANGE
FIRST THREE QUARTERS 1950-1990

	1st month	2nd month	3rd month
First Q	1.5%	− 0.1%	1.1%
Second Q	1.3	− 0.3	0.3
Third Q	1.1	0.5	− 0.5
Total	**3.9%**	**0.1%**	**0.9%**
Average	**1.30%**	**0.03%**	**0.30%**

DJI % CHANGES FOR MOST RECENT YEARS

First Quarter

	Jan	Feb	Mar
1991	3.9%	5.3%	1.1%
1992	1.7	1.4	− 1.0
1993	0.3	1.8	1.9
1994	6.0	− 3.7	− 5.1
1995	0.2	4.3	3.7
1996	5.4	1.7	1.9
1997	5.7	0.9	− 4.3
1998	− 0.02	8.1	3.0
1999	4.1	− 3.2	3.9
2000	− 4.8	− 7.4	7.8
2001	0.9	− 3.6	− 8.7
2002	− 1.0	1.9	2.9
2003	− 3.5	− 2.0	1.3

Second Quarter

	Apr	May	Jun
1991	− 0.9%	4.8%	− 4.0%
1992	3.8	1.1	− 2.3
1993	− 0.2	2.9	− 0.3
1994	1.3	2.1	− 3.5
1995	3.9	3.3	2.0
1996	− 0.3	1.3	0.2
1997	6.5	4.6	4.7
1998	0.9	− 1.9	3.9
1999	3.8	− 2.5	5.4
2000	− 1.7	− 2.0	− 0.7
2001	8.7	1.6	− 3.8
2002	− 4.4	− 0.2	− 6.9
2003	6.1	4.4	1.5

Third Quarter

	Jul	Aug	Sep
1991	4.1%	0.6%	− 0.9%
1992	2.3	− 4.0	0.4
1993	0.7	3.2	− 2.6
1994	3.8	4.0	− 1.8
1995	3.3	− 2.1	3.9
1996	− 2.2	1.6	4.7
1997	7.2	− 7.3	4.2
1998	− 1.2	− 14.6	6.2
1999	− 2.9	1.6	− 4.5
2000	0.7	6.6	− 5.0
2001	0.2	− 5.4	− 11.1
2002	− 5.5	− 0.8	− 12.4
Total	**56.9%**	**8.4%**	**—14.3%**
Average	**1.50%**	**0.22%**	**— 0.38%**

AUGUST

August worst month last 15 years on Dow –1.9% and S&P –1.6%
Second worst on NASDAQ –0.6%

MONDAY

Love your enemies, for they tell you your faults.
— Benjamin Franklin

TUESDAY

*The highest reward for a person's toil is not
what they get for it, but what they become by it.*
— John Ruskin (English writer)

WEDNESDAY

*Moses Shapiro (of General Instrument) told me,
"Son, this is Talmudic wisdom. Always ask the question 'If not?'
Few people have good strategies for when their assumptions
are wrong." That's the best business advice I ever got.*
— John Malone (CEO of cable giant TCI, *Fortune*, February 16, 1998)

THURSDAY

*The universal line of distinction between the strong
and the weak is that one persists, while the other
hesitates, falters, trifles and at last collapses or caves in.*
— Edwin Percy Whipple (American essayist, 1819-1886)

FRIDAY

*The task of leadership is not to put greatness into humanity,
but to elicit it, for the greatness is already there.*
— Sir John Buchan (Former Governor-General of Canada)

SATURDAY
7

SUNDAY
8

DOWN TRIPLE-WITCHING WEEKS
TRIGGER MORE WEAKNESS WEEK AFTER

	DOW POINT CHANGES	
	Expiration Week	Week After
1991	— 6.93	— 89.36
	— 34.98	— 58.81
	33.54	— 13.19
	20.12	167.04
1992	40.48	— 44.95
	— 69.01	— 2.94
	21.35	— 76.73
	9.19	12.97
1993	43.76	— 31.60
	— 10.24	— 3.88
	— 8.38	— 70.14
	10.90	6.15
1994	32.95	—120.92
	3.33	—139.84
	58.54	—101.60
	116.08	26.24
1995	38.04	65.02
	86.80	75.05
	96.85	— 33.42
	19.87	— 78.76
1996	114.52	51.67
	55.78	— 50.60
	49.94	— 15.54
	179.53	76.51
1997	— 130.67	— 64.20
	14.47	—108.79
	174.30	4.91
	— 82.01	— 76.98
1998	303.91	—110.35
	— 102.07	231.67
	100.16	133.11
	81.87	314.36
1999	27.20	— 81.31
	365.05	—303.00
	— 224.80	—524.30
	32.73	148.33
2000	666.41	517.49
	— 164.76	— 44.55
	— 293.65	— 79.63
	— 277.95	200.60
2001	— 821.21	—318.63
	— 353.36	— 19.05
	—1369.70	611.75
	224.19	101.65
2002	34.74	—179.56
	— 220.42	— 10.53
	— 326.67	—284.57
	77.61	—207.54
2003	662.26	—376.20
	83.63	—211.70
Up	33	17
Down	17	33

Since the S&P index futures began trading in June 1982, traders have analyzed what the market does prior, during and following their expirations in hopes of finding the "Holy Grail." Locating a consistent trading pattern is never easy. For as soon as a pattern becomes obvious, the market almost always tends to "move the goal posts."

Triple-witching week (TWW) refers to expirations in all three categories: S&P futures; put and call options on other indices; and options on stocks. They occur in weeks ending third Fridays in March, June, September and December. Here are some TWW patterns:

• TWWs became more bullish in the last decade, except in the second quarter.

• Following weeks became more bearish. (Last six in a row were down.)

• TWWs have tended to be down in flat periods and dramatically so during the 2000-2002 bear market.

• "DOWN WEEKS TEND TO FOLLOW DOWN TRIPLE-WITCHING WEEKS" is the most interesting pattern. Since 1991, of 17 down TWWs, 14 following weeks were also down. This is surprising inasmuch as the previous decade had an exactly opposite pattern: There were 13 down TWWs then, but 12 UP WEEKS followed them.

Jan. 1991 to 2Q 2003 (50 Qs)
Dow 2633.66 to 8985.44 up 241.2%

	Triple Witching		Following Week	
	Up	Down	Up	Down
1Q	10	3	3	10
2Q	6	7	2	11
3Q	7	5	3	9
4Q	10	2	9	3
Totals	33	17	17	33

June 1982 to 1990 (35 Qs)
Dow 819.54 to 2633.66 up 221.4%

	Triple Witching		Following Week	
	Up	Down	Up	Down
1Q	5	2	4	4
2Q	6	3	7	2
3Q	4	5	7	2
4Q	6	3	7	1
Totals	21	13	25	9

AUGUST

MONDAY
9

*The greatest lie ever told: Build a better mousetrap
and the world will beat a path to your door.*
— Yale Hirsch

FOMC Meeting

TUESDAY
10

*In order to be great writer [or "investor"]
a person must have a built-in, shockproof crap detector.*
— Ernest Hemingway

WEDNESDAY
11

*You have to find something that you love enough to be able to take risks,
jump over the hurdles and break through the brick walls that are always
going to be placed in front of you. If you don't have that kind of feeling
for what it is you're doing, you'll stop at the first giant hurdle.*
— George Lucas (*Star Wars* director)

THURSDAY
12

*The average bottom-of-the-ladder person is potentially as
creative as the top executive who sits in the big office.
The problem is that the person on the bottom of the
ladder doesn't trust his own brilliance and doesn't,
therefore, believe in his own ideas.*
— Robert Schuller (Minister)

Mid-August stronger than beginning

FRIDAY
13

*Towering genius disdains a beaten path.
It scorns to tread in the footsteps of any predecessor,
however illustrious. It thirsts for distinction.*
— Abraham Lincoln

SATURDAY
14

SUNDAY
15

CAN THE REPUBLICANS BEAT THE ODDS IN 2004?

The recurring quadrennial political/stock market cycle going back 170 years has been a lodestone in publishing the *Almanac*. Some of its most significant patterns have been the start of wars and bear markets mostly in the first and second years of presidential terms and the bullishness of third years—with not one losing third year of a presidential term since 1939 (see page 127).

If we could predict the outcome of the fourth-year presidential election twelve to eighteen months ahead of time, it sure would provide insight as to what the market might do in 2004. As we can't, we added up the sixteen times since 1900 that parties retained the White House and find the **Dow gained 15.8 percent** in the average election year. The ten other times "ins" were ousted the **Dow lost 1.4 percent** on average.

ELECTION YEAR MARKETS SINCE 1900

	16 Wins	10 Losses
DJI Gains	253.2%	– 14.2%
Average	15.8%	– 1.4%

What are the prospects for the incumbent Republicans in 2004? One obstacle for the GOP is that no president who failed to win the popular vote won a second term. John Quincy Adams, a son of a former president, and Benjamin Harrison both failed in their bids for reelection. Rutherford B. Hayes chose not to run in 1880.

PRESIDENTS WHO LOST THE POPULAR VOTE

Election Year	Elected President	Next Election	What Happened
1824	John Quincy Adams	1828	*Not Reelected*
1876	Rutherford B. Hayes	1880	*Chose not to run*
1888	Benjamin Harrison	1892	*Not Reelected*
2000	George W. Bush	2004	**??**

Another negative facing the Administration is that popularity during wartime often fades by the time the war ends, or seems to be ending, and the next presidential election rolls around.

The Democrats lost power after WWI (1920), Korea (1952), and Vietnam (1968); the Republicans gave up the White House in 1992, despite their very high ratings during and after Desert Storm. (Even the greatest leader of the century, England's Sir Winston Churchill, lost power in July 1945 shortly after the Allies' overwhelming defeat of the enemy.)

In the modern era only Truman, in 1948, managed to retain power for the Democrats when he ran against a candidate (Dewey), who was heavily favored to win. Stocks did not run away during these five election years.

HOW WARS AFFECT POLITICAL PARTIES

Election Year	War	Party Ousted	Retains Power	Dow % Elec Day	Dow % Full Year
1920	WWI	Dem		– 20.3%	– 32.9%
1948	WWII		Dem	4.7%	– 2.1%
1952	Korea	Dem		0.4%	8.4%
1968	Vietnam	Dem		4.5%	4.3%
1992	Gulf War	Rep		2.9%	4.2%
2004	Iraq				

To beat the odds in 2004 the Republicans will need a growing economy and a peaceful Middle East.

AUGUST

Monday before expiration day Dow up 9 of last 13

MONDAY

16

The mind is not a vessel to be filled but a fire to be kindled.
— Plutarch (Greek biographer and philosopher,
Parallel Lives, 46-120 AD)

TUESDAY

*The greatest good you can do for another is not just
to share your riches, but to reveal to him his own.*
— Benjamin Disraeli (British prime minister, 1804-1881)

WEDNESDAY

*In this game, the market has to keep pitching, but you
don't have to swing. You can stand there with the bat on
your shoulder for six months until you get a fat pitch.*
— Warren Buffett

THURSDAY

*Follow the course opposite to custom
and you will almost always do well.*
— Jean Jacques Rousseau

Expiration day Dow down 10 of last 13

FRIDAY

*It's a buy when the 10-week moving average crosses the 30-week
moving average and the slope of both averages is up.*
— Victor Sperandeo (*Trader Vic—Methods of a Wall Street Master*)

SATURDAY

21

SUNDAY

MARKET ACTS AS A BAROMETER BETWEEN THE LAST CONVENTION AND ELECTION DAY

Another election-year phenomenon, one with an outstanding track record, is the Post-Convention-to-Election-Day Forecaster. Here the direction of the Dow, between the close of the last presidential convention and Election Day, reflects voter sentiment.

Of the sixteen presidential elections since 1900 where the incumbent parties were victorious, fourteen were foretold by rising stock prices. The two exceptions were minor (–2.3% in 1956 and –0.6% in 1984). Gains for the period averaged 8.6%. Conversely, dissatisfaction with an incumbent party is most times reflected by a decline between the last convention and Election Day. Here, seven out of ten election years produced declines.

Though an average change when incumbent parties lose is +3.4%, it reflects the Dow hitting bottom in 1932 (losing 89.2% since 1929) then moving up over 100% intraday in 60 days before giving back half by Election Day. Excluding 1932 changes the average to –1.6%.

Even 1968's post-convention gain is suspect because riots and two assassinations disrupted the market and depressed it prior to the last convention.

POST-CONVENTION-TO-ELECTION MARKETS

Year Incumbent Party Won	% Change	Year Incumbent Party Lost	% Change
1900	7.7%	1912	— 1.4%
1904	30.7	1920	— 9.1
1908	10.0	1932	48.6
1916	16.7	1952	— 2.8
1924	7.5	1960	— 3.1
1928	22.4	1968	5.6
1936	11.8	1976	— 0.8
1940	10.7	1980	— 3.1
1944	1.6	1992	1.1
1948	1.1*	2000	— 0.6
1956	— 2.5**	**Average**	**3.4%**
1964	4.3	**Excluding 1932**	**— 1.6%**
1972	2.8		
1984	— 0.6	*% change based on Dow Jones Industrials*	
1988	5.4	**Truman upsets Dewey*	
1996	7.6	*** Russian tanks in Hungary in October*	
Average	**8.6%**		

I PREDICT THE CANDIDATES WILL BE

Democrat _____ **Republican** _____

I predict the next President wil be _____

	Dow Close After Last Convention Sept. 3, 2004	Dow Close Day Before The Election Nov. 1, 2004	

AUGUST

Beware the "Summer Rally" hype, historically the weakest rally of all seasons
Averages 9.2% on the Dow (page 70), 2002 only 2.8%

MONDAY

23

News on stocks is not important.
How the stock reacts to it is important.
— Michael Burke (*Investors Intelligence*)

TUESDAY

24

Keep away from people who try to belittle your
ambitions. Small people always do that, but the really
great make you feel that you, too, can become great.
— Mark Twain

End of August murderous 6 of the last 7 years
Average loss last 5 days of August
Dow −4.0% S&P −3.8% NAS −3.5%

WEDNESDAY

25

The heights by great men reached and kept
Were not attained by sudden flight,
But they, while their companions slept,
Were toiling upward in the night.
— Henry Wadsworth Longfellow

THURSDAY

26

In democracies, nothing is more great or brilliant than commerce;
it attracts the attention of the public and fills the imagination of
the multitude; all passions of energy are directed towards it.
— Alexis de Tocqueville
(Author, *Democracy in America* 1840, 1805-1859)

FRIDAY

27

I was in search of a one-armed economist so that the guy
could never make a statement and then say: "on the other hand."
— Harry S. Truman

SATURDAY

28

September Sector Seasonalities:
Bullish: Pharmaceutical; Bearish: Semiconductor (page 118)

SUNDAY

29

SEPTEMBER ALMANAC

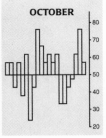

AUGUST   SEPTEMBER   OCTOBER

SEPTEMBER						
S	M	T	W	T	F	S
				1	2	3	4
5	6	7	8	9	10	11
12	13	14	15	16	17	18
19	20	21	22	23	24	25
26	27	28	29	30		

OCTOBER						
S	M	T	W	T	F	S
					1	2
3	4	5	6	7	8	9
10	11	12	13	14	15	16
17	18	19	20	21	22	23
24	25	26	27	28	29	30
31						

Market Probability Chart above is a graphic representation of the Market Probability Calendar on page 123.

◆ Start of business year, end of vacations, and back to school made September a leading barometer month in first 60 years of the century, now portfolio managers back after Labor Day tend to clean house ◆ Biggest % loser on the S&P, Dow and NASDAQ (pages 48 & 54) ◆ Streak of four great Septembers averaging 4.2% gains ended with four big losers in a row (see below) ◆ Day after Labor Day up 7 of last 9 ◆ Opened strong seven of last eight years but tends to close weak due to end-of-quarter mutual fund portfolio restructuring ◆ Only 3 losses last 10 Election Year Septembers, 1972 and 1984 incumbents ran and won, 2000 down over 5% on three major averages during incumbentless fuzzy campaigns

SEPTEMBER DAILY POINT CHANGES DOW JONES INDUSTRIALS

Previous Month	1993	1994	1995	1996	1997	1998	1999	2000	2001	2002
Close	3651.25	3913.42	4610.56	5616.21	7622.42	7539.07	10829.28	11215.10	9949.75	8663.50
1	− 6.15	− 11.98	36.98	—	H	288.36	108.60	23.68	—	—
2	− 19.00	− 15.86	—	H	257.36	− 45.06	− 94.67	—	—	H
3	7.83	—	—	32.18	14.86	−100.15	235.24	—	H	− 355.45
4	—	—	H	8.51	− 27.40	− 41.97	—	H	47.74	117.07
5	—	H	22.54	− 49.94	− 44.83	—	—	21.83	35.78	− 141.42
6	H	13.12	13.73	52.90	—	—	H	50.03	− 192.43	143.50
7	− 26.83	− 12.45	− 14.09	—	—	H	− 44.32	− 50.77	− 234.99	—
8	− 18.17	22.21	31.00	—	12.77	380.53	2.21	− 39.22	—	—
9	0.56	− 33.65	—	73.98	16.73	−155.76	43.06	—	—	92.18
10	32.14	—	—	− 6.66	−132.63	−249.48	− 50.97	—	—	83.23
11	—	—	4.22	27.74	− 58.30	179.96	—	− 25.16	Closed*	− 21.44
12	—	− 14.47	42.27	17.02	81.99	—	—	37.74	Closed*	− 201.76
13	12.58	19.52	18.31	66.58	—	—	1.90	− 51.05	Closed*	− 66.72
14	− 18.45	15.47	36.28	—	—	149.85	− 120.00	− 94.71	Closed*	—
15	17.89	58.55	− 4.23	—	− 21.83	79.04	−108.91	− 160.41	—	—
16	− 2.80	− 20.53	—	50.68	174.78	65.39	− 63.96	—	—	67.49
17	− 17.60	—	—	− 0.37	− 9.48	−216.01	66.17	—	− 684.81	− 172.63
18	—	—	− 17.16	− 11.47	36.28	21.89	—	− 118.54	− 17.30	− 35.10
19	—	3.37	− 13.37	− 9.62	− 5.45	—	—	− 19.23	− 144.27	− 230.06
20	− 37.45	− 67.63	25.65	20.72	—	—	20.27	−101.37	− 382.92	43.63
21	− 38.56	− 17.49	− 25.29	—	—	37.59	− 225.43	77.60	− 140.40	—
22	9.78	− 14.47	− 3.25	—	79.56	− 36.05	− 74.40	81.85	—	—
23	− 7.27	− 5.38	—	6.28	− 26.77	257.21	− 205.48	—	—	− 113.87
24	3.36	—	—	− 20.71	− 63.35	−152.42	− 39.26	—	368.05	− 189.02
25	—	—	5.78	3.33	− 58.70	26.78	—	− 39.22	56.11	158.69
26	—	17.49	− 4.33	− 8.51	74.17	—	—	− 176.83	92.58	155.30
27	24.59	13.80	− 3.25	4.07	—	—	24.06	− 2.96	114.03	− 295.67
28	− 1.68	15.14	25.29	—	—	80.07	− 27.86	195.70	166.14	—
29	0.28	− 23.55	1.44	—	69.25	− 28.32	− 62.05	−173.14	—	—
30	− 11.18	− 11.44	—	9.25	− 46.17	−237.90	123.47	—	—	− 109.52
Close	3555.12	3843.19	4789.08	5882.17	7945.26	7842.62	10336.95	10650.92	8847.56	7591.93
Change	− 96.13	− 70.23	178.52	265.96	322.84	303.55	− 492.33	− 564.18	−1102.19	− 1071.57

* Market closed for four days after 9/11 terrorist attack

September is when leaves and stocks tend to fall
On Wall Street it's the worst month of all

AUGUST/SEPTEMBER

Republican Convention begins

*There are very few instances in history
when any government has ever paid off debt.*
— Walter Wriston (Retired CEO of Citicorp and Citibank)

TUESDAY

31

*A good new chairman of the Federal Reserve Bank
is worth a $10 billion tax cut.*
— Paul H. Douglas (U.S. Senator 1949-1967)

*September opened strong 7 of last 8 years
But still worst month for Dow, S&P and NASDAQ (pages 48, 54)*

WEDNESDAY

1

*An entrepreneur tends to lie some of the time.
An entrepreneur in trouble tends to lie most of the time.*
— Anonymous

Republican Convention ends

THURSDAY

2

*There is always plenty of capital for those
who can create practical plans for using it.*
— Napoleon Hill (Author, *Think and Grow Rich*, 1883-1970)

*Average September losses last 32 years
NAS −1.1% Dow −1.6% S&P −1.3%*

FRIDAY

3

*In business, the competition will bite you if you keep running;
if you stand still, they will swallow you.*
— William Knudsen (Former president of GM)

SATURDAY

SUNDAY

5

A CORRECTION FOR ALL SEASONS

While there's a rally for every season (page 70), almost always there's a decline or correction, too. Fortunately, corrections tend to be smaller than rallies, and that's what gives the stock market its long-term upward bias. In each season the average bounce outdoes the average setback. On average the net gain between the rally and the correction is smallest in summer and fall.

The summer setback tends to be slightly outdone by the average correction in the fall. Tax selling and portfolio cleaning are the usual explanations—individuals sell to register a tax loss and institutions like to get rid of their losers before preparing year-end statements. The October jinx also plays a major part. Since 1964, there have been 16 fall declines of over 10%, and in nine of them (1966, 1974, 1978, 1979, 1987, 1990, 1997, 2000 and 2002) much damage was done in October, where so many bear markets end. Important October lows were also seen in 1998 and 1999. Most often, it has paid to buy after fourth quarter or late third quarter "waterfall declines" for a rally that may continue into January or even beyond.

SEASONAL CORRECTIONS IN DOW JONES INDUSTRIALS

	WINTER Nov/Dec High to 1 Q. Low	SPRING Feb/Mar High to 2 Q. Low	SUMMER May/Jun High to 3 Q. Low	FALL Aug/Sep High to 4 Q. Low
1964	− 0.2%	− 2.4%	− 1.0%	− 2.1
1965	− 2.5	− 7.3	− 8.3	− 0.9
1966	− 6.0	− 13.2	− 17.7	− 12.7
1967	− 4.2	− 3.9	− 5.5	− 9.9
1968	− 8.8	− 0.3	− 5.5	+ 0.4
1969	− 8.7	− 8.7	− 17.2	− 8.1
1970	− 13.8	− 20.2	− 8.8	− 2.5
1971	− 1.4	− 4.8	− 10.7	− 13.4
1972	− 0.5	− 2.6	− 6.3	− 5.3
1973	− 11.0	− 12.8	− 10.9	− 17.3
1974	− 15.3	− 10.8	− 29.8	− 27.6
1975	− 6.3	− 5.6	− 9.9	− 6.7
1976	− 0.2	− 5.1	− 4.7	− 8.9
1977	− 8.5	− 7.2	− 11.5	− 10.2
1978	− 12.3	− 4.0	− 7.0	− 13.5
1979	− 2.5	− 5.8	− 3.7	− 10.9
1980	− 10.0	− 16.0	− 1.7	− 6.8
1981	− 6.9	− 5.1	− 18.6	− 12.9
1982	− 10.9	− 7.5	− 10.6	− 3.3
1983	− 4.1	− 2.8	− 6.8	− 3.6
1984	− 11.9	− 10.5	− 8.4	− 6.2
1985	− 4.8	− 4.4	− 2.8	− 2.3
1986	− 3.3	− 4.7	− 7.3	− 7.6
1987	− 1.5	− 6.6	− 1.7	− 36.1
1988	− 6.7	− 7.0	− 7.6	− 4.5
1989	− 1.7	− 2.4	− 3.1	− 6.6
1990	− 7.9	− 4.0	− 17.3	− 18.4
1991	− 6.3	− 3.6	− 4.5	− 6.3
1992	+ 0.1	− 3.3	− 5.4	− 7.6
1993	− 2.7	− 3.1	− 3.0	− 2.0
1994	− 4.4	− 9.6	− 4.4	− 7.1
1995	− 0.8	− 0.1	− 0.2	− 2.0
1996	− 3.5	− 4.6	− 7.5	+ 0.2
1997	− 1.8	− 9.8	− 2.2	− 13.3
1998	− 7.0	− 0.4	− 18.2	− 13.1
1999	− 2.7	− 1.7	− 8.1	− 11.5
2000	− 14.8	− 7.4	− 4.1	− 11.8
2001	− 14.5	− 13.6	− 27.4	− 16.2
2002	− 5.1	− 14.2	− 26.7	− 19.5
2003	− 15.8	− 5.3		
Totals	− 250.9%	− 262.4%	− 356.0%	− 368.2%
Average	− 6.3%	− 6.6%	− 9.1%	− 9.4%

SEPTEMBER

Labor Day
(Market Closed)

MONDAY

6

*All the features and achievements of modern civilization are,
directly or indirectly, the products of the capitalist process.*
— Joseph A. Schumpeter (Austrian-American economist,
Theory of Economic Development, 1883-1950)

Day after Labor Day Dow up 7 of last 9

TUESDAY
7

*The political problem of mankind is to combine three things:
economic efficiency, social justice, and individual liberty.*
— John Maynard Keynes

WEDNESDAY

8

The only thing that saves us from the bureaucracy is its inefficiency.
— Eugene McCarthy

THURSDAY
9

*The most valuable executive is one who is
training somebody to be a better man than he is.*
— Robert G. Ingersoll (American lawyer and orator,
"the Great Agnostic," 1833-1899)

FRIDAY

10

You know you're right when the other side starts to shout.
— I. A. O'Shaughnessy

*In memory of our comrades and colleagues
lost on September 11, 2001*

"In Memory"

SATURDAY
11

SUNDAY

12

MARKET BEHAVIOR THREE DAYS BEFORE AND THREE DAYS AFTER HOLIDAYS

We have kept track of holiday seasonality annually in the *Stock Trader's Almanac* since the first edition in 1968. Over the years the market tended to go up on the day before holidays and sell off the day after, but a transformation has taken place. Some holidays seem to be favored by the bulls, while others are not.

Eight holidays are separated into three groups: those positive the day after, those negative the day after, and the sole holiday that's negative both the day before and after. Notice we show average percent changes for the Dow, S&P 500, and the Zweig Unweighted Price Index.

Bear in mind that the Dow and S&P are both blue chip indices, whereas the Zweig would be more representative of smaller cap stocks. This is evident on the last day of the year with ZUPI smaller stocks having a field day, while their larger brethren in the Dow and S&P are showing losses on average. The best six-day span can be seen for ZUPI stocks on the three days before and three days after New Year's Day, a gain of about 2.2% on average. Thanks to the Santa Claus Rally, the six days around Christmas are up solidly as well.

The worst day after a holiday is the day after Easter. Surprisingly, the following day is the best second day after a holiday.

Presidents' Day is the least bullish of all the holidays, bearish the day before and three days after. The Dow has dropped 11 of the last 12 days before Presidents' Day.

HOLIDAYS: 3 DAYS BEFORE, 3 DAYS AFTER (Average % Change 1980 - July 28, 2003)

	− 3	− 2	− 1		+1	+2	
				Positive Day After			
S&P 500	0.05	0.31	− 0.18	**New Year's**	0.03	0.49	0.13
DJIA	0.03	0.24	− 0.30	**Day**	0.25	0.49	0.32
ZUPI	0.07	0.31	0.53	*1.1.04*	0.36	0.53	0.37
S&P 500	0.15	− 0.08	0.04	**Memorial**	0.40	0.16	0.22
DJIA	0.15	− 0.14	− 0.02	**Day**	0.49	0.18	0.16
ZUPI	− 0.09	0.05	0.18	*5.31.04*	0.14	0.11	0.23
S&P 500	− 0.17	− 0.35	0.23	**Labor**	0.03	0.04	− 0.13
DJIA	− 0.17	− 0.38	0.22	**Day**	0.12	0.05	− 0.19
ZUPI	N/C	− 0.06	0.25	*9.6.04*	− 0.03	N/C	0.14
S&P 500	− 0.10	− 0.01	0.23	**Thanksgiving**	0.24	− 0.28	0.20
DJIA	0.03	0.02	0.32	*11.25.04*	0.18	− 0.28	0.26
ZUPI	− 0.19	− 0.16	0.18		0.32	− 0.23	0.13
S&P 500	0.17	0.17	0.25	**Christmas**	0.21	0.01	0.37
DJIA	0.24	0.26	0.33	*12.25.04 (Closed 12.24)*	0.26	− 0.01	0.32
ZUPI	0.03	0.16	0.37		0.12	0.08	0.38
				Negative Day After			
S&P 500	0.26	− 0.02	0.25	**Good Friday**	− 0.48	0.61	0.11
DJIA	0.20	− 0.07	0.23	*4.9.04*	− 0.34	0.61	0.08
ZUPI	0.09	0.10	0.19		− 0.40	0.32	0.11
S&P 500	− 0.01	0.17	0.08	**Independence**	− 0.17	− 0.03	0.15
DJIA	− 0.01	0.16	0.06	**Day**	− 0.11	0.02	0.11
ZUPI	0.10	0.09	0.11	*7.4.04 (Closed 7.5)*	− 0.07	− 0.06	0.08
				Negative Before & After			
S&P 500	0.21	N/C	− 0.36	**Presidents'**	− 0.19	− 0.10	− 0.04
DJIA	0.21	0.04	− 0.30	**Day**	− 0.10	− 0.16	− 0.07
ZUPI	0.15	− 0.01	− 0.06	*2.16.04*	− 0.26	− 0.15	− 0.05

Data courtesy of Martin Zweig/Catherine Nolan

SEPTEMBER

MONDAY

13

*If you bet on a horse, that's gambling. If you bet you can
make three spades, that's entertainment. If you bet cotton
will go up three points, that's business. See the difference?*
— Blackie Sherrod

TUESDAY

14

Life is an illusion. You are what you think you are.
— Yale Hirsch

WEDNESDAY

15

*What the superior man seeks, is in himself.
What the inferior man seeks, is in others.*
— Confucius

Rosh Hashanah

THURSDAY

16

*During the first period of a man's life,
the greatest danger is: not to take the risk.*
— Soren Kierkegaard

September Triple-Witching day Dow down 8 of last 13

FRIDAY

17

*In the realm of ideas, everything depends on enthusiasm;
in the real world, all rests on perseverance.*
— Goethe

SATURDAY

18

SUNDAY

19

END-OF-MONTH BULLISH SEASONALITY SHIFTING

Trading patterns have changed dramatically. For many years the last day plus the first four days were the best days of the month. Thousands took advantage of this anomaly and thrived. The market currently exhibits greater bullish bias from the last three trading days of the previous month through the first two days of the current month and now shows significant bullishness during the middle three trading days nine to eleven, due to 401(k) cash inflows (see pages 136 and 137). From 1995 to 1999 this pattern was not as pronounced with market strength all month long. But the last four years have experienced monthly bullishness at the ends, beginnings and middles of months versus losses during the rest of the month. Was 1999's "rest of month" bullishness a bearish omen?

SUPER EIGHT DAYS* DOW % CHANGES VS. REST OF MONTH

	Super 8 Days	Rest of Month	Super 8 Days	Rest of Month	Super 8 Days	Rest of Month
	1995		**1996**		**1997**	
Jan	1.75%	− 1.50%	2.10%	1.12%	0.80%	0.91%
Feb	1.20	2.19	1.07	4.46	4.19	1.46
Mar	− 0.52	4.21	0.65	1.24	− 3.83	1.58
Apr	0.75	2.81	2.44	− 4.20	− 4.50	2.66
May	1.41	1.18	0.71	1.86	5.49	3.81
Jun	1.85	1.08	− 1.04	1.22	1.63	2.55
Jul	0.73	2.88	− 2.91	− 1.36	2.85	2.64
Aug	− 0.42	− 2.00	3.09	1.25	− 2.39	− 1.76
Sep	1.97	1.73	1.07	1.84	4.51	− 3.57
Oct	0.70	− 1.99	2.37	− 0.74	2.45	− 6.73
Nov	3.30	4.29	2.46	6.86	6.56	− 2.84
Dec	1.39	− 0.60	− 3.70	3.82	2.53	− 3.57
Totals	**14.13%**	**14.29%**	**8.31%**	**17.36%**	**20.27%**	**− 2.84%**
Average	**1.18%**	**1.19%**	**0.69%**	**1.45%**	**1.69%**	**− 0.24%**
	1998		**1999**		**2000**	
Jan	4.18%	− 2.30%	0.98%	0.08%	− 4.09%	0.46%
Feb	5.43	1.55	0.76	1.62	0.43	− 9.10
Mar	3.06	2.53	− 0.68	3.74	2.76	5.62
Apr	2.29	− 1.47	2.84	7.09	− 2.79	4.77
May	2.37	− 1.79	− 0.83	− 1.92	0.70	− 7.86
Jun	− 4.64	4.47	0.20	0.01	5.99	− 4.10
Jul	3.55	− 3.43	5.87	− 1.74	− 0.65	0.83
Aug	− 4.75	0.17	− 0.35	2.41	3.08	3.75
Sep	− 4.92	− 0.59	− 5.83	− 2.32	− 3.27	− 2.34
Oct	0.68	3.59	− 2.86	2.97	− 0.85	− 1.47
Nov	6.19	4.57	4.25	2.45	5.81	− 4.06
Dec	− 2.75	2.11	0.29	3.92	− 2.96	4.44
Totals	**10.69%**	**9.42%**	**4.63%**	**18.32%**	**4.15%**	**− 9.06%**
Average	**0.89%**	**0.78%**	**0.39%**	**1.53%**	**0.35%**	**− 0.76%**
	2001		**2002**		**2003**	
Jan	2.13%	− 2.36%	− 1.92%	− 0.23%	1.00%	− 4.86%
Feb	1.41	− 3.36	− 1.41	4.27	2.71	− 4.82
Mar	− 1.50	− 3.30	4.11	− 2.64	5.22	− 0.90
Apr	− 2.61	9.56	− 2.46	0.08	2.87	− 1.91
May	2.02	1.53	3.62	− 4.06	3.17	2.46
Jun	− 2.46	− 2.45	− 2.22	− 6.51	3.09	− 0.38
Jul	2.16	− 2.29	− 5.04	− 4.75		
Aug	0.24	− 2.48	2.08	4.59		
Sep	− 3.62	− 12.05	− 6.58	− 5.00		
Oct	4.51	5.36	8.48	− 1.50		
Nov	1.01	2.48	4.74	0.99		
Dec	0.19	1.99	− 0.76	− 4.02		
Totals	**3.47%**	**− 7.37%**	**2.64%**	**− 18.78%**	**18.07%**	**− 10.42%**
Average	**0.29%**	**− 0.61%**	**0.22%**	**− 1.57%**	**3.01%**	**− 1.74%**

	Super 8 Days*		**Rest of Month (13 Days)**	
101	Net % Changes	86.36%	Net % Changes	10.92%
Month	Average Period	0.87%	Average Period	0.004%
Totals	Average Day	0.11%	Average Day	0.0003%

* Super 8 Days = Last 3 + First 2 + Middle 3

SEPTEMBER

MONDAY
20

*For a country, everything will be lost when the jobs of an
economist and a banker become highly respected professions.*
— Montesquieu

FOMC Meeting

TUESDAY
21

*Those heroes of finance are like beads on a string,
when one slips off, the rest follow.*
— Henrik Ibsen

WEDNESDAY
22

Every man is the architect of his own fortune.
— Appius Claudius

THURSDAY
23

All a parent can give a child is roots and wings.
— Chinese proverb

FRIDAY
24

*The worse a situation becomes the less it takes
to turn it around, the bigger the upside.*
— George Soros

Yom Kippur

SATURDAY
25

*Bullish October Sector Seasonalities: Airline, Internet, Cyclical,
High-Tech, Telecomm, NASDAQ 100, Banking, Forest/Paper,
Gold/Silver, Semiconductor, Broker/Dealer (page 118)*

SUNDAY
26

OCTOBER ALMANAC

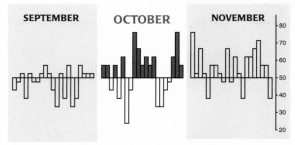

OCTOBER							NOVEMBER					
S	M	T	W	T	F	S	S	M	T	W	T	F	S

OCTOBER

S	M	T	W	T	F	S
					1	2
3	4	5	6	7	8	9
10	11	12	13	14	15	16
17	18	19	20	21	22	23
24	25	26	27	28	29	30
31						

NOVEMBER

S	M	T	W	T	F	S
		1	2	3	4	5	6
7	8	9	10	11	12	13
14	15	16	17	18	19	20
21	22	23	24	25	26	27
28	29	30				

Market Probability Chart above is a graphic representation of the Market Probability Calendar on page 123.

◆ Known as the jinx month because of crashes in 1929, 1987, the 554-point drop on October 27, 1997, back-to-back massacres in 1978 and 1979 and Friday the 13th in 1989 ◆ Yet October is a "bear killer" and turned the tide in eleven post-WWII bear markets: 1946, 1957, 1960, 1962, 1966, 1974, 1987, 1990, 1998, 2001 and 2002 ◆ Worst six months of the year ends with October (page 50) ◆ No longer worst month (pages 48 & 54) ◆ October is a great time to buy stocks, especially high-tech stocks (page 118) ◆ Big October gains in 2001 and 2002 after atrocious Septembers ◆ Can get into Best Six Months earlier using MACD (page 52) ◆ Election Year Octobers are just average

OCTOBER DAILY POINT CHANGES DOW JONES INDUSTRIALS

Previous Month	1993	1994	1995	1996	1997	1998	1999	2000	2001	2002
Close	3555.12	3843.19	4789.08	5882.17	7945.26	7842.62	10336.95	10650.92	8847.56	7591.93
1	25.99	—	—	22.73	70.24	−210.09	− 63.95	—	− 10.73	346.86
2	—	—	− 27.82	29.07	12.03	152.16	—	49.21	113.76	− 183.18
3	—	3.70	− 11.56	− 1.12	11.05	—	—	19.61	173.19	− 38.42
4	− 3.35	− 45.76	− 9.03	60.01	—	—	128.23	64.74	− 62.90	− 188.79
5	9.50	− 13.79	22.04	—	—	− 58.45	− 0.64	− 59.56	58.89	—
6	11.73	− 11.78	6.50	—	61.64	16.74	187.75	− 128.38	—	—
7	− 15.36	21.87	—	− 13.05	78.09	− 1.29	− 51.29	—	—	− 105.56
8	1.11	—	—	− 13.04	− 83.25	− 9.78	112.71	—	− 51.83	78.65
9	—	—	− 42.99	− 36.15	− 33.64	167.61	—	− 28.11	− 15.50	− 215.22
10	—	23.89	− 5.42	− 8.95	− 16.21	—	—	− 44.03	188.42	247.68
11	8.67	55.51	14.45	47.71	—	—	1.58	− 110.61	169.59	316.34
12	− 0.28	− 1.68	29.63	—	—	101.95	− 231.12	− 379.21	− 66.29	—
13	10.06	14.80	28.90	—	27.01	− 63.33	− 184.90	157.60	—	—
14	18.44	20.52	—	40.62	24.07	30.64	54.45	—	—	27.11
15	8.10	—	—	− 5.22	− 38.31	330.58	− 266.90	—	3.46	378.28
16	—	—	− 9.40	16.03	− 119.10	117.40	—	46.62	36.61	− 219.65
17	—	13.46	11.56	38.39	− 91.85	—	—	− 149.09	− 151.26	239.01
18	12.58	− 6.39	− 18.42	35.03	—	—	96.57	− 114.69	− 69.75	47.36
19	− 6.99	18.50	24.93	—	—	49.69	88.65	167.96	40.89	—
20	9.78	− 24.89	− 7.59	—	74.41	39.40	187.43	83.61	—	—
21	− 8.94	− 19.85	—	− 3.36	139.00	13.38	− 94.67	—	—	215.84
22	13.14	—	—	− 29.07	− 25.79	13.91	172.56	—	172.92	− 88.08
23	—	—	− 39.38	− 25.34	− 186.88	− 80.85	—	45.13	− 36.95	44.11
24	—	− 36.00	28.18	− 43.98	− 132.36	—	—	121.35	5.54	− 176.93
25	24.31	− 4.71	− 29.98	14.54	—	—	− 120.32	− 66.59	117.28	126.65
26	− 1.12	− 2.36	− 49.86	—	—	− 20.08	− 47.80	53.64	82.27	—
27	− 7.83	26.92	37.93	—	− 554.26	− 66.17	92.76	210.50	—	—
28	23.20	55.51	—	− 34.29	337.17	5.93	227.64	—	—	− 75.95
29	− 7.27	—	—	34.29	8.35	123.06	107.33	—	− 275.67	0.90
30	—	—	14.82	− 13.79	− 125.00	97.07	—	245.15	− 147.52	58.47
31	—	− 22.54	− 1.09	36.15	61.13	—	—	135.37	− 46.84	− 30.38
Close	3680.59	3908.12	4755.48	6029.38	7442.80	8592.10	10729.86	10971.14	9075.14	8397.03
Change	125.47	64.93	− 33.60	147.21	− 502.46	749.48	392.91	320.22	227.58	805.10

October has killed many a bear
Buy tech stocks and you'll soon wear a grin ear to ear

SEPTEMBER/OCTOBER

Septembers close weak (pages 82 and 123)

MONDAY

27

There is only one side of the market and it is not the bull side or the bear side, but the right side.
— Jesse Livermore

TUESDAY

28

Patriotism is when love of your own people comes first. Nationalism is when hate for people other than your own comes first.
— Charles De Gaulle (French president and WWII general, 1890-1970, May 1969)

WEDNESDAY

29

I don't know where speculation got such a bad name, since I know of no forward leap which was not fathered by speculation.
— John Steinbeck

THURSDAY

30

To affect the quality of the day, that is the highest of the arts.
— Henry David Thoreau

October no longer worst month (pages 48 and 54)
End of "Worst Six Months" and "Worst Four" (pages 50 and 58)

FRIDAY

1

Early in March (1960), Dr. Arthur F. Burns called on me... Burns' conclusion was that unless some decisive action was taken, and taken soon, we were heading for another economic dip which would hit its low point in October, just before the elections.
— Richard M. Nixon (37th US President, *Six Crises*, 1913-1994)

SATURDAY

2

SUNDAY

3

CERTAIN STOCKS SOAR, OTHERS TUMBLE DURING CERTAIN MONTHS OF THE YEAR

On page 118 of the *Almanac* we list Sector Seasonality: Selected Percentage Plays. These are from Jon D. Markman's previous book, *Online Investing*.

Many individual stocks also have recurring bullish or bearish patterns during certain months of the year. Markman's excellent *Swing Trading*, one of this Year's Top Investment Books (see page 98), lists a total of 1200 stocks with these tendencies.

Each of the 1200 stocks started their respective historical month with a split-adjusted price greater than $2, a minimum price of $5 on June 2002 and average daily volume greater than 25,000 shares.

The table shown here presents a sampling of just 24 of them. We selected one from each month that had a fairly recognizable name, a high batting average over a decent length of years, and a solid mean change.

BEST LONG CANDIDATES BY MONTH (12 SELECTED FROM 600)

Month	Symbol	Stock	Mean % Change	Months Up	Months Down
January	ASCA	Ameristar Casinos	24.7%	8	0
February	MEDC	Med Design	35.5	6	0
March	HOTT	Hot Topic	32.6	5	0
April	Rwy	Rent Way	21.9	8	0
May	MAT	Mattel	7.2	14	1
June	ORCL	Oracle	18.2	7	0
July	SYK	Stryker	9.5	13	1
August	KRON	Kronos	7.1	10	0
September	AMHC	American Healthways	15.5	10	1
October	MLNM	Millennium Pharma.	13.2	6	0
November	IMCL	Imclone Systems	21.9	7	1
December	PSTI	Per Se Technologies	17.7	11	0

BEST SHORT CANDIDATES BY MONTH (12 SELECTED FROM 600)

Month	Symbol	Stock	Mean % Change	Months Up	Months Down
January	TSA	Sports Authority	− 17.0%	0	5
February	SCHL	Scholastic	− 9.5	1	8
March	VICL	Vical	− 20.0	0	8
April	APSG	Applied Signal Tech	− 12.6	1	8
May	SNIC	Sonic Solutions	− 10.9	0	7
June	SNIC	Sonic Solutions	− 12.0	0	7
July	CACI	CACI International	− 9.0	0	10
August	IT	Gartner	− 7.5	0	8
September	BDK	Black & Decker	− 7.6	2	14
October	FRC	First Republic Bank	− 7.1	2	14
November	CRK	Comstock Resources	− 11.3	1	12
December	TSA	Sports Authority	− 13.2	0	7

From Swing Trading *by Jon Markman, John Wiley & Sons*
Source: Camelback Research Alliance

OCTOBER

Average October gains last 32 years
NAS 0.2% Dow 0.5% S&P 0.9%

MONDAY

Imagination is more important than knowledge.
— Albert Einstein

Start looking for MACD seasonal BUY Signal (pages 52 and 58)
Almanac Investor subscribers will be emailed
Visit stocktradersalmanac.com for details

TUESDAY

He who knows nothing is confident of everything.
— Anonymous

WEDNESDAY

I just wait until the fourth year, when the business cycle bottoms,
and buy whatever I think will have the biggest bounce.
— Larry Tisch's investment style

THURSDAY

Spend at least as much time researching a stock
as you would choosing a refrigerator.
— Peter Lynch

FRIDAY

The first rule is not to lose.
The second rule is not to forget the first rule.
— Warren Buffett

SATURDAY

SUNDAY

2004 PRESIDENTIAL ELECTION YEAR PERSPECTIVES

Guessing which party will win an election can help get one on the right side of the market. Of course, guessing right isn't the easiest thing. What if the economy doesn't really pick up? What if things get ugly in the Middle East? What does Bush have to do to win reelection in November 2004? Remember, Bush Sr. was fairly popular after Persian Gulf in 1991 but blew it in 1992.

PRESIDENTS ARE REELECTED DURING WARS OR THREATS OF WAR

Voters usually "rally round the flag" when wars are in progress or threatening. During the twentieth century, elected presidents successfully running for second terms included Wilson (1916) prior to World War I and Roosevelt (1940) for a third term prior to America being involved in the Second World War. Roosevelt was elected again (1944) for a fourth term and Nixon (1972) won his second term, as wars were in progress. The Dow declined in the first two instances and climbed in the latter two. In the previous century Madison was reelected during the War of 1812 and Lincoln (1864) in the midst of the Civil War.

ELECTED PRESIDENTS RUNNING FOR 2ND TERM

Year	President		Reelected Dow %	Ousted Dow %	Reason for Loss
1912	Taft	R		7.6%	Party Split
1916	**Wilson**	**D**	– 4.2%		
1932	Hoover	R		– 23.1	Depression
1936	Roosevelt	D	24.8		
1940	**Roosevelt**	**D**	– 12.7		
1944	**Roosevelt**	**D**	12.1		
1956	Eisenhower	R	2.3		
1972	**Nixon**	**R**	14.6		
1980	Carter	D		14.9	Iran Hostage Crisis
1984	Reagan	R	– 3.7		
1992	Bush	R		4.2	Post– Kuwait Recession
1996	Clinton	D	26.0		
2004	Bush GW	R			
	Totals		**59.2%**	**3.6%**	
	Average		**7.4%**	**0.9%**	

Bold: War in progress

THE STOCK MARKET AS A POPULARITY POLL

Excepting exogenous events, markets tend to do better when incumbent presidents are reelected, rather than ousted. If you tally up the twelve occasions in the last 100 years when elected presidents ran for reelection, you get an average gain of 7.4 percent on the Dow when incumbents are reelected, compared to a 0.9 percent loss on average when they lose.

DEMOCRATS LOSE OVERSEAS, REPUBLICANS HERE, TILL 1992

Power in Washington has changed hands ten times since 1900. For most of the century Democrats gave up the White House after foreign entanglements were over or turned sour, while Republicans had to move out after things went awry on our own shores. Democrats lost power in 1920 (WWI), 1952 (Korea), 1968 (Vietnam), and 1980 (Iran hostage crisis). Republicans lost it domestically in 1912 (party split), 1932 (Depression), 1960 (recession), and 1976 (Watergate).

Did the two parties trade places in the last two switches? Obviously, the Democrats lost in 2000 because of the domestic scandal, in spite of the biggest bull market on record. But, did the Republicans lose it in 1992 because of, "It's the economy, stupid," fading popularity after the Persian Gulf War, or Ross Perot siphoning off almost 20 million votes as a third-party candidate?

OCTOBER

Columbus Day
(Bond Market Closed)
One of the two (July 19) worst trading days of the year (page 123)
Monday before expiration up 11 of last 13

MONDAY
11

> *Press on. Nothing in the world can take the place of persistence. Talent will not: nothing is more common than unrewarded talent. Education alone will not: the world is full of educated failures. Persistence alone is omnipotent.*
> — Calvin Coolidge

TUESDAY
12

> *Companies already dominant in a field rarely produce the breakthroughs that transform it.*
> — George Gilder

WEDNESDAY

13

> *With enough inside information and a million dollars, you can go broke in a year.*
> — Warren Buffett

THURSDAY

14

> *The greatest discovery of my generation is that human beings can alter their lives by altering their attitudes.*
> — William James

Options expiration day up 7 of last 13

FRIDAY

15

> *If all the economists in the world were laid end to end, they still wouldn't reach a conclusion.*
> — George Bernard Shaw

SATURDAY
16

SUNDAY
17

THE RIGHT STOCK AT THE RIGHT TIME
By Larry Williams
THE BEST INVESTMENT BOOK OF THE YEAR
Reviewed by Yale Hirsch

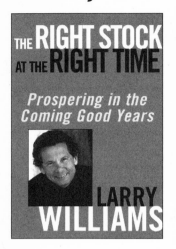

We received a copy of the original manuscript of this book back in 2001. The title then was, *Blast Off*, and it predicted the market would bottom in October 2002, which it did. The rationale was based on three major patterns featured in past editions of the *Stock Trader's Almanac*: Second years of decades tend to launch bull markets; mid-term years of presidential terms are the best buying times of the Four-Year Presidential Cycle; and October most often has been the "bear-killing" month.

Now, manuscripts are usually double-spaced on one side of 8½" x 11" sheets. This makes for a heavy mass and an awesome pile of paper to wade through. Somehow or other I put it aside. Was it the shock of 9/11 that overshadowed everything else, the brashness of the title, or the weight of the manuscript?

When I stumbled across the manuscript in the spring of 2002, I suddenly realized that I had overlooked the importance of what Williams had done. He was sticking his neck out in the midst of the biggest NASDAQ crash ever and calling for the market to turn around in October of 2002. I was simply awed to see someone as bold as I had been back in the seventies. Our newsletter headline in June 1974 urged, "Start preparing for the big bull market ahead." On the exact day of the market bottom in October, our headline had "BUY!" 20 times in two rows. And in December with the Dow at 600, our headline was, "Dow 800 by April." A call for a 33% leap in four months was right on the nose!

Of course, it's just impossible for any publisher to get out a book with a stunning forecast six months down the road, so the book had to be restructured. Nevertheless, it is quite impressive when one of the stock market's major talents analyzing past patterns can make such a breathtaking forecast. Williams discusses examples of recurring patterns familiar to Almanac readers:

DECENNIAL PATTERN

Fifth years of the last twelve decades have all been up and have averaged a 30% annual gain in the Dow.

Eighth years. Buying in the eighth week of these years and holding till year-end produced an average gain of 15.6%.

Seventh years are the second worst. Buying at lows late in these years and selling in September of **Ninth years** have produced 28.3% average gains over 13 decades.

RESERVE YOUR *2005 ALMANAC*

As a special service to *Almanac* readers, we offer you the opportunity to purchase the *2005 Stock Trader's Almanac* at a pre-publication discount. To order, call Toll-Free 877-762-2974 (in Canada call 800-567-4797) and **Save 20%** off the regular price. You may also fax your order to 800-597-3299 or email customer@wiley.com. **Refer to promo code ALMA5.**

RESERVE YOUR *2005 STOCK TRADER'S ALMANAC* NOW!

☐ Please reserve _____ copies of your *2005 Stock Trader's Almanac.*

$27.96 (regularly $34.95) plus shipping *(US: first item $5.00, each additional $3.00; International: first item $10.50, each additional $7.00).* Bulk discounts for 5 or more copies available. Call 201-748-6037.

☐ $_____ payment enclosed
(US Funds only, drawn on a US bank)

☐ Charge Credit Card (check one):
☐ Visa   ☐ Mastercard   ☐ AmEx

Name

Address

City

State   Zip

Account #

Expiration Date

Signature

BECOME A SUBSCRIBER!

☐ *I want to stay up-to-date!* Please send me future editions of the *Stock Trader's Almanac* at the yearly pre-publication discount.

You will automatically be shipped (along with the bill) future editions of the *Stock Trader's Almanac.* It's so easy and convenient!

ISBN: 0-471-64936-8   PROMO CODE ALMA5

SEND ME MORE OF THE *2004 STOCK TRADER'S ALMANAC* !

☐ Send _____ additional copies of the 2004 *Stock Trader's Almanac.*

$34.95 for single copies plus shipping *(US: first item $5.00, each additional $3.00; International: first item $10.50, each additional $7.00).* Bulk discounts for 5 or more copies available. Call 201-748-6037.

☐ $_____ payment enclosed
(US Funds only, drawn on a US bank)

☐ Charge Credit Card (check one):
☐ Visa   ☐ Mastercard   ☐ AmEx

Name

Address

City

State   Zip

Account #

Expiration Date

Signature

ISBN: 0-471-47754-0

RESERVE YOUR *2005 STOCK TRADER'S ALMANAC* NOW AND RECEIVE 20% OFF.

Mail the postage paid card below to reserve your copy.

NO POSTAGE
NECESSARY
IF MAILED
IN THE
UNITED STATES

BUSINESS REPLY MAIL
FIRST-CLASS MAIL   PERMIT NO. 2277   HOBOKEN NJ

POSTAGE WILL BE PAID BY ADDRESSEE

F REID
WILEY
111 RIVER ST.
HOBOKEN, NJ 07030-9442

NO POSTAGE
NECESSARY
IF MAILED
IN THE
UNITED STATES

BUSINESS REPLY MAIL
FIRST-CLASS MAIL   PERMIT NO. 2277   HOBOKEN NJ

POSTAGE WILL BE PAID BY ADDRESSEE

F REID
WILEY
111 RIVER ST.
HOBOKEN, NJ 07030-9442

Zero years have been the worst with the NASDAQ bubble bursting in 2000 (anticipation of new decades, or centuries, pump up prior years, leaving nothing for the zero year).

FOUR-YEAR PHENOMENON

Second years of presidential terms, since 1858, have seen stocks bottom 86% of the time, in perfect harmony with this four-year repetitive Presidential/Stock Market Cycle.

Third years (pre-election years) have been the best, with no losers since 1939.

DARLINGS OF THE DOW

Williams dresses up the "Dogs of the Dow" with his **"Darlings of the Dow"** concept and expands it to the Utility averages as well. He would buy the five lowest-priced, high-yielding Dow industrials in the last week of October of each year, and then exit on the first Friday of April the next year. At that time he would switch into the five lowest-priced, high-yielding Dow utilities and hold them till the first trading week the following October. Over a recent 25-year period this strategy produced about 30% per year. This is a very interesting addition to the "Best Six Months" switching strategy I discovered in 1986.

When it comes to market performance, the Darlings recently beat the Dogs, hands down. His web site (*larrywms.com*) listed the Darlings in October 2002 and they were up 27.4% at this writing, triple what the Dow did.

Market timing—when investors should start buying into a bear market—is always a problem. Williams answers this in a unique way, using the bond market to time his stock positions. As the book shows, the technique has an excellent record of buying shortly before or slightly after the turn has come.

Gold bugs will be driven buggy by Larry discussing when gold will rally— and why. Gold rallies, contrary to what the average investor thinks, are not stock market crash-driven as he details in the book.

In *The Right Stock at the Right Time,* Williams also covers:

- How to instantly tell if your stock is a good value
- The key stock market patterns every investor should know
- The unique relationship between seasonality and stock prices
- Gauging crucial investor sentiment
- Focusing on value while avoiding chasing high-flyers, buying rumor or concept stocks
- How to buy stocks at a discount
- Finding an approach to money management that works for you
- Why entertainment and transportation will be the industries to watch

If interested in buying the book, use the "Wiley" link on our website ***www.stocktradersalmanac.com*** and enter the **Promo Code W4448** to receive a 15% discount.

YEAR'S TOP INVESTMENT BOOKS

The Right Stock at the Right Time, Larry Williams, John Wiley & Sons, $27.95. Best Investment Book of the Year. Predicted the market would "blast off" in October 2002, one year ahead of time, but unfortunately it couldn't get to press fast enough. A perfect book for Almanac readers! (See page 96.)

Swing Trading: Power Strategies to Cut Risk and Boost Profits, Jon D. Markman, John Wiley & Sons, $29.95. Markman identifies 1200 stocks that have a definite bullish or bearish seasonal bias during certain months of the year. Also, describes the unusual strategies of five other money managers. (See page 92.)

Ahead of the Market, Mitch Zacks, HarperBusiness, $26.95. Earnings or anticipated earnings are what drive a stock's price. No ifs, ands, or buts about it. Expert from Zacks Research shows how the earnings game (they cover 30,000 analyst recommendations) is played, and how you can play it yourself. Wonder why only 8.3% of ratings are SELL recommendations? Tells how to interpret and predict future earnings announcements and revisions.

Uncommon Stock Market Strategies, David G. Funk, Ph.D, Info Publications, $29.95. Explains a rarely used technique with which investors may purchase a common stock at a price LESS than the current market price, and sell a common stock at MORE than the current market price, then benefit from price movements in either direction. These savvy investors likely outperform 98% of all investors over the years.

New Insights on Covered Call Writing: The Powerful Technique that Enhances Return and Lowers Risk in Stock Investing, Richard Lehman and Lawrence G. McMillan, Bloomberg Press, $39.95. Everything about covered call writing from two of the world's leading experts. This strategy should be part of every sophisticated investor's M.O.

Dean LeBaron's Book of Investment Quotations, Dean LeBaron, Romesh Vaitilingam & Marilyn Pitchford, John Wiley & Sons, $24.95. This is probably one of the best quotation books ever. Enjoyed it immensely and found a slew of new quotes for this year's edition. "Amongst democratic nations, each generation is a new people." Alexis de Tocqueville stated this back in the 1850s. Brilliant!

Confessions of a Street Addict, James J. Cramer, Simon & Schuster, $26. Quite a story from TheStreet.com's and CNBC's Jim Cramer (Kudlow & Cramer). Includes a number of different strategies he has developed. Very enjoyable reading.

Triumph of the Optimists: 101 Years of Global Investment Returns, Elroy Dimson, Paul Marsh, & Mike Staunton, Princeton University Press, $99.50. Analyzes returns of equities, bonds, and treasuries in 16 countries over the century. Only work of its kind, very complete and impressive, with many charts and tables.

Screening the Market: A Four-Step Method to Find, Analyze, Buy, and Sell Stocks, Marc H. Gerstein, John Wiley & Sons, $49.95. Screening data to: 1. Find a group of stocks worthy of study; 2. Analyze specific companies and their stocks; 3. Buy the best of the stocks that pass muster; and 4. Sell stocks that, after review, are no longer suitable. Most people are seat-of-the-pants investors. This is much better!

(continued on page 100)

OCTOBER

MONDAY
 18

The best minds are not in government.
If any were, business would hire them away.
— Ronald Reagan

1987 Crash Dow down 22.6% in one day

TUESDAY
19

It is a funny thing about life; if you refuse to
accept anything but the best, you very often get it.
— W. Somerset Maugham

WEDNESDAY
 20

Capitalism without bankruptcy is like Christianity without hell.
— Frank Borman (CEO Eastern Airlines, April 1986)

THURSDAY
21

I'm always turned off by an overly optimistic
letter from the president in the annual report. If his
letter is mildly pessimistic, to me that's a good sign.
— Philip Carret (Centenarian,
founded Pioneer Fund in 1928, 1896-1998)

FRIDAY
22

When I talk to a company that tells me the last analyst showed
up three years ago, I can hardly contain my enthusiasm.
— Peter Lynch

SATURDAY
23

SUNDAY
24

Less Is More: How Great Companies Use Productivity as a Competitive Tool in Business, Jason Jennings, Portfolio (a member of Penguin Putnam), $24.95. For this Number One business Best Seller, Jennings, a top keynote speaker, traveled the globe with a research team to find the most productive companies. Pick companies this way and investment success is assured.

The Complete Idiot's Guide to Market Timing, Scott Barrie, Alpha Books, $19.95. Don't let the title fool you! This is a wonderful book with more wisdom than most investment books. The author is a very savvy trader and tracker of investment strategies and recurring seasonal patterns.

The Ideas That Conquered the World: Peace, Democracy, and Free Markets in the 21st Century, Michael Mandelbaum, Public Affairs, $30.00. Three simple concepts changed the world from 100 years ago: Wars between major powers don't occur; one-eighth of the world's population lived in democracies in 1900, now two-thirds do; and free trade is rapidly spreading. Imagine how different things will be in 2103.

The Hydrogen Economy: The Creation of the World-Wide Energy Web and the Redistribution of Power on Earth, Jeremy Rifkin, J. P. Tarcher (a member of Penguin Putnam), $24.95. A very fascinating book. Things are moving rapidly. Ford's Chairman, Bill Ford, stated two years ago, "I believe fuel cells will finally end the 100-year reign of the internal combustion engine." Traces energy sources from wood to coal to oil to gas, and soon, to hydrogen.

Why Stock Markets Crash: Critical Events in Complex Financial Systems, Didier Sornette, Princeton University Press, $29.95. A specialist in catastrophe predictions uses the science of complex systems and historical precedents to calculate a market collapse. Author is a professor of geophysics at UCLA and presents some controversial concepts.

How Technical Analysis Works, Bruce M. Kamich, Prentice Hall Press (a member of Penguin Putnam), $30. A former president of the Market Technicians Association explains the basics of charting and analysis to identify trends, tops and bottoms.

Professional Stock Trading: System Design and Automation, Mark R. Conway & Aaron N. Behle, Acme Trader, $64.95. Presents a diversity of trading systems as an integrated, scientific approach to professional stock trading. Requires computer skills.

Acme Trader
237 Moody Street #565
Waltham MA 02453

Alpha Books
201 West 103rd Street
Indianapolis IN 46290

Bloomberg Press
100 Business Park Drive
Princeton NJ 08542

HarperBusiness
10 East 53rd Street
New York NY 10022

Info Publications
P.O. Box 811414
Boca Raton FL 33481

Penguin Putnam
375 Hudson Street
New York NY 10014

Princeton University Press
41 William Street
Princeton NJ 08540

Public Affairs Books
250 West 57th Street #1321
New York NY 10107

Simon & Schuster
1230 Ave. of the Americas
New York NY 10020

John Wiley & Sons
111 River Street
Hoboken NJ 07030

OCTOBER

Late October is time to buy depressed high tech stocks (page 90)

MONDAY

25

*Analysts are supposed to be critics of corporations.
They often end up being public relations spokesmen for them.*
— Ralph Wanger (Chief Investment Officer, Acorn Fund)

TUESDAY

26

*It's a lot of fun finding a country nobody knows about. The only thing
better is finding a country everybody's bullish on and shorting it.*
— Jim Rogers

WEDNESDAY

27

*Short-term volatility is greatest at turning points
and diminishes as a trend becomes established.*
— George Soros

1929 Crash Dow down 23.9% in two days

THURSDAY

28

The bigger a man's head gets, the easier it is to fill his shoes.
— Anonymous

FRIDAY

29

*The test of success is not what you do when you are on top.
Success is how high you bounce when you hit bottom.*
— General George S. Patton

SATURDAY

30

Halloween
Daylight Savings Time ends

*Bullish November Sector Seasonalities:
NASDAQ, Russell 2000 (page 118)*

SUNDAY

31

NOVEMBER ALMANAC

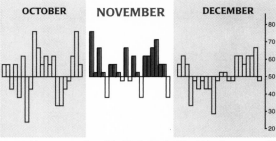

NOVEMBER							DECEMBER						
S	M	T	W	T	F	S	S	M	T	W	T	F	S
	1	2	3	4	5	6				1	2	3	4
7	8	9	10	11	12	13	5	6	7	8	9	10	11
14	15	16	17	18	19	20	12	13	14	15	16	17	18
21	22	23	24	25	26	27	19	20	21	22	23	24	25
28	29	30					26	27	28	29	30	31	

Market Probability Chart above is a graphic representation of the Market Probability Calendar on page 123.

◆ Top S&P month and #2 on Dow since 1950, #3 on NASDAQ since 1971 (pages 48 & 54) ◆ Also start of the "best six months" of the year (page 50) and NASDAQ's best three and eight months ◆ Simple timing indicator almost triples "best six months" strategy (page 52) doubles NASDAQ's best eight (page 58) ◆ RECORD S&P up 35, down 18, Dow 36/17 ◆ Day before and after Thanksgiving Day combined, only 9 losses in 51 years (page 108) ◆ 2000 worst Election Year November since Truman upsets Dewy in 1948 following first undecided Presidential Election since 1888 ◆ Previous 7 Republican victories averaged 2.8% on S&P, 7 Democrats, 0.4% (page 36)

NOVEMBER DAILY POINT CHANGES DOW JONES INDUSTRIALS

Previous Month	1993	1994	1995	1996	1997	1998	1999	2000	2001	2002
Close	3680.59	3908.12	4755.48	6029.38	7442.80	8592.10	10729.86	10971.14	9075.14	8397.03
1	12.02	− 44.75	11.20	− 7.45	—	—	− 81.35	− 71.67	188.76	120.61
2	5.03	− 26.24	41.91	—	—	114.05	− 66.67	− 18.96	59.64	—
3	− 35.77	8.75	16.98	—	231.59	N/C	27.22	− 62.56	—	—
4	− 36.89	− 38.36	—	19.75	14.74	76.99	30.58	—	—	53.96
5	18.45	—	—	39.50	3.44	132.33	64.84	—	117.49	106.67
6	—	—	− 11.56	96.53	− 9.33	59.99	—	159.26	150.09	92.74
7	—	1.35	− 16.98	28.33	− 101.92	—	—	− 25.03	− 36.75	− 184.77
8	4.47	21.87	55.64	13.78	—	—	14.37	− 45.12	33.15	− 49.11
9	− 7.83	1.01	11.56	—	—	− 77.50	− 101.53	− 72.81	20.48	—
10	23.48	− 9.76	6.14	—	− 28.73	− 33.98	− 19.58	− 231.30	—	—
11	− 1.12	− 20.52	—	35.78	6.14	− 40.16	− 2.44	—	—	− 178.18
12	22.08	—	—	10.44	− 157.41	5.92	174.02	—	− 53.63	27.05
13	—	—	2.53	8.20	86.44	89.85	—	− 85.70	196.58	12.49
14	—	28.26	− 1.09	38.76	84.72	—	—	163.81	72.66	143.64
15	− 6.99	− 3.37	50.94	35.03	—	—	8.57	26.54	48.78	36.96
16	33.25	18.84	46.61	—	—	91.66	171.58	− 51.57	− 5.40	—
17	− 6.42	− 17.15	20.59	—	125.74	− 24.97	− 49.24	− 26.16	—	—
18	− 19.01	− 12.79	—	− 1.12	− 47.40	54.83	152.61	—	—	− 92.52
19	8.67	—	—	50.69	73.92	14.94	− 31.81	—	109.47	− 11.79
20	—	—	− 6.86	32.42	101.87	103.50	—	− 167.22	− 75.08	148.23
21	—	− 45.75	40.46	− 11.55	54.46	—	—	31.85	− 66.70	222.14
22	− 23.76	− 91.52	18.06	53.29	—	—	85.63	− 95.18	H	− 40.31
23	3.92	− 3.36	H	—	—	214.72	− 93.89	H	125.03*	—
24	13.41	H	7.23*	76.03	− 113.15	− 73.12	12.54	70.91*	—	—
25	H	33.64*	—	76.03	41.03	13.13	H	—	23.04	44.56
26	− 3.63*	—	− 19.38	− 14.17	H	− 19.26*	—	23.04	− 172.98
27	—	—	22.04	− 29.07	H	18.80*	—	75.84	− 110.15	255.26
28	—	31.29	7.22	H	28.35*	—	—	− 38.49	− 60.74	H
29	− 6.15	− 1.01	27.46	22.36*	—	—	− 40.99	121.53	117.56	− 35.59*
30	6.15	0.68	− 31.07	—	—	− 216.53	− 70.11	− 214.62	22.14	—
Close	3683.95	3739.23	5074.49	6521.70	7823.13	9116.55	10877.81	10414.49	9851.56	8896.09
Change	3.36	− 168.89	319.01	492.32	380.33	524.45	147.95	− 556.65	776.42	499.06

Shortened trading day

*Astute investors always smile and remember
When stocks seasonally start soaring, and salute November*

NOVEMBER

"Best Six Months" begin Dow and S&P
"Best Eight" on NASDAQ (pages 50 and 58)

MONDAY

1

When an old man dies, a library burns down.
— African proverb

Election Day

TUESDAY

2

You try to be greedy when others are fearful,
and fearful when others are greedy.
— Warren Buffett

Average November gains last 32 years
NAS 1.9% Dow 1.4% S&P 1.4%

WEDNESDAY

3

I never hired anybody who wasn't smarter than me.
— Don Hewett (Producer, *60 Minutes*)

THURSDAY

4

Chance favors the informed mind.
— Louis Pasteur

FRIDAY

5

Drawing on my fine command of language, I said nothing.
— Robert Benchley

SATURDAY

6

SUNDAY

7

ANNOUNCING A NEW TOOL FOR ALMANAC INVESTORS

Try It FREE Along with a FREE Issue of
Almanac Investor Newsletter

Investment success is a never-ending challenge. After 37 years of publishing *The Stock Trader's Almanac,* we are still working hard at monitoring market changes and incorporating them into our strategies, developing new indicators, updating the major and minor cycles—and of course, finding new opportunities in the ever-churning universe of 10,000 active stocks.

In addition to the annual *Almanac*, we have long published newsletters that kept subscribers abreast of our current research and thinking on the market. These efforts culminated two years ago in the launch of *Almanac Investor Newsletter*, a 16-page monthly guide to market patterns, cycles, fundamental developments, strategies and stock selection.

This newsletter combines our previous monthly publications in one comprehensive but easily understandable package. It is specifically designed to update and expand the proven strategies outlined in *The Stock Trader's Almanac*—and do much more besides. **As of this writing, *Almanac Investor* holds the number three performance ranking of all newsletters reviewed by the independent *Hulbert Financial Digest* for the last 12 months.**

How to Get *Inside* the Market

Now, we can tell you about a *new* tool that is available to traders and investors who want to do their own research and explore the market in depth. We began the development of this tool—basically an interactive database—five years ago. The original idea was to make our own research quicker, more accurate and more comprehensive. We also thought about making the research tool available to subscribers, but first wanted to work out the kinks and make it easy to use.

While we shall be adding new features and much more data to this resource, we feel it is finally ready to be unveiled. *Almanac Investor* subscribers can have unlimited use of the **Online Almanac Research Tool** for a small additional fee. But as a *Stock Trader's Almanac* reader, you are invited to try out the Research Tool, as well as our monthly newsletter, FOR FREE, as explained below.

The Research Tool will integrate data and studies assembled over the 37-year history of the *Almanac* plus ongoing research and more. It's designed to be of value to the beginning investor seeking to expand his skills as well as experienced traders wanting to do their own in-depth research.

Comparable databases—if they are available at all—present users with a mass of difficult-to-use data and may cost thousands of dollars. Our Online Research Tool guides users through the process, opening the needed data step by step, graphing or calculating the results in an easily understood way.

Just go to *stocktradersalmanac.com* and try the site—FREE for one month. We do not want or need your personal information. All that is required is a valid email address. Refer to the insert card after page 96 in this book for more details. Peruse the archives of our newsletter, *Almanac Investor*. You will also receive one new issue emailed to you (The newsletter is generally emailed the third Thursday of each month). Then, subscribe online using promotional code STA4 for a 10% discount off the coupon prices. We want to make this website the best research tool available on the Internet, and in order to do that we need your comments and feedback.

NOVEMBER

MONDAY
8

I've never been poor, only broke. Being poor is a frame of mind.
Being broke is only a temporary situation.
— Mike Todd (Movie producer, 1903-1958)

TUESDAY
9

The measure of success is not whether you have a tough problem
to deal with, but whether it's the same problem you had last year.
— John Foster Dulles (Secretary of State under Eisenhower,
1888-1959)

FOMC Meeting

WEDNESDAY
10

Don't be scared to take big steps—
you can't cross a chasm in two small jumps.
— David Lloyd George (British Prime Minister, 1916-1922)

Veteran's Day
(Bond Market Closed)

THURSDAY
11

I cannot give you a formula for success but I can
give you a formula for failure: Try to please everybody.
— Herbert Swope (American journalist, 1882-1958)

FRIDAY
 # 12

Under capitalism, the seller chases after the buyer,
and that makes both of them work better; under socialism,
the buyer chases the seller, and neither has time to work.
— Andrei Sakharov's Uncle Ivan

SATURDAY
13

SUNDAY
14

MOST OF THE SO-CALLED "JANUARY EFFECT" TAKES PLACE IN DECEMBER'S LAST TWO WEEKS

Over the years we reported annually on the fascinating January Effect, showing that Standard and Poor's Low-Priced Stock Index during January handily outperformed the S&P 500 Index 40 out of 43 years between 1953 and 1995. Readers saw that "Cats and Dogs" on average quadrupled the returns of blue chips in this period. Then, the January Effect disappeared over the next four years.

In addition, S&P decided to discontinue their Low-Priced Index. S&P's SmallCap 600 index was launched October 17, 1994, not giving us an historically significant set of data. Looking at the graph on page 114, which shows small cap stocks beginning to outperform the blue chips in mid-December, made the decision simple; just compare the Russell 1000 index of large capitalization stocks to the Russell 2000 smaller capitalization stocks. Doing it in half-month segments was an inspiration and proved to be quite revealing, as you can see in the table.

16-YEAR AVERAGE RATES OF RETURN (DEC 1987- FEB 2003)

From 12/15	Russell 1000		Russell 2000	
	Change	Annualized	Change	Annualized
12/15-12/31	2.1%	69.9%	3.7%	159.2%
12/15-01/15	2.3	31.8	4.4	67.6
12/15-01/31	3.3	30.2	5.4	52.7
12/15-02/15	4.0	26.8	7.0	50.0
12/15-02/28	3.3	17.8	7.7	44.8
From 12/31				
12/31-01/15	0.3	3.2	0.6	7.7
12/31-01/31	1.3	10.6	1.6	13.7
12/31-02/15	1.9	12.2	3.1	20.2
12/31-02/28	1.4	7.0	3.6	19.6

24-YEAR AVERAGE RATES OF RETURN (DEC 1979- FEB 2003)

From 12/15	Russell 1000		Russell 2000	
	Change	Annualized	Change	Annualized
12/15-12/31	1.7%	55.6%	3.0%	118.3%
12/15-01/15	2.4	33.7	4.7	74.0
12/15-01/31	3.4	31.2	5.7	55.7
12/15-02/15	4.0	26.8	7.2	51.5
12/15-02/28	3.7	19.7	7.7	45.0
From 12/31				
12/31-01/15	0.7	9.1	1.6	21.4
12/31-01/31	1.7	14.7	2.6	22.4
12/31-02/15	2.3	14.7	4.0	26.5
12/31-02/28	2.0	10.5	4.4	24.2

Small-cap strength in December's last two weeks becomes even more magnified after the 1987 market crash. Note the dramatic shift in the gains the last two weeks of December during the 16-year period starting in 1987 versus the 24 years from 1979 to 2003. With all the beaten-down small stocks being dumped for tax loss purposes, it pays to get a head start on the January Effect in mid-December.

NOVEMBER

Monday before Expiration
Dow down 7 of last 12 (down 4 in row)

MONDAY
15

Get inside information from the president and you will probably lose half your money. If you get it from the chairman of the board, you will lose all your money.
— Jim Rogers

Week before Thanksgiving Week,
S&P up 11 years in a row

TUESDAY
16

Things may come to those who wait, but only the things left by those who hustle.
— Abraham Lincoln

WEDNESDAY
17

There is one thing stronger than all the armies in the world, and this is an idea whose time has come.
— Victor Hugo

THURSDAY
18

He who wants to persuade should put his trust not in the right argument, but in the right word. The power of sound has always been greater than the power of sense.
— Joseph Conrad

Options Expiration Dow up 7 of last 12

FRIDAY
19

There have been three great inventions since the beginning of time: The fire, the wheel, and central banking.
— Will Rogers

SATURDAY
20

SUNDAY
21

TRADING THE THANKSGIVING MARKET

For 35 years the combination of the Wednesday before Thanksgiving and the Friday after had a great track record, except for two occasions. Attributing this phenomenon to the warm "holiday spirit" was a no-brainer. But, publishing it in the 1987 Almanac was the "kiss of death." Since then it has been up nine of the last sixteen times. However, going long into weakness Tuesday or Wednesday and staying in through the following Monday improves the record.

DOW JONES INDUSTRIALS BEFORE AND AFTER THANKSGIVING

	Tuesday Before	Wednesday Before		Friday After	Total Gain Dow Points	Dow Close	Next Monday
1952	− 0.18	1.54		1.22	2.76	283.66	0.04
1953	1.71	0.65		2.45	3.10	280.23	1.14
1954	3.27	1.89		3.16	5.05	387.79	0.72
1955	4.61	0.71		0.26	0.97	482.88	− 1.92
1956	− 4.49	− 2.16		4.65	2.49	472.56	− 2.27
1957	− 9.04	10.69		3.84	14.53	449.87	− 2.96
1958	− 4.37	8.63		8.31	16.94	557.46	2.61
1959	2.94	1.41	T	1.42	2.83	652.52	6.66
1960	− 3.44	1.37		4.00	5.37	606.47	− 1.04
1961	− 0.77	1.10		2.18	3.28	732.60	− 0.61
1962	6.73	4.31		7.62	11.93	644.87	− 2.81
1963	32.03	− 2.52	H	9.52	7.00	750.52	1.39
1964	− 1.68	− 5.21		− 0.28	− 5.49	882.12	− 6.69
1965	2.56	N/C	A	− 0.78	− 0.78	948.16	− 1.23
1966	− 3.18	1.84		6.52	8.36	803.34	− 2.18
1967	13.17	3.07	N	3.58	6.65	877.60	4.51
1968	8.14	− 3.17		8.76	5.59	985.08	− 1.74
1969	− 5.61	3.23	K	1.78	5.01	812.30	− 7.26
1970	5.21	1.98		6.64	8.62	781.35	12.74
1971	− 5.18	0.66	S	17.96	18.62	816.59	13.14
1972	8.21	7.29		4.67	11.96	1025.21	− 7.45
1973	− 17.76	10.08	G	− 0.98	9.10	854.00	− 29.05
1974	5.32	2.03		− 0.63	1.40	618.66	− 15.64
1975	9.76	3.15	I	2.12	5.27	860.67	− 4.33
1976	− 6.57	1.66		5.66	7.32	956.62	− 6.57
1977	6.41	0.78		1.12	1.90	844.42	− 4.85
1978	− 1.56	2.95	V	3.12	6.07	810.12	3.72
1979	− 6.05	− 1.80		4.35	2.55	811.77	16.98
1980	3.93	7.00	I	3.66	10.66	993.34	− 23.89
1981	18.45	7.90		7.80	15.70	885.94	3.04
1982	− 9.01	9.01	N	7.36	16.37	1007.36	− 4.51
1983	7.01	− 0.20		1.83	1.63	1277.44	− 7.62
1984	9.83	6.40	G	18.78	25.18	1220.30	− 7.95
1985	0.12	18.92		− 3.56	15.36	1472.13	− 14.22
1986	6.05	4.64		− 2.53	2.11	1914.23	− 1.55
1987	40.45	− 16.58		− 36.47	− 53.05	1910.48	− 76.93
1988	11.73	14.58		− 17.60	− 3.02	2074.68	6.76
1989	7.25	17.49		18.77	36.26	2675.55	19.42
1990	− 35.15	9.16	D	− 12.13	− 2.97	2527.23	5.94
1991	14.08	− 16.10		− 5.36	− 21.46	2894.68	40.70
1992	25.66	17.56	A	15.94	33.50	3282.20	22.96
1993	3.92	13.41		− 3.63	9.78	3683.95	− 6.15
1994	− 91.52	− 3.36	Y	33.64	30.28	3708.27	31.29
1995	40.46	18.06		7.23*	25.29	5048.84	22.04
1996	− 19.38	− 29.07		22.36*	− 6.71	6521.70	N/C
1997	41.03	− 14.17		28.35*	14.18	7823.13	189.98
1998	− 73.12	13.13		18.80*	31.93	9333.08	− 216.53
1999	− 93.89	12.54		− 19.26*	− 6.72	10988.91	− 40.99
2000	31.85	− 95.18		70.91*	− 24.27	10470.23	75.84
2001	− 75.08	− 66.70		125.03*	58.33	9959.71	23.04
2002	−172.98	255.26		− 35.59*	219.67	8896.09	− 33.52

*Shortened trading day

NOVEMBER

MONDAY 22

I measure what's going on, and I adapt to it.
I try to get my ego out of the way.
The market is smarter than I am so I bend.
— Martin Zweig

TUESDAY 23

The market is a voting machine, whereon countless
individuals register choices which are the
product partly of reason and partly of emotion.
— Graham & Dodd

(Bond Market Closes Early) ## WEDNESDAY 24

Your emotions are often a reverse indicator
of what you ought to be doing.
— John F. Hindelong (Dillon, Reed)

Thanksgiving
(Market Closed) ## THURSDAY 25

To me, the "tape" is the final arbiter
of any investment decision.
I have a cardinal rule: Never fight the tape!
— Martin Zweig

(Shortened Trading Day) ## FRIDAY 26

Every successful enterprise requires three people—
a dreamer, a businessman, and a son-of-a-bitch.
— Peter McArthur (1904)

SATURDAY 27

Bullish December Sector Seasonalities: Oil, Gold/Silver ## SUNDAY 28

DECEMBER ALMANAC

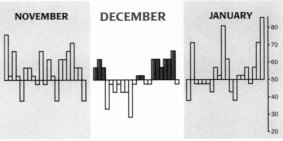

Market Probability Chart above is a graphic representation of the Market Probability Calendar on page 123.

◆ #2 month; average S&P gain 1.6%, Dow 1.7% since 1950 (page 48); NASDAQ 2.1% since 1971 ◆ 2002 worst December since 1931, down over 6% Dow and S&P, –9.7% on NASDAQ (pages 141, 145 & 151) ◆ "Free lunch" served on Wall Street at month end (page 112) ◆ Small-caps start to outperform larger caps near middle of month (page 114) ◆ "Santa Claus Rally" visible in graph above and on page 116 ◆ In 1998 was part of best fourth quarter since 1928 ◆ Election Year Decembers fare well; S&P averages 1.1%, up 10, down 3; NASDAQ, +1.1%, up 5, down 3

DECEMBER DAILY POINT CHANGES DOW JONES INDUSTRIALS

Previous Month Close	1993 3683.95	1994 3739.23	1995 5074.49	1996 6521.70	1997 7823.13	1998 9116.55	1999 10877.81	2000 10414.49	2001 9851.56	2002 8896.09
1	13.13	–38.36	12.64	—	189.98	16.99	120.58	– 40.95	—	—
2	5.03	44.75	—	N/C	5.72	– 69.00	40.67	—	—	– 33.52
3	1.96	—	—	– 79.01	13.18	–184.86	247.12	—	– 87.60	–119.64
4	—	—	52.39	– 19.75	18.15	136.46	—	186.56	129.88	– 5.08
5	—	– 3.70	37.93	14.16	98.97	—	—	338.62	220.45	–114.57
6	6.14	4.03	21.68	– 55.16	—	—	– 61.17	–234.34	– 15.15	22.49
7	8.67	–10.43	– 39.74	—	—	54.33	–118.36	– 47.02	– 49.68	—
8	15.65	–49.79	– 2.53	—	– 38.29	– 42.49	– 38.53	95.55	—	—
9	– 4.75	5.38	—	82.00	– 61.18	– 18.79	66.67	—	—	–172.36
10	10.89	—	—	9.31	– 70.87	–167.61	89.91	—	–128.01	100.85
11	—	—	27.46	– 70.73	–129.80	– 19.82	—	12.89	– 33.08	14.88
12	—	27.26	– 9.40	– 98.81	– 10.69	—	—	42.47	6.44	– 50.74
13	23.76	– 3.03	41.55	1.16	—	—	– 32.11	26.17	–128.36	–104.69
14	–21.80	30.95	– 34.32	—	—	–126.16	– 32.42	–119.45	44.70	—
15	–25.71	19.18	– 5.42	—	84.29	127.70	65.15	–240.04	—	—
16	9.22	41.72	—	– 36.52	53.72	– 32.70	19.57	—	—	193.69
17	25.43	—	—	39.98	– 18.90	85.22	12.54	—	80.82	– 92.01
18	—	—	–101.52	38.44	–110.91	27.81	—	210.47	106.42	– 88.04
19	—	–16.49	34.68	126.87	– 90.21	—	—	– 61.05	72.10	– 82.55
20	3.64	–23.55	– 50.57	10.76	—	—	–113.16	–265.44	– 85.31	146.52
21	–10.06	34.65	37.21	—	—	85.22	56.27	168.36	50.16	—
22	17.04	13.12	1.44	—	63.02	55.61	3.06	148.27	—	—
23	– 4.47	18.51	—	4.62	–127.54	157.57	202.16*	—	—	– 18.03
24	Closed	—	—	33.83*	– 31.64*	15.96*	Closed	—	N/C*	– 45.18*
25	H	H	H	H	H	H	H	H	H	H
26	—	Closed	12.29	23.83	19.18*	—	—	56.88	52.80	– 15.50
27	35.21	28.26	– 4.34	14.23	—	—	– 14.68	110.72	43.17	–128.83
28	0.84	–22.20	– 10.12	—	—	8.76	85.63	65.60	5.68	—
29	0.56	– 6.06	21.32	—	113.10	94.23	7.95	– 81.91	—	—
30	–18.45	1.01	—	– 11.54	123.56	– 46.34	– 31.80	—	—	29.07
31	–21.79	—	—	–101.10	– 7.72	– 93.21	44.26	—	–115.49	8.78
Close	3754.09	3834.44	5117.12	6448.27	7908.25	9181.43	11497.12	10786.85	10021.50	8341.63
Change	70.14	95.21	42.63	– 73.43	85.12	64.88	619.31	372.36	169.94	– 554.46

* Shortened trading day

If Santa Claus should fail to call
Bears may come to Broad and Wall

NOVEMBER/DECEMBER

MONDAY
29

I always keep these seasonal patterns in the back of my mind.
My antennae start to purr at certain times of the year.
— Kenneth Ward

TUESDAY
30

To find one man in a thousand who is your true friend from
unselfish motives is to find one of the great wonders of the world.
— Leopold Mozart (Quoted by Maynard Solomon, *Mozart*)

December first trading day Dow up 6 of last 12 (down 3 in a row)

WEDNESDAY
1

Averaging down in a bear market is tantamount
to taking a seat on the down escalator at Macy's.
— Richard Russell (*Dow Theory Letters*, 1984)

Average December gains last 32 years
NAS 2.1% Dow 1.6% S&P 1.6%

THURSDAY
2

The possession of gold has ruined fewer men than the lack of it.
— Thomas Bailey Aldridge (1903)

FRIDAY
3

A man will fight harder for his interests than his rights.
— Napoleon Bonaparte (1815)

SATURDAY
4

SUNDAY
5

WALL STREET'S ONLY "FREE LUNCH" NOW SERVED IN LATE DECEMBER

As investors normally tend to get rid of their losers near year-end for tax purposes, these stocks are often hammered down to bargain levels. Over the years the Almanac has shown that New York Stock Exchange stocks selling at their lows on December 15 will usually outperform the market by February 15 in the following year. Preferred stocks, closed-end funds, splits and new issues are eliminated. When there are a huge number of new lows, stocks down the most are selected, even though there are usually good reasons why some stocks have been battered.

BARGAIN STOCKS VS. THE MARKET**

Short Span Late Dec - Jan/Feb	New Lows Late Dec	% Change Jan/Feb	% Change NYSE Composite	Bargain Stocks Advantage
1974-75	112	48.9%	22.1%	26.8%
1975-76	21	34.9	14.9	20.0
1976-77	2	1.3	— 3.3	4.6
1977-78	15	2.8	— 4.5	7.3
1978-79	43	11.8	3.9	7.9
1979-80	5	9.3	6.1	3.2
1980-81	14	7.1	— 2.0	9.1
1981-82	21	— 2.6	— 7.4	4.8
1982-83	4	33.0	9.7	23.3
1983-84	13	— 3.2	— 3.8	0.6
1984-85	32	19.0	12.1	6.9
1985-86	4	— 22.5	3.9	— 26.4
1986-87	22	9.3	12.5	— 3.2
1987-88	23	13.2	6.8	6.4
1988-89	14	30.0	6.4	23.6
1989-90	25	— 3.1	— 4.8	1.7
1990-91	18	18.8	12.6	6.2
1991-92	23	51.1	7.7	43.4
1992-93	9	8.7	0.6	8.1
1993-94	10	— 1.4	2.0	— 3.4
1994-95	25	14.6	5.7	8.9
1995-96	5	— 11.3	4.5	—15.8
1996-97	16	13.9	11.2	2.7
1997-98	29	9.9	5.7	4.2
1998-99	40	— 2.8	4.3	— 7.1
1999-00	26[*]	8.9	— 5.4	14.3
2000-01	51[1]	44.4	0.1	44.3
2001-02	12[2]	31.4	— 2.3	33.7
2002-03	33[3]	28.7	3.9	24.8
29-Year Totals		**404.1%**	**123.2%**	**280.9%**
Average		**13.9%**	**4.2%**	**9.7%**

Chosen 12/29/99 [1] Chosen 12/27/00 [2] Chosen 12/26/01, incl NAS stocks, % chg thru 1/16/02
*[3] Chosen 12/26/02, incl NAS & AMEX stocks, % chg thru 1/14/03 ** Dec 15 - Feb 15 (1974-1999)*

However, as tax selling in recent years seems to be continuing down to the last few days of the year, "scavengers" have been given an even better opportunity. So, we've altered the strategy the last four years to make our selections from NYSE stocks making new lows on the fourth-to-last trading day of the year. We tweaked the strategy further in 2002 and 2003. With few NYSE stocks left after our screens in 2002 and 2003 we turned to the NASDAQ and AMEX and selected more stocks using the same criteria and emailed them to our *Almanac Investor* newsletter subscribers. And, noticing the tendency over the past few years for these stocks to start giving back their gains in January, we advised subscribers to sell in mid-January. To receive a free copy of the *Almanac Investor* newsletter send an email to **service@hirschorg.com** or visit **www.stocktradersalmanac.com**. Subscribers will receive the list of stocks selected December 26, 2003 via email.

Examination of December trades by NYSE members through the years shows they tend to buy on balance during this month, contrary to other months.

DECEMBER

MONDAY
6

*In all recorded history, there has not been one economist who
has had to worry about where the next meal would come from.*
— Peter Drucker

TUESDAY
7

*The less a man knows about the past and the present the more
insecure must be his judgment of the future.*
— Sigmund Freud

Chanukah

WEDNESDAY
8

The first stocks to double in a bull market will usually double again.
— Michael Burke (*Investors Intelligence*)

THURSDAY
9

*Marx's great achievement was to place
the system of capitalism on the defensive.*
— Charles A. Madison (1977)

FRIDAY
10

*The word "crisis" in Chinese is composed of two characters:
the first, the symbol of danger; the second, opportunity.*
— Anonymous

SATURDAY
11

SUNDAY
12

JANUARY EFFECT STARTS IN MID-DECEMBER

We always hear about the January Effect, but now we have a graph revealing that it does indeed exist. Ned Davis Research has taken the 24 years of daily data for the Russell 2000 index of smaller companies and divided it by the Russell 1000 index of largest companies. Then they compressed the 24 years into a single year to show an idealized yearly pattern. When the graph is descending, big blue chips are outperforming smaller companies; when the graph is rising, smaller companies are moving up faster than their larger brethren.

In a typical year the smaller fry stay on the sidelines while the big boys are on the field; suddenly, in mid-December, the smaller fry take over and take off. This is known as the "January Effect." So many year-end dividends, payouts and bonuses could be a factor. Another major move is quite evident just before Labor Day. Possibly because individual investors are back from vacations. Also note the moves off the low points in late October and November.

RUSSELL 2000/RUSSELL 1000 ONE-YEAR SEASONAL PATTERN

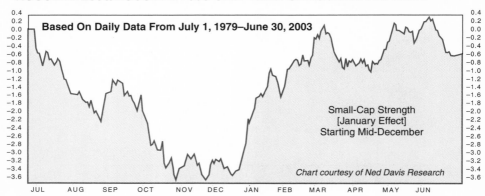

The data for the bottom graph was provided by Global Financial Data and shows the actual ratio of the Russell 2000 divided by the Russell 1000 from 1979. We see the smaller companies having the upper hand for five years into 1983; then falling behind for about seven years, coming back after the Persian Gulf War and moving up more until 1994. For six years the picture had been bleak for small fry as the blue chips and tech stocks moved to stratospheric PE ratios. But note the small-cap spikes in late 1999, 2000, 2001 and the continuing uptrend into mid-2002. After the bear market ended in October 2002 and the successful test in March 2003 small caps resumed trumping the big caps. Stocks with lower market capitalizations should outperform for more years to come.

RUSSELL 2000/RUSSELL 1000 (1979–JUNE 2003)

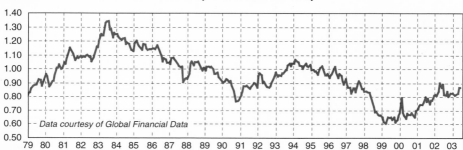

DECEMBER

Monday before Triple-Witching Dow up 8 of last 12

MONDAY

13

In the course of evolution and a higher civilization we might be able to get along comfortably without Congress, but without Wall Street, never.
— Henry Clews (1900)

FOMC Meeting

TUESDAY

14

Let us have the courage to stop borrowing to meet the continuing deficits. Stop the deficits.
— Franklin D. Roosevelt (1932)

Small cap strength starts In mid-December

WEDNESDAY

15

If I had my life to live over again, I would elect to be a trader of goods rather than a student of science. I think barter is a noble thing.
— Albert Einstein (1934)

THURSDAY

16

You must automate, emigrate, or evaporate.
— James A. Baker (General Electric)

December Triple Witching up 9 of last 12

FRIDAY

17

If you don't know who you are, the stock market is an expensive place to find out.
— George Goodman (1959)

SATURDAY

18

SUNDAY

19

IF SANTA CLAUS SHOULD FAIL TO CALL
BEARS MAY COME TO BROAD & WALL

Santa Claus tends to come to Wall Street nearly every year, bringing a short, sweet, respectable rally within the last five days of the year and the first two in January. This has been good for an average 1.7% gain since 1969 (1.5% since 1950). Santa's failure to show tends to precede bear markets, or times stocks could be purchased later in the year at much lower prices. Such occasions provide opportunities for long-term players to at least write options on their stocks. We discovered this phenomenon in 1972.

DAILY % CHANGE IN S&P COMPOSITE INDEX AT YEAR END

	Trading Days Before Year-End						First Days in January			Rally % Change
	6	5	4	3	2	1	1	2	3	
1969	— 0.4	1.1	0.8	— 0.7	0.4	0.5	1.0	0.5	— 0.7	3.6
1970	0.1	0.6	0.5	1.1	0.2	— 0.1	— 1.1	0.7	0.6	1.9
1971	— 0.4	0.2	1.0	0.3	— 0.4	0.3	— 0.4	0.4	1.0	1.3
1972	— 0.3	— 0.7	0.6	0.4	0.5	1.0	0.9	0.4	— 0.1	3.1
1973	— 1.1	— 0.7	3.1	2.1	— 0.2	0.01	0.1	2.2	— 0.9	6.7
1974	— 1.4	1.4	0.8	— 0.4	0.03	2.1	2.4	0.7	0.5	7.2
1975	0.7	0.8	0.9	— 0.1	— 0.4	0.5	0.8	1.8	1.0	4.3
1976	0.1	1.2	0.7	— 0.4	0.5	0.5	— 0.4	— 1.2	— 0.9	0.8
1977	0.8	0.9	N/C	0.1	0.2	0.2	— 1.3	— 0.3	— 0.8	— 0.3
1978	0.03	1.7	1.3	— 0.9	— 0.4	— 0.2	0.6	1.1	0.8	3.3
1979	— 0.6	0.1	0.1	0.2	— 0.1	0.1	— 2.0	— 0.5	1.2	— 2.2
1980	— 0.4	0.4	0.5	— 1.1	0.2	0.3	0.4	1.2	0.1	2.0
1981	— 0.5	0.2	— 0.2	— 0.5	0.5	0.2	0.2	— 2.2	— 0.7	— 1.8
1982	0.6	1.8	— 1.0	0.3	— 0.7	0.2	— 1.6	2.2	0.4	1.2
1983	— 0.2	— 0.03	0.9	0.3	— 0.2	0.05	— 0.5	1.7	1.2	2.1
1984	— 0.5	0.8	— 0.2	— 0.4	0.3	0.6	— 1.1	— 0.5	— 0.5	— 0.6
1985	— 1.1	— 0.7	0.2	0.9	0.5	0.3	— 0.8	0.6	— 0.1	1.1
1986	— 1.0	0.2	0.1	— 0.9	— 0.5	— 0.5	1.8	2.3	0.2	2.4
1987	1.3	— 0.5	— 2.6	— 0.4	1.3	— 0.3	3.6	1.1	0.1	2.2
1988	— 0.2	0.3	— 0.4	0.1	0.8	— 0.6	— 0.9	1.5	0.2	0.9
1989	0.6	0.8	— 0.2	0.6	0.5	0.8	1.8	— 0.3	— 0.9	4.1
1990	0.5	— 0.6	0.3	— 0.8	0.1	0.5	— 1.1	— 1.4	— 0.3	— 3.0
1991	2.5	0.6	1.4	0.4	2.1	0.5	0.04	0.5	— 0.3	5.7
1992	— 0.3	0.2	— 0.1	— 0.3	0.2	— 0.7	— 0.1	— 0.2	0.04	— 1.1
1993	0.01	0.7	0.1	— 0.1	— 0.4	— 0.5	— 0.2	0.3	0.1	— 0.1
1994	0.01	0.2	0.4	— 0.3	0.1	— 0.4	— 0.03	0.3	— 0.1	0.2
1995	0.8	0.2	0.4	0.04	— 0.1	0.3	0.8	0.1	— 0.6	1.8
1996	— 0.3	0.5	0.6	0.1	— 0.4	— 1.7	— 0.5	1.5	— 0.1	0.1
1997	— 1.5	— 0.7	0.4	1.8	1.8	— 0.04	0.5	0.2	— 1.1	4.0
1998	2.1	— 0.2	— 0.1	1.3	— 0.8	— 0.2	— 0.1	1.4	2.2	1.3
1999	1.6	— 0.1	0.04	0.4	0.1	0.3	— 1.0	— 3.8	0.2	— 4.0
2000	0.8	2.4	0.7	1.0	0.4	— 1.0	— 2.8	5.0	— 1.1	5.7
2001	0.4	— 0.02	0.4	0.7	0.3	— 1.1	0.6	0.9	0.6	1.8
2002	— 0.2	— 0.5	— 0.2	— 1.5	0.4	0.1	3.2	— 0.1	2.0	1.3
Avg	**0.07**	**0.37**	**0.35**	**0.09**	**0.21**	**0.05**	**0.08**	**0.53**	**0.10**	**1.7**

The couplet above was certainly on the mark in 2000, as the period suffered a horrendous 4.0% loss. On January 14, 2000 the Dow started its 33-month 37.8% slide to the October 2002 midterm election year bottom. NASDAQ cracked eight weeks later, falling 37.3% in 10 weeks, eventually dropping 77.9% by October 2002. This is reminiscent of the Dow during the Depression, when the Dow initially fell 47.9% in just over two months from 381.17 September 3, 1929, only to end down 89.2% at its 20th century low of 41.22 on July 8, 1932. Perhaps October 9, 2002 will prove to be the low for the 21st century. Saddam Hussein cancelled Christmas by invading Kuwait in 1990. Less bullishness on last day is due to last-minute portfolio restructuring. Pushing gains and losses into the next tax year affects year's first trading day.

DECEMBER

MONDAY
20

*The worst trades are generally when people freeze
and start to pray and hope rather than take some action.*
— Robert Mnuchin (Goldman, Sachs)

TUESDAY
21

*A good trader has to have three things:
a chronic inability to accept things at face value,
to feel continuously unsettled, and to have humility.*
— Michael Steinhardt

Watch for Santa Claus Rally (page 116)

WEDNESDAY
 22

*The pursuit of gain is the only way in which people
can serve the needs of others whom they do not know.*
— Friedrich von Hayek (*Counterrevolution of Science*)

Last trading day before Christmas Dow up 8 of last 12 (pages 86 & 110)

THURSDAY
23

*Cheapening the cost of necessities and conveniences of life
is the most powerful agent of civilization and progress.*
— Thomas Elliott Perkins (1888)

(Market Closed)

FRIDAY
24

*In the market, yesterday is a memory and tomorrow is a vision.
And looking back is a lot easier than looking ahead.*
— Frankie Joe

Christmas Day

SATURDAY
25

SUNDAY
26

SECTOR SEASONALITY: SELECTED PERCENTAGE PLAYS

Sector seasonality, a study by Merrill Lynch, was featured in the first 1968 Almanac. It showed that buying aerospace, agriculture, air conditioning, eastern railroads, fire/casualty insurance, machine tools, and meatpacking sectors around September or October and selling in the first few months of the 1954-1964 years gained more than triple the profit than holding them for ten years. This didn't include interest or profits made the rest of the year.

From the seasonality studies on sectors by Jon D. Markman, senior investment strategist and portfolio manager at Pinnacle Investment Advisors, in his book, *Online Investing*, and his online *SuperModels* on CNBC on MSN Money, we have fashioned the sector index seasonality table below. It is similar in style to the "Best Six Months" on page 50 and hypothetically offers even greater possibilities. Also, see Exchange Traded Funds on page 189.

SECTOR INDEX SEASONALITY TABLE

Symbol	Sector Index		Months of Streak Start	End	Avg.% Return
XNG	Natural Gas	(Bearish)	January	January	− 3.4%
BKX	PHLX Banking		January	May	8.8
SOX	PHLX Semiconductor		January	January	9.0
UTY	PHLX Utility	(Bearish)	January	March	− 2.9
IIX	Internet	(Bearish)	February	February	− 5.8
XNG	Natural Gas		February	May	16.9
XAL	Airline		March	June	16.9
BTK	Biotechnology	(Bearish)	March	March	− 5.6
XBD	Securities Broker/Dealer		March	June	12.3
BTK	Biotechnology		April	June	8.5
FPP	PHLX Forest/Pap		April	April	7.0
SOX	PHLX Semiconductor		April	April	6.9
UTY	PHLX Utility		April	December	6.8
FPP	PHLX Forest/Pap	(Bearish)	May	September	− 10.7
XNG	Natural Gas	(Bearish)	June	July	− 7.0
XAL	Airline	(Bearish)	July	September	− 21.9
IIX	Internet	(Bearish)	July	August	− 7.2
RUT	Russell 2000	(Bearish)	July	October	− 5.4
BTK	Biotechnology		August	February	29.7
CYC	Morgan Stanley Cyclical	(Bearish)	August	September	− 6.2
DRG	Pharmaceutical		September	January	13.5
SOX	PHLX Semiconductor	(Bearish)	September	September	− 7.4
XAL	Airline		October	December	16.6
IIX	Internet		October	January	21.7
CYC	Morgan Stanley Cyclical		October	April	12.8
MSH	Morgan/Stanley High-Tech		October	January	18.9
XTC	N. Amer Telecomm		October	January	13.9
NDX	Nasdaq 100		October	June	18.7
NDX	Nasdaq 100		October	January	12.4
BKX	PHLX Banking		October	May	14.3
FPP	PHLX Forest/Pap		October	April	13.8
XAU	PHLX Gold/Silver	(Bearish)	October	October	− 6.7
SOX	PHLX Semiconductor		October	April	31.7
XBD	Securities Broker/Dealer		October	January	18.2
COMP	Nasdaq Composite		November	June	14.9
COMP	Nasdaq Composite		November	January	10.5
PSE	Pacfic SE High-Tech		November	February	15.0
RUT	Russell 2000		November	May	12.9
XOI	Oil		December	May	11.0
XAU	PHLX Gold/Silver		December	May	7.7

DECEMBER/JANUARY 2004

First trading day after Christmas Dow up 10 of last 12

MONDAY

27

*If you don't profit from your investment mistakes,
someone else will.*
— Yale Hirsch

*New Lows perform better when selected last
settlement day of year (page 112)*

TUESDAY

28

*Major bottoms are usually made when analysts cut their earnings estimates
and companies report earnings which are below expectations.*
— Edward Babbitt, Jr. (Avatar Associates)

*Almanac Investor FREE LUNCH Menu of
New Lows served to subscribers, visit
stocktradersalmanac.com for details*

WEDNESDAY

29

*The worst bankrupt in the world is
the person who has lost his enthusiasm.*
— H.W. Arnold

THURSDAY

30

*Man's mind, once stretched by a new idea,
never regains its original dimensions.*
— Oliver Wendell Holmes

(Shortened Trading Day)
*Last day of year NASDAQ up 29 of 32, but down 3 in a row
Dow down 7 of last 11*

FRIDAY

31

*It's no coincidence that three of the top five stock option traders
in a recent trading contest were all former Marines.*
— Robert Prechter, Jr. (*Elliott Wave Theorist*)

New Year's Day

SATURDAY

1

*January Sector Seasonalities:
Bullish: Banking, Semiconductor;
Bearish: Natural Gas, Utilities (page 118)*

SUNDAY

2

NASDAQ COMPOSITE MARKET PROBABILITY CALENDAR 2004
THE % CHANCE OF THE MARKET RISING ON ANY TRADING DAY OF THE YEAR

(Based on the number of times the NASDAQ rose on a particular trading day during January 1972-December 2002)

Date	Jan	Feb	Mar	Apr	May	Jun	Jul	Aug	Sep	Oct	Nov	Dec
1	H	S	67.7	35.5	S	58.1	51.6	S	51.6	45.2	71.0	61.3
2	48.4	64.5	61.3	58.1	S	77.4	48.4	51.6	64.5	S	51.6	61.3
3	S	71.0	74.2	S	58.1	61.3	S	41.9	58.1	S	74.2	64.5
4	S	64.5	54.8	S	71.0	58.1	S	51.6	S	61.3	51.6	S
5	77.4	64.5	54.8	61.3	67.7	S	H	67.7	S	51.6	45.2	S
6	58.1	54.8	S	54.8	54.8	S	41.9	64.5	H	61.3	S	58.1
7	64.5	S	S	51.6	58.1	58.1	48.4	S	58.1	61.3	S	45.2
8	51.6	S	61.3	64.5	S	48.4	61.3	S	54.8	64.5	54.8	48.4
9	58.1	48.4	61.3	H	S	45.2	61.3	41.9	45.2	S	67.7	41.9
10	S	51.6	51.6	S	61.3	58.1	S	51.6	45.2	S	64.5	41.9
11	S	67.7	71.0	S	54.8	61.3	S	51.6	S	45.2	51.6	S
12	51.6	54.8	48.4	67.7	38.7	S	61.3	61.3	S	48.4	58.1	S
13	61.3	58.1	S	58.1	58.1	S	74.2	61.3	58.1	77.4	S	45.2
14	67.7	S	S	54.8	61.3	64.5	77.4	S	54.8	64.5	S	35.5
15	74.2	S	54.8	64.5	S	51.6	71.0	S	35.5	51.6	41.9	45.2
16	77.4	H	64.5	51.6	S	61.3	48.4	54.8	38.7	S	41.9	58.1
17	S	54.8	51.6	S	48.4	38.7	S	67.7	35.5	S	51.6	51.6
18	S	51.6	64.5	S	51.6	45.2	S	41.9	S	67.7	45.2	S
19	H	54.8	41.9	54.8	45.2	S	29.0	35.5	S	48.4	54.8	S
20	51.6	38.7	S	51.6	54.8	S	48.4	71.0	58.1	64.5	S	54.8
21	45.2	S	S	54.8	45.2	64.5	41.9	S	58.1	38.7	S	51.6
22	51.6	S	38.7	51.6	S	51.6	45.2	S	61.3	41.9	71.0	54.8
23	54.8	51.6	61.3	51.6	S	51.6	54.8	54.8	45.2	S	61.3	67.7
24	S	54.8	58.1	S	58.1	51.6	S	51.6	48.4	S	54.8	H
25	S	58.1	35.5	S	48.4	41.9	S	51.6	S	32.3	H	S
26	41.9	51.6	51.6	48.4	54.8	S	58.1	54.8	S	38.7	71.0	S
27	64.5	58.1	S	51.6	48.4	S	48.4	51.6	51.6	54.8	S	71.0
28	58.1	S	S	67.7	71.0	58.1	51.6	S	45.2	58.1	S	71.0
29	64.5	S	54.8	58.1	S	71.0	51.6	S	45.2	71.0	64.5	51.6
30	71.0		48.4	80.6	S	77.4	58.1	61.3	51.6	S	67.7	71.0
31	S		71.0		H		S	74.2		S		90.3

Based on NASDAQ composite, prior to February 5, 1971, based on National Quotation Bureau indices

DOW JONES INDUSTRIALS MARKET PROBABILITY CALENDAR 2004

THE % CHANCE OF THE MARKET RISING ON ANY TRADING DAY OF THE YEAR

(Based on the number of times the DJIA rose on a particular trading day during January 1954-December 2002)

Date	Jan	Feb	Mar	Apr	May	Jun	Jul	Aug	Sep	Oct	Nov	Dec
1	H	S	67.3	55.1	S	57.1	63.3	S	61.2	51.0	63.3	46.9
2	55.1	53.1	71.4	55.1	S	51.0	63.3	44.9	57.1	S	53.1	57.1
3	S	55.1	59.2	S	55.1	57.1	S	44.9	61.2	S	69.4	61.2
4	S	40.8	51.0	S	65.3	57.1	S	46.9	S	61.2	55.1	S
5	75.5	53.1	44.9	53.1	57.1	S	H	53.1	S	51.0	44.9	S
6	49.0	44.9	S	59.2	49.0	S	61.2	57.1	H	59.2	S	59.2
7	57.1	S	S	53.1	44.9	51.0	55.1	S	42.9	49.0	S	46.9
8	49.0	S	57.1	63.3	S	40.8	61.2	S	44.9	53.1	63.3	40.8
9	46.9	40.8	61.2	H	S	34.7	55.1	46.9	42.9	S	55.1	55.1
10	S	44.9	51.0	S	49.0	59.2	S	49.0	53.1	S	59.2	61.2
11	S	63.3	57.1	S	49.0	59.2	S	51.0	S	36.7	46.9	S
12	44.9	42.9	49.0	67.3	46.9	S	55.1	46.9	S	40.8	51.0	S
13	46.9	51.0	S	63.3	51.0	S	34.7	65.3	57.1	55.1	S	38.8
14	59.2	S	S	59.2	55.1	55.1	65.3	S	44.9	59.2	S	49.0
15	57.1	S	59.2	71.4	S	49.0	49.0	S	53.1	53.1	57.1	46.9
16	57.1	H	61.2	63.3	S	59.2	46.9	57.1	49.0	S	61.2	55.1
17	S	49.0	57.1	S	49.0	46.9	S	53.1	44.9	S	49.0	51.0
18	S	40.8	67.3	S	44.9	42.9	S	44.9	S	57.1	36.7	S
19	H	46.9	46.9	57.1	51.0	S	28.6	44.9	S	55.1	61.2	S
20	44.9	59.2	S	40.8	46.9	S	49.0	59.2	36.7	51.0	S	59.2
21	38.8	S	S	55.1	30.6	55.1	49.0	S	44.9	38.8	S	57.1
22	59.2	S	40.8	46.9	S	49.0	44.9	S	44.9	49.0	69.4	55.1
23	51.0	36.7	49.0	49.0	S	42.9	49.0	49.0	40.8	S	59.2	46.9
24	S	44.9	36.7	S	59.2	40.8	S	51.0	51.0	S	65.3	H
25	S	61.2	46.9	S	38.8	49.0	S	53.1	S	26.5	H	S
26	59.2	46.9	51.0	51.0	42.9	S	59.2	44.9	S	49.0	57.1	S
27	57.1	53.1	S	59.2	53.1	S	55.1	53.1	55.1	55.1	S	65.3
28	46.9	S	S	51.0	63.3	42.9	51.0	S	46.9	61.2	S	71.4
29	65.3	S	59.2	44.9	S	57.1	61.2	S	46.9	53.1	51.0	53.1
30	61.2		40.8	57.1	S	55.1	55.1	40.8	42.9	S	51.0	61.2
31	S		44.9		H		S	61.2		S		59.2

S&P 500 MARKET PROBABILITY CALENDAR 2004

THE % CHANCE OF THE MARKET RISING ON ANY TRADING DAY OF THE YEAR*

(Based on the number of times the S&P 500 rose on a particular trading day during January 1954-December 2002)

Date	Jan	Feb	Mar	Apr	May	Jun	Jul	Aug	Sep	Oct	Nov	Dec
1	H	S	61.2	61.2	S	57.1	69.4	S	63.3	46.9	63.3	46.9
2	46.9	55.1	67.3	55.1	S	61.2	61.2	46.9	55.1	S	57.1	53.1
3	S	57.1	63.3	S	55.1	57.1	S	42.9	61.2	S	71.4	61.2
4	S	53.1	46.9	S	71.4	55.1	S	49.0	S	69.4	51.0	S
5	75.5	49.0	46.9	55.1	59.2	S	H	55.1	S	55.1	42.9	S
6	51.0	51.0	S	57.1	42.9	S	53.1	59.2	H	61.2	S	59.2
7	49.0	S	S	55.1	42.9	51.0	59.2	S	42.9	49.0	S	42.9
8	44.9	S	61.2	63.3	S	40.8	65.3	S	49.0	55.1	63.3	46.9
9	51.0	42.9	61.2	H	S	40.8	55.1	42.9	49.0	S	65.3	55.1
10	S	40.8	49.0	S	51.0	61.2	S	53.1	53.1	S	57.1	49.0
11	S	63.3	61.2	S	49.0	61.2	S	46.9	S	34.7	44.9	S
12	51.0	49.0	44.9	65.3	51.0	S	53.1	49.0	S	46.9	55.1	S
13	55.1	42.9	S	51.0	51.0	S	44.9	67.3	61.2	53.1	S	44.9
14	61.2	S	S	53.1	55.1	55.1	73.5	S	49.0	51.0	S	40.8
15	65.3	S	65.3	63.3	S	53.1	59.2	S	53.1	51.0	51.0	49.0
16	61.2	H	61.2	61.2	S	61.2	42.9	61.2	49.0	S	57.1	55.1
17	S	49.0	51.0	S	55.1	42.9	S	69.4	46.9	S	57.1	53.1
18	S	38.8	69.4	S	44.9	42.9	S	44.9	S	63.3	38.8	S
19	H	51.0	46.9	55.1	46.9	S	26.5	44.9	S	55.1	59.2	S
20	51.0	51.0	S	42.9	55.1	S	44.9	61.2	42.9	49.0	S	49.0
21	49.0	S	S	55.1	40.8	53.1	40.8	S	51.0	34.7	S	51.0
22	59.2	S	44.9	49.0	S	55.1	42.9	S	55.1	42.9	65.3	51.0
23	63.3	44.9	42.9	44.9	S	42.9	46.9	46.9	38.8	S	61.2	46.9
24	S	38.8	53.1	S	53.1	38.8	S	51.0	49.0	S	67.3	H
25	S	59.2	40.8	S	42.9	40.8	S	46.9	S	32.7	H	S
26	53.1	49.0	53.1	46.9	44.9	S	59.2	42.9	S	59.2	57.1	S
27	53.1	61.2	S	59.2	53.1	S	55.1	53.1	53.1	59.2	S	63.3
28	44.9	S	S	51.0	61.2	49.0	53.1	S	55.1	59.2	S	73.5
29	67.3	S	57.1	44.9	S	65.3	65.3	S	49.0	53.1	55.1	55.1
30	67.3		34.7	63.3	S	53.1	67.3	49.0	46.9	S	51.0	67.3
31	S		44.9		H		S	65.3		S		69.4

* See new trends developing on pages 60, 88 and 136

RECENT S&P 500 MARKET PROBABILITY CALENDAR 2004

THE % CHANCE OF THE MARKET RISING ON ANY TRADING DAY OF THE YEAR*

(Based on the number of times the S&P 500 rose on a particular trading day during January 1982-December 2002**)

Date	Jan	Feb	Mar	Apr	May	Jun	Jul	Aug	Sep	Oct	Nov	Dec
1	H	S	52.4	57.1	S	57.1	76.2	S	42.9	57.1	76.2	57.1
2	38.1	42.9	61.9	52.4	S	71.4	47.6	47.6	47.6	S	52.4	61.9
3	S	61.9	57.1	S	61.9	52.4	S	38.1	52.4	S	66.7	57.1
4	S	66.7	47.6	S	71.4	47.6	S	47.6	S	57.1	52.4	S
5	71.4	42.9	47.6	42.9	57.1	S	H	47.6	S	42.9	38.1	S
6	47.6	52.4	S	61.9	28.6	S	38.1	57.1	H	57.1	S	33.3
7	47.6	S	S	47.6	33.3	47.6	52.4	S	38.1	38.1	S	47.6
8	47.6	S	61.9	66.7	S	28.6	61.9	S	52.4	61.9	57.1	42.9
9	47.6	42.9	52.4	H	S	42.9	42.9	42.9	47.6	S	57.1	47.6
10	S	38.1	42.9	S	52.4	52.4	S	38.1	47.6	S	52.4	42.9
11	S	76.2	57.1	S	61.9	57.1	S	47.6	S	23.8	47.6	S
12	42.9	61.9	38.1	57.1	47.6	S	61.9	42.9	S	42.9	66.7	S
13	57.1	42.9	S	42.9	66.7	S	61.9	71.4	52.4	76.2	S	42.9
14	52.4	S	S	52.4	66.7	66.7	85.7	S	57.1	66.7	S	28.6
15	81.0	S	71.4	61.9	S	52.4	52.4	S	52.4	57.1	47.6	47.6
16	61.9	H	61.9	66.7	S	61.9	52.4	57.1	42.9	S	61.9	52.4
17	S	52.4	61.9	S	52.4	52.4	S	61.9	33.3	S	52.4	52.4
18	S	33.3	71.4	S	42.9	38.1	S	66.7	S	61.9	38.1	S
19	H	47.6	42.9	42.9	57.1	S	23.8	47.6	S	57.1	61.9	S
20	42.9	42.9	S	38.1	47.6	S	38.1	61.9	52.4	61.9	S	47.6
21	38.1	S	S	66.7	33.3	52.4	33.3	S	38.1	33.3	S	47.6
22	52.4	S	47.6	38.1	S	71.4	33.3	S	57.1	33.3	61.9	61.9
23	52.4	52.4	42.9	52.4	S	33.3	38.1	52.4	33.3	S	66.7	61.9
24	S	38.1	57.1	S	71.4	33.3	S	61.9	38.1	S	71.4	H
25	S	57.1	47.6	S	47.6	28.6	S	47.6	S	42.9	H	S
26	57.1	52.4	47.6	38.1	42.9	S	76.2	57.1	S	47.6	57.1	S
27	47.6	57.1	S	61.9	52.4	S	57.1	47.6	57.1	61.9	S	57.1
28	57.1	S	S	52.4	52.4	52.4	47.6	S	52.4	76.2	S	61.9
29	71.4	S	61.9	52.4	S	71.4	66.7	S	52.4	57.1	57.1	61.9
30	85.7		28.6	71.4	S	47.6	66.7	42.9	52.4	S	38.1	66.7
31	S		47.6		H		S	52.4		S		47.6

* See new trends developing on pages 60, 88 and 136   ** Based on most recent 21-year period

2005 STRATEGY CALENDAR
(Option expiration dates encircled)

	MONDAY	TUESDAY	WEDNESDAY	THURSDAY	FRIDAY	SATURDAY	SUNDAY
	27	28	29	30	31	1 JANUARY New Year's Day	2
JANUARY	3	4	5	6	7	8	9
	10	11	12	13	14	15	16
	17 Martin Luther King Day	18	19	20	(21)	22	23
	24	25	26	27	28	29	30
FEBRUARY	31	1 FEBRUARY	2	3	4	5	6
	7	8	9 Ash Wednesday	10	11	12	13
	14 ♥	15	16	17	(18)	19	20
	21 Presidents' Day	22	23	24	25	26	27
MARCH	28	1 MARCH	2	3	4	5	6
	7	8	9	10	11	12	13
	14	15	16	17 ♣ St. Patrick's Day	(18)	19	20
	21	22	23	24	25 Good Friday	26	27 Easter
APRIL	28	29	30	31	1 APRIL	2	3 Daylight Savings Time Begins
	4	5	6	7	8	9	10
	11	12	13	14	(15)	16	17
	18	19	20	21	22	23	24 Passover
MAY	25	26	27	28	29	30	1 MAY
	2	3	4	5	6	7	8 Mother's Day
	9	10	11	12	13	14	15
	16	17	18	19	(20)	21	22
	23	24	25	26	27	28	29
JUNE	30 Memorial Day	31	1 JUNE	2	3	4	5
	6	7	8	9	10	11	12
	13	14	15	16	(17)	18	19 Father's Day
	20	21	22	23	24	25	26

Market closed on shaded weekdays; closes early when half-shaded.

2005 STRATEGY CALENDAR
(Option expiration dates encircled)

MONDAY	TUESDAY	WEDNESDAY	THURSDAY	FRIDAY	SATURDAY	SUNDAY	
27	28	29	30	1 JULY	2	3	
4 Independence Day	5	6	7	8	9	10	JULY
11	12	13	14	⑮	16	17	
18	19	20	21	22	23	24	
25	26	27	28	29	30	31	
1 AUGUST	2	3	4	5	6	7	
8	9	10	11	12	13	14	AUGUST
15	16	17	18	⑲	20	21	
22	23	24	25	26	27	28	
29	30	31	1 SEPTEMBER	2	3	4	
5 Labor Day	6	7	8	9	10	11	
12	13	14	15	⑯	17	18	SEPTEMBER
19	20	21	22	23	24	25	
26	27	28	29	30	1 OCTOBER	2	
3	4 Rosh Hashanah	5	6	7	8	9	
10 Columbus Day	11	12	13 Yom Kippur	14	15	16	OCTOBER
17	18	19	20	㉑	22	23	
24	25	26	27	28	29	30 Daylight Savings Time Ends	
31 🎃	1 NOVEMBER	2	3	4	5	6	
7	8 Election Day	9	10	11 Veteran's Day	12	13	NOVEMBER
14	15	16	17	⑱	19	20	
21	22	23	24 Thanksgiving	25	26	27	
28	29	30	1 DECEMBER	2	3	4	
5	6	7	8	9	10	11	
12	13	14	15	⑯	17	18	DECEMBER
19	20	21	22	23	24	25 Christmas	
26 Chanukah	27	28	29	30	31		

DECENNIAL CYCLE: A MARKET PHENOMENON

By arranging each year's market gain or loss so the first and succeeding years of each decade fall into the same column, certain interesting patterns emerge—strong fifth and eighth years, weak seventh and zero years.

This fascinating phenomenon was first presented by Edgar Lawrence Smith in *Common Stocks and Business Cycles* (William-Frederick Press, 1959). Anthony Gaubis co-pioneered the decennial pattern with Smith.

When Smith first cut graphs of market prices into ten-year segments and placed them above one another, he observed that each decade tended to have three bull market cycles and that the longest and strongest bull markets seem to favor the middle years of a decade.

Don't place too much emphasis on the decennial cycle nowadays, other than the extraordinary fifth and zero years, as the stock market is more influenced by the quadrennial presidential election cycle, shown on page 127. Also, the last half-century, which has been the most prosperous in US history, has distributed the returns among most years of the decade. Interestingly, NASDAQ suffered its worst bear market ever in a zero year, giving us the rare experience of witnessing a bubble burst.

With a solid midterm to pre-election rally already underway from the October 2002 bottom, a timid economic recovery, and potential sticky situations overseas, returns for election year 2004 will likely be more tame. (See Election Year column on page 127.)

THE TEN-YEAR STOCK MARKET CYCLE

Annual % Change In Dow Jones Industrial Average
Year Of Decade

DECADES	1st	2nd	3rd	4th	5th	6th	7th	8th	9th	10th
1881-1890	3.0	− 2.9	− 8.5	−18.8	20.1	12.4	− 8.4	4.8	5.5	−14.1
1891-1900	17.6	− 6.6	−24.6	− 0.6	2.3	− 1.7	21.3	22.5	9.2	7.0
1901-1910	− 8.7	− 0.4	−23.6	41.7	38.2	− 1.9	−37.7	46.6	15.0	−17.9
1911-1920	0.4	7.6	−10.3	− 5.4	81.7	− 4.2	−21.7	10.5	30.5	−32.9
1921-1930	12.7	21.7	− 3.3	26.2	30.0	0.3	28.8	48.2	−17.2	−33.8
1931-1940	−52.7	−23.1	66.7	4.1	38.5	24.8	−32.8	28.1	− 2.9	−12.7
1941-1950	−15.4	7.6	13.8	12.1	26.6	− 8.1	2.2	− 2.1	12.9	17.6
1951-1960	14.4	8.4	− 3.8	44.0	20.8	2.3	−12.8	34.0	16.4	− 9.3
1961-1970	18.7	−10.8	17.0	14.6	10.9	−18.9	15.2	4.3	−15.2	4.8
1971-1980	6.1	14.6	−16.6	−27.6	38.3	17.9	−17.3	− 3.1	4.2	14.9
1981-1990	− 9.2	19.6	20.3	− 3.7	27.7	22.6	2.3	11.8	27.0	− 4.3
1991-2000	20.3	4.2	13.7	2.1	33.5	26.0	22.6	16.1	25.2	− 6.2
2001–2010	− 7.1	−16.8								

Total % Change	0.1%	23.1%	40.8%	88.7%	368.6%	71.5%	−38.3%	221.7%	110.6%	−86.9%
Up Years	8	7	5	7	12	7	6	10	9	4
Down Years	5	6	7	5	0	5	6	2	3	8

Based on annual close   *Cowles indices 1881–1885*

PRESIDENTIAL ELECTION/STOCK MARKET CYCLE
THE 170-YEAR SAGA CONTINUES

It is no mere coincidence that the last two years (pre-election year and election year) of the 43 administrations since 1833 produced a total net market gain of 717.5%, dwarfing the 227.6% gain of the first two years of these administrations.

Presidential elections every four years have a profound impact on the economy and the stock market. Wars, recessions and bear markets tend to start or occur in the first half of the term; prosperous times and bull markets, in the latter half.

STOCK MARKET ACTION SINCE 1833
Annual % Change In Dow Jones Industrial Average[1]

4-Year Cycle Beginning	Elected President	Post-Election Year	Mid-Term Year	Pre-Election Year	Election Year
1833	Jackson (D)	− 0.9	13.0	3.1	− 11.7
1837	Van Buren (D)	− 11.5	1.6	− 12.3	5.5
1841*	W.H. Harrison (W)**	− 13.3	− 18.1	45.0	15.5
1845*	Polk (D)	8.1	− 14.5	1.2	− 3.6
1849*	Taylor (W)	N/C	18.7	− 3.2	19.6
1853*	Pierce (D)	− 12.7	− 30.2	1.5	4.4
1857	Buchanan (D)	− 31.0	14.3	− 10.7	14.0
1861*	Lincoln (R)	− 1.8	55.4	38.0	6.4
1863	Lincoln (R)	− 8.5	3.6	1.6	10.8
1869	Grant (R)	1.7	5.6	7.3	6.8
1873	Grant (R)	− 12.7	2.8	− 4.1	− 17.9
1877	Hayes (R)	− 9.4	6.1	43.0	18.7
1881	Garfield (R)**	3.0	− 2.9	− 8.5	− 18.8
1885*	Cleveland (D)	20.1	12.4	− 8.4	4.8
1889*	B. Harrison (R)	5.5	− 14.1	17.6	− 6.6
1893*	Cleveland (D)	− 24.6	− 0.6	2.3	− 1.7
1897*	McKinley (R)	21.3	22.5	9.2	7.0
1901	McKinley (R)**	− 8.7	− 0.4	− 23.6	41.7
1905	T. Roosevelt (R)	38.2	− 1.9	− 37.7	46.6
1909	Taft (R)	15.0	− 17.9	0.4	7.6
1913*	Wilson (D)	− 10.3	− 5.4	81.7	− 4.2
1917	Wilson (D)	− 21.7	10.5	30.5	− 32.9
1921*	Harding (R)	12.7	21.7	− 3.3	26.2
1925	Coolidge (R)	30.0	0.3	28.8	48.2
1929	Hoover (R)	− 17.2	− 33.8	− 52.7	− 23.1
1933*	F. Roosevelt (D)	66.7	4.1	38.5	24.8
1937	F. Roosevelt (D)	− 32.8	28.1	− 2.9	− 12.7
1941	F. Roosevelt (D)	− 15.4	7.6	13.8	12.1
1945	F. Roosevelt (D)	26.6	− 8.1	2.2	− 2.1
1949	Truman (D)	12.9	17.6	14.4	8.4
1953*	Eisenhower (R)	− 3.8	44.0	20.8	2.3
1957	Eisenhower (R)	− 12.8	34.0	16.4	− 9.3
1961*	Kennedy (D)**	18.7	− 10.8	17.0	14.6
1965	Johnson (D)	10.9	− 18.9	15.2	4.3
1969*	Nixon (R)	− 15.2	4.8	6.1	14.6
1973	Nixon (R)***	− 16.6	− 27.6	38.3	17.9
1977*	Carter (D)	− 17.3	− 3.1	4.2	14.9
1981*	Reagan (R)	− 9.2	19.6	20.3	− 3.7
1985	Reagan (R)	27.7	22.6	2.3	11.8
1989	G. H. W. Bush (R)	27.0	− 4.3	20.3	4.2
1993*	Clinton (D)	13.7	2.1	33.5	26.0
1997	Clinton (D)	22.6	16.1	25.2	− 6.2
2001*	G. W. Bush (R)	− 7.1	− 16.8		
Total % Gain		**67.9 %**	**159.7%**	**432.3%**	**285.2%**
# Up		19	25	31	28
# Down		23	18	11	14

*Party in power ousted   **Death in office   ***Resigned   **D**—Democrat, **W**—Whig, **R**—Republican

[1]Based on annual close, prior to 1886 based on Cowles and other indices

BULL AND BEAR MARKETS SINCE 1900

— Beginning —		— Ending —		Bull		Bear	
Date	DJIA	Date	DJIA	% Gain	Days	% Change	Days
9/24/00	38.80	6/17/01	57.33	47.8%	266	− 46.1%	875
11/9/03	30.88	1/19/06	75.45	144.3	802	− 48.5	665
11/15/07	38.83	11/19/09	73.64	89.6	735	− 27.4	675
9/25/11	53.43	9/30/12	68.97	29.1	371	− 24.1	668
7/30/14	52.32	11/21/16	110.15	110.5	845	− 40.1	393
12/19/17	65.95	11/3/19	119.62	81.4	684	− 46.6	660
8/24/21	63.90	3/20/23	105.38	64.9	573	− 18.6	221
10/27/23	85.76	9/3/29	381.17	344.5	2138	− 47.9	71
11/13/29	198.69	4/17/30	294.07	48.0	155	− 86.0	813
7/8/32	41.22	9/7/32	79.93	93.9	61	− 37.2	173
2/27/33	50.16	2/5/34	110.74	120.8	343	− 22.8	171
7/26/34	85.51	3/10/37	194.40	127.3	958	− 49.1	386
3/31/38	98.95	11/12/38	158.41	60.1	226	− 23.3	147
4/8/39	121.44	9/12/39	155.92	28.4	157	− 40.4	959
4/28/42	92.92	5/29/46	212.50	128.7	1492	− 23.2	353
5/17/47	163.21	6/15/48	193.16	18.4	395	− 16.3	363
6/13/49	161.60	1/5/53	293.79	81.8	1302	− 13.0	252
9/14/53	255.49	4/6/56	521.05	103.9	935	− 19.4	564
10/22/57	419.79	1/5/60	685.47	63.3	805	− 17.4	294
10/25/60	566.05	12/13/61	734.91	29.8	414	− 27.1	195
6/26/62	535.76	2/9/66	995.15	85.7	1324	− 25.2	240
10/7/66	744.32	12/3/68	985.21	32.4	788	− 35.9	539
5/26/70	631.16	4/28/71	950.82	50.6	337	− 16.1	209
11/23/71	797.97	1/11/73	1051.70	31.8	415	− 45.1	694
12/6/74	577.60	9/21/76	1014.79	75.7	655	− 26.9	525
2/28/78	742.12	9/8/78	907.74	22.3	192	− 16.4	591
4/21/80	759.13	4/27/81	1024.05	34.9	371	− 24.1	472
8/12/82	776.92	11/29/83	1287.20	65.7	474	− 15.6	238
7/24/84	1086.57	8/25/87	2722.42	150.6	1127	− 36.1	55
10/19/87	1738.74	7/17/90	2999.75	72.5	1002	− 21.2	86
10/11/90	2365.10	7/17/98	9337.97	294.8	2836	− 19.3	45
8/31/98	7539.07	1/14/00	11722.98	55.5	501	− 29.7	616
9/21/01	8235.81	3/19/02	10635.25	29.1	179	− 31.5	204
10/9/02	7286.27	6/17/03	9323.02	28.0*	251*	* At Press Time	

Based on Dow Jones industrial average
The NYSE was closed from 7/31/1914 to 12/11/1914 due to World War I.
DJIA figures were then adjusted back to reflect the composition change from 12 to 20 stock in September 1916.

1900-2000 Data: Ned Davis Research

Bear markets begin at the end of one bull market and end at the start of the next bull market (July 17, 1990 to October 11, 1990 as an example). The high at Dow 3978.36 on January 31, 1994 was followed by a 9.7 percent correction. A 10.3 percent correction occurred between the May 22, 1996 closing high of 5778 and the intraday low on July 16, 1996. The longest bull market on record ended on July 17, 1998 and the shortest bear market on record ended on August 31, 1998 when the new bull market began. The greatest bull super cycle in history, that began August 12, 1982, ended in 2000 after the Dow gained 1409% and NASDAQ climbed 3072%. The Dow gained only 497% in the eight-year super bull from 1921 to the top in 1929. NASDAQ suffered its worst loss ever, down 77.9%, nearly as much as the 89.2% drop in the Dow from 1929 to the bottom in 1932.

DIRECTORY OF TRADING PATTERNS & DATABANK

CONTENTS

A TYPICAL DAY IN THE MARKET

Half-hourly data became available for the Dow Jones industrial average starting in January 1987. The NYSE switched 10:00am openings to 9:30am in October 1985. Below is the comparison between half-hourly performance 1987-April 2003 and hourly November 1963-June 1985. Stronger openings and closings in a more bullish climate are evident. Morning and afternoon weakness appear an hour earlier.

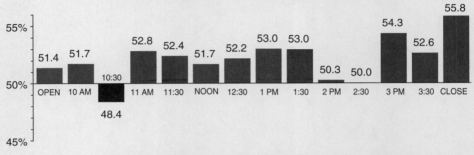

MARKET % PERFORMANCE EACH HALF-HOUR OF THE DAY (JANUARY 1987 - APRIL 2003)

Based on the number of times the Dow Jones Industrial Average increased over previous half-hour

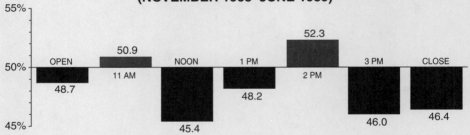

MARKET % PERFORMANCE EACH HOUR OF THE DAY (NOVEMBER 1963–JUNE 1985)

Based on the number of times the Dow Jones Industrial Average increased over previous hour

On the opposite page, half-hourly movements since January 1987 are separated by day of the week. From 1953 to 1989 Monday was the worst day of the week, especially during long bear markets, but times changed. Monday reversed positions and became the best day of the week, and on the plus side twelve years in a row from 1990 to 2000. With the market back to normal Monday has been a net loser in 2001 and 2002 and mixed in 2003 so far. (See pages 60, 66, 132-135.) Fridays were down 2000-2002 on the S&P and 2001-2002 on NASDAQ during the bear, but up solidly so far in 2003. On all days stocks do tend to firm up near the close.

THROUGH THE WEEK ON A HALF-HOURLY BASIS

From the chart showing the percentage of times the Dow Jones Industrial Average rose over the preceding half-hour (January 1987—April 2003*) the typical week unfolds.

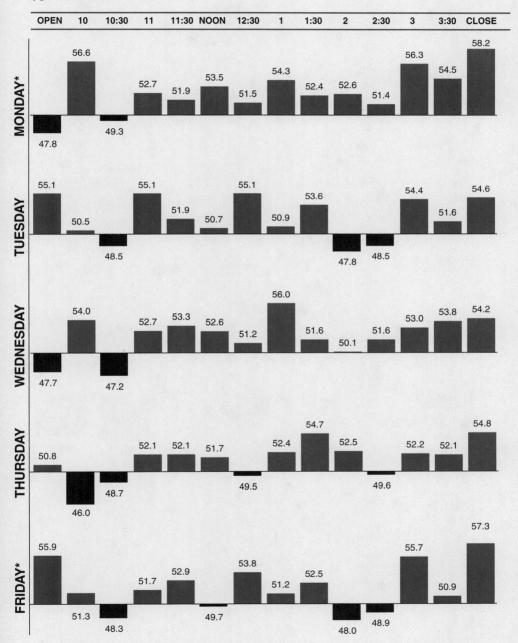

*Research indicates that where Tuesday is the first trading day of the week, it follows the Monday pattern. Therefore, all such Tuesdays were combined with the Mondays here. Thursdays that are the final trading day of a given week behave like Fridays, and were similarly grouped with Fridays.

MONDAY REVERTS TO ITS OLD BEAR PATTERN
WORST DAY OF WEEK LAST THREE YEARS

Between 1952 and 1989 Monday was the worst trading day of the week. The first trading day of the week (including Tuesday, when Monday is a holiday) rose only 44.5% of the time, while the other trading days closed higher 54.7% of the time. (NYSE Saturday trading discontinued June 1952.)

MARKET % PERFORMANCE EACH DAY OF THE WEEK
(JUNE 1952-DECEMBER 1989)

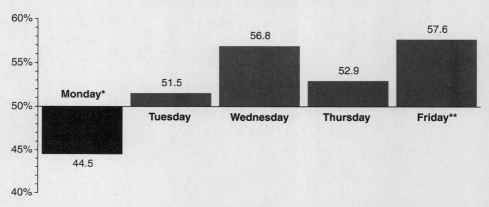

A dramatic reversal occurred during the 1990-2000 bull years—Monday became the most powerful day of the week. Throughout the recent bear market (2000-2002) Monday has returned to its old ways and Friday has become a day to avoid, as traders are not inclined to stay long over the weekend during uncertain market times. See pages 60 and 134.

MARKET % PERFORMANCE EACH DAY OF THE WEEK
(JANUARY 1990-MAY 2003)

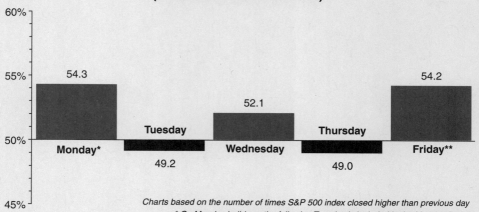

Charts based on the number of times S&P 500 index closed higher than previous day
* On Monday holidays, the following Tuesday is included in the Monday figure
** On Friday holidays, the preceding Thursday is included in the Friday figure

NASDAQ DAYS OF THE WEEK

Despite 20 years less data, daily trading patterns on NASDAQ through 1989 appear to be fairly similar to the S&P across on page 132 except for more bullishness on Thursdays. During the mostly flat markets of the 1970s and early 1980s, it would appear that apprehensive investors decided to throw in the towel over weekends and sell on Mondays and Tuesdays.

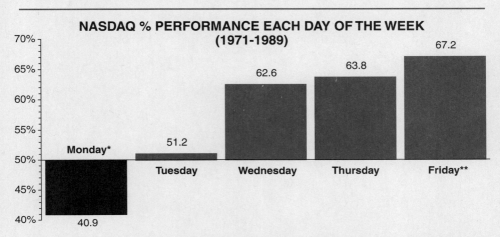

NASDAQ % PERFORMANCE EACH DAY OF THE WEEK (1971-1989)

Notice the vast difference in the daily trading pattern between NASDAQ and S&P from January 1, 1990 to recent times. The reason for so much more bullishness is that NASDAQ moved up 1010%, over three times as much during the 1990-2000 period. The gain for the S&P was 332% and for the Dow Jones industrials, 326%. NASDAQ's weekly patterns are beginning to move in step with the rest of the market. Notice on page 135 Monday's weakness during the 2000 to 2002 bear market.

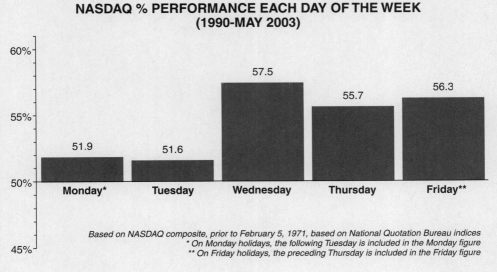

NASDAQ % PERFORMANCE EACH DAY OF THE WEEK (1990-MAY 2003)

Based on NASDAQ composite, prior to February 5, 1971, based on National Quotation Bureau indices
* On Monday holidays, the following Tuesday is included in the Monday figure
** On Friday holidays, the preceding Thursday is included in the Friday figure

S&P DAILY PERFORMANCE EACH YEAR SINCE 1952

To determine if market trend alters performance of different days of the week, we separated the seventeen bear years of 1953, '57, '60, '62, '66, '69, '70, '73, '74, '77, '81, '84, '90, '94, 2000, 2001 and 2002 from the 34 bull market years. While Tuesday and Thursday did not vary much on average between bull and bear years, Mondays and Fridays were sharply affected. There was a swing of 10.3 percentage points in Monday's and 11.1 in Friday's performance. Mondays were much stronger during the bullish period 1990-2000.

PERCENTAGE OF TIMES MARKET CLOSED HIGHER THAN PREVIOUS DAY
(JUNE 1952 - MAY 2003)

	Monday*	Tuesday	Wednesday	Thursday	Friday**
1952	48.4%	55.6%	58.1%	51.9%	66.7%
1953	34.6	52.1	54.9	59.6	54.7
1954	50.0	57.4	63.5	59.2	73.1
1955	50.0	45.7	63.5	60.0	78.8
1956	37.7	39.6	45.8	50.0	59.6
1957	26.9	54.0	66.7	48.9	44.2
1958	59.6	52.0	58.8	68.1	73.1
1959	40.4	53.1	55.8	48.9	69.8
1960	34.6	50.0	44.2	54.0	59.6
1961	53.8	52.2	64.0	56.0	63.5
1962	28.3	52.1	54.0	53.1	48.1
1963	46.2	63.3	51.0	57.4	69.2
1964	40.4	48.0	61.5	58.7	77.4
1965	46.2	57.4	55.8	51.0	71.2
1966	36.5	47.8	53.8	42.0	57.7
1967	38.5	50.0	60.8	64.0	69.2
1968[1]	49.1	55.3	63.0	40.4	55.8
1969	32.7	45.8	50.0	67.4	50.0
1970	40.4	44.0	65.4	46.8	52.8
1971	44.2	62.5	55.8	57.1	50.0
1972	38.5	60.9	57.7	51.0	67.3
1973	32.1	51.1	52.9	44.9	44.2
1974	32.7	57.1	51.0	36.7	30.8
1975	53.8	38.8	61.5	56.3	55.8
1976	55.8	55.3	55.8	40.8	58.5
1977	40.4	40.4	46.2	53.1	53.8
1978	51.9	43.5	59.6	54.0	48.1
1979	54.7	53.2	58.8	66.0	44.2
1980	55.8	56.3	69.8	35.4	55.8
1981	44.2	38.8	55.8	53.2	47.2
1982	46.2	39.6	44.2	44.9	50.0
1983	55.8	46.8	61.5	50.0	55.8
1984	39.6	63.8	31.4	46.0	44.2
1985	44.2	61.2	54.9	56.3	53.8
1986	51.9	44.9	67.3	58.3	55.8
1987	51.9	57.1	63.5	61.7	49.1
1988	51.9	61.7	51.9	48.0	59.6
1989	51.9	47.8	69.2	58.0	69.2
1990	67.9	53.2	52.9	40.0	51.9
1991	44.2	46.9	52.9	49.0	51.9
1992	51.9	49.0	53.8	56.3	45.3
1993	65.4	41.7	55.8	44.9	48.1
1994	55.8	46.8	52.9	48.0	59.6
1995	63.5	56.5	63.5	62.0	63.5
1996	54.7	44.9	51.0	57.1	63.5
1997	67.3	69.4	42.3	41.7	57.7
1998	57.7	62.5	57.7	37.5	61.5
1999	46.2	29.8	66.7	53.1	59.6
2000	51.9	43.5	40.4	56.0	46.2
2001	45.3	51.1	44.0	59.2	43.1
2002	40.4	37.5	56.9	38.8	48.1
2003[2]	47.6	55.6	38.1	42.9	59.1
Average	**47.1**	**50.8**	**55.9**	**52.0**	**56.6**
34 Bull Years	**50.6**	**51.8**	**58.1**	**53.1**	**60.3**
17 Bear Years	**40.3**	**48.8**	**51.4**	**49.9**	**49.2**

Based on S&P 500

[1] Excludes last six months of four-day market weeks. [2] Five months only. Not included in averages.
* On Monday holidays, the following Tuesday is included in the Monday figure
** On Friday holidays, the preceding Thursday is included in the Friday figure

134

NASDAQ DAILY PERFORMANCE EACH YEAR SINCE 1971

After dropping a hefty 77.9% from their 2000 high (versus -37.8% on the Dow and -49.1% on the S&P 500), NASDAQ tech stocks still outpace the blue chips and big caps—but not by nearly as much as they did. From January 1, 1971 through June 23, 2003, NASDAQ moved up an impressive 1698%. The S&P (up 965%) and the Dow (up 982%) gained just over half as much.

Monday's performance on NASDAQ returned to its bearish ways during the three-year bear market of 2000-2002. On page 68 another important daily performance pattern is detailed. When major stocks become overextended for some period of time, nervous traders will sell off positions on Friday. And when the world does not collapse over the weekend, they come back in and push up Mondays. Conversely, when Fridays close down and those traders that sold don't come back in on Monday, watch out. This can lead to further declines, especially when a cluster of "Down Fridays, Down Mondays" develops.

PERCENTAGE OF TIMES NASDAQ CLOSED HIGHER THAN PREVIOUS DAY
(1971-MAY 2003)

	Monday*	Tuesday	Wednesday	Thursday	Friday**
1971	51.9%	52.1%	59.6%	65.3%	71.2%
1972	30.8	60.9	63.5	57.1	78.8
1973	34.0	48.9	52.9	53.1	48.1
1974	30.8	46.9	51.0	49.0	42.3
1975	42.3	42.9	63.5	64.6	63.5
1976	50.0	63.8	67.3	59.2	58.5
1977	50.0	42.6	53.8	61.2	73.1
1978	48.1	47.8	71.2	72.0	84.6
1979	45.3	53.2	64.7	86.0	82.7
1980	44.2	64.6	84.9	52.1	73.1
1981	42.3	32.7	67.3	76.6	69.8
1982	36.5	47.9	61.5	51.0	61.5
1983	42.3	42.6	67.3	68.0	73.1
1984	22.6	53.2	35.3	52.0	51.9
1985	36.5	59.2	62.7	68.8	67.3
1986	38.5	55.1	65.4	72.9	75.0
1987	42.3	49.0	65.4	68.1	66.0
1988	50.0	55.3	61.5	66.0	63.5
1989	38.5	54.3	71.2	70.0	73.1
1990	54.7	42.6	60.8	46.0	55.8
1991	51.9	59.2	66.7	65.3	51.9
1992	46.2	53.1	59.6	60.4	45.3
1993	55.8	56.3	69.2	57.1	67.3
1994	51.9	46.8	54.9	52.0	55.8
1995	50.0	52.2	63.5	62.0	63.5
1996	50.9	57.1	64.7	61.2	63.5
1997	65.4	59.2	53.8	52.1	55.8
1998	59.6	58.3	63.5	46.8	58.5
1999	61.5	40.4	63.5	57.1	65.4
2000	40.4	41.3	42.3	60.0	57.7
2001	41.5	57.8	52.0	55.1	47.1
2002	44.2	37.5	56.9	46.9	46.2
2003[1]	52.4	61.1	33.3	57.1	54.5
Average	**45.3%**	**51.1%**	**61.3%**	**60.5%**	**62.8%**
22 Bull Years	**47.6%**	**53.5%**	**64.7%**	**62.6%**	**66.8%**
10 Bear Years	**40.5%**	**45.7%**	**53.9%**	**55.9%**	**54.1%**

Based on NASDAQ composite, prior to February 5, 1971, based on National Quotation Bureau indices
[1] *Five months only. Not included in averages.*
* *On Monday holidays, the following Tuesday is included in the Monday figure*
** *On Friday holidays, the preceding Thursday is included in the Friday figure*

MONTHLY CASH INFLOWS INTO S&P STOCKS

For many years, the last trading day of the month plus the first four of the following month were the best market days of the month. This pattern is quite clear in the first chart showing these five consecutive trading days towering above the other 16 trading days of the average month in the 1953-1981 period. The rationale was that individuals and institutions tended to operate similarly, causing a massive flow of cash into stocks near beginnings of months.

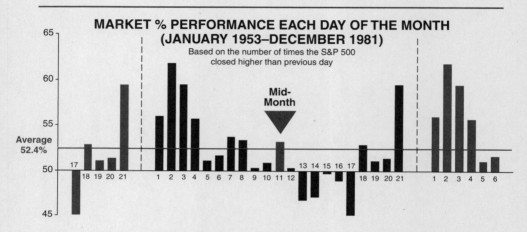

Clearly, "front-running" traders took advantage of this phenomenon, drastically altering the previous pattern. The second chart from 1982 onward shows the trading shift caused by these "anticipators" to the last three trading days of the month plus the first two. Another astonishing development shows the ninth, tenth, and eleventh trading days rising strongly as well. Perhaps the enormous growth of 401(k) retirement plans (participants' salaries are usually paid twice monthly) is responsible for this new mid-month bulge. First trading days of the month have produced the greatest gains in recent years (see page 62).

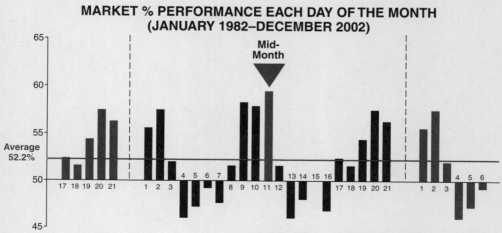

TRADING DAYS (excluding Saturdays, Sundays, and holidays)

MONTHLY CASH INFLOWS INTO NASDAQ STOCKS

NASDAQ stocks moved up 57.9% of the time through 1981 compared to 52.4% for the S&P across the page. Ends and beginnings of the month are fairly similar, specifically the last plus the first four trading days. But notice how investors kept piling into NASDAQ stocks for six additional days. NASDAQ rose 118.5% from January 1, 1971 to December 31, 1981 compared to 33.0% for the S&P.

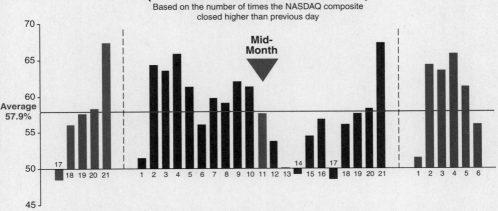

NASDAQ % PERFORMANCE EACH DAY OF THE MONTH (JANUARY 1971–DECEMBER 1981)

Based on the number of times the NASDAQ composite closed higher than previous day

After three years of the bear, the S&P is now slightly ahead of NASDAQ posting a 617.9% gain to NASDAQ's 581.9% over the next 21 years. Last three, first three and middle three days rose the most. Where the S&P has seven days of the month that go down more often than up, NASDAQ only has one. NASDAQ still exhibits the most strength on the last trading day of the month, and the last trading day of December has only been down thrice in 32 years.

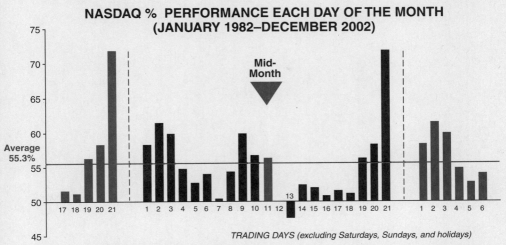

NASDAQ % PERFORMANCE EACH DAY OF THE MONTH (JANUARY 1982–DECEMBER 2002)

TRADING DAYS (excluding Saturdays, Sundays, and holidays)

Based on NASDAQ composite, prior to February 5, 1971, based on National Quotation Bureau indices

NOVEMBER, DECEMBER, AND JANUARY
YEAR'S BEST THREE-MONTH SPAN

The most important observation to be made from a chart showing the average monthly percent change in market prices since 1950 is that institutions (mutual funds, pension funds, banks, etc.) determine the trading patterns in today's market.

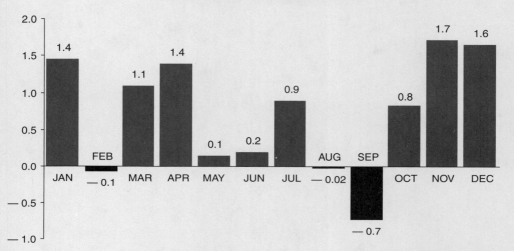

S&P 500 MONTHLY % PERFORMANCE
JANUARY 1950-JUNE 2003

Average month-to-month % change in S&P 500
(Based on monthly closing prices)

The "investment calendar" reflects the annual, semi-annual and quarterly operations of institutions during January, April and July. October, besides being a "tight money" month, and the last campaign month before elections, is also the time when most bear markets seem to end, as in 1946, 1957, 1960, 1966, 1974, 1987, 1990, 1998 and 2002. (August and September tend to combine to make the worst consecutive two-month period.)

Unusual year-end strength comes from corporate and private pension funds, producing a 4.7% gain on average between November 1 and January 31. September's dismal performance makes it the worst month of the year. In the last nineteen years it has only been up six times.

Best months in election years since 1950: June +1.9% (11-2), December +1.1% (10-3), March +1.0% (9-4).

See page 48 for monthly performance tables for the S&P 500 and the Dow Jones industrials. See pages 50 and 52 for unique six-month switching strategies.

On page 74 you can see how the first month of the first three quarters far out-performs the second and the third months since 1950. Individual monthly performance is also shown for each year starting with 1991.

NOVEMBER THROUGH JUNE
NASDAQ'S EIGHT-MONTH RUN

The two and a half year plunge of 77.9% in NASDAQ stocks between March 10, 2000 and October 9, 2002 brought several horrendous monthly losses. The two greatest were in November 2000 (-22.9%) and February 2001 (-22.4), which severely affected those months' average performance over the 32-year period of NASDAQ trading. Two huge turnaround Octobers in 2001 (+12.8%) and 2002 (+13.5%) have put bear-killing October in the black. January's 4.0% average gain is still awesome, and 2.9 times better than what the S&P did in January.

Bear in mind when comparing NASDAQ to the S&P across the page that there are 21 fewer years of data here. During this 32-year (1971-June 2003) period NASDAQ gained 1711%, while the S&P and the Dow rose only 957% and 971%, respectively. On page 54 you can see a statistical monthly comparison between NASDAQ and the Dow.

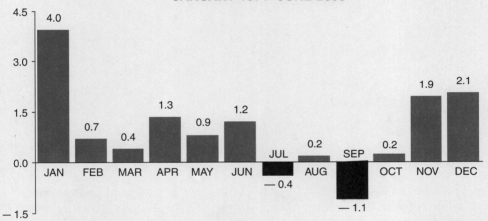

NASDAQ MONTHLY % PERFORMANCE
JANUARY 1971- JUNE 2003

Average month-to-month % change in NASDAQ composite,
prior to February 5, 1971, based on National Quotation Bureau indices
(Based on monthly closing prices)

Year-end strength is even more pronounced in NASDAQ, producing an 8.0% gain on average between November 1 and January 31—nearly twice that of the S&P 500 across the page. September is the worst month of the year for the over-the-counter index as well posting a deeper average loss of -1.1%. These extremes underscore the NAS's higher volatility—and potential for moves of greater magnitude.

Best months in election years since 1971: February +4.1% (6-2), August +3.5% (5-3), January +3.4% (6-2), June +2.9% (5-3).

See page 54 for monthly performance tables for the NASDAQ Composite and the Dow Jones Industrials. See page 58 for NASDAQ's impressive eight-month switching strategy using MACD timing.

STANDARD & POOR'S 500
MONTHLY PERCENT CHANGES

	JAN	FEB	MAR	APR	MAY	JUN
1950	1.7%	1.0%	0.4%	4.5%	3.9%	— 5.8%
1951	6.1	0.6	— 1.8	4.8	— 4.1	— 2.6
1952	1.6	— 3.6	4.8	— 4.3	2.3	4.6
1953	— 0.7	— 1.8	— 2.4	— 2.6	— 0.3	— 1.6
1954	5.1	0.3	3.0	4.9	3.3	0.1
1955	1.8	0.4	— 0.5	3.8	— 0.1	8.2
1956	— 3.6	3.5	6.9	— 0.2	— 6.6	3.9
1957	— 4.2	— 3.3	2.0	3.7	3.7	— 0.1
1958	4.3	— 2.1	3.1	3.2	1.5	2.6
1959	0.4	— 0.02	0.1	3.9	1.9	— 0.4
1960	— 7.1	0.9	— 1.4	— 1.8	2.7	2.0
1961	6.3	2.7	2.6	0.4	1.9	— 2.9
1962	— 3.8	1.6	— 0.6	— 6.2	— 8.6	— 8.2
1963	4.9	— 2.9	3.5	4.9	1.4	— 2.0
1964	2.7	1.0	1.5	0.6	1.1	1.6
1965	3.3	— 0.1	— 1.5	3.4	— 0.8	— 4.9
1966	0.5	— 1.8	— 2.2	2.1	— 5.4	— 1.6
1967	7.8	0.2	3.9	4.2	— 5.2	1.8
1968	— 4.4	— 3.1	0.9	8.2	1.1	0.9
1969	— 0.8	— 4.7	3.4	2.1	— 0.2	— 5.6
1970	— 7.6	5.3	0.1	— 9.0	— 6.1	— 5.0
1971	4.0	0.9	3.7	3.6	— 4.2	0.1
1972	1.8	2.5	0.6	0.4	1.7	— 2.2
1973	— 1.7	— 3.7	— 0.1	— 4.1	— 1.9	— 0.7
1974	— 1.0	— 0.4	— 2.3	— 3.9	— 3.4	— 1.5
1975	12.3	6.0	2.2	4.7	4.4	4.4
1976	11.8	— 1.1	3.1	— 1.1	— 1.4	4.1
1977	— 5.1	— 2.2	— 1.4	0.02	— 2.4	4.5
1978	— 6.2	— 2.5	2.5	8.5	0.4	— 1.8
1979	4.0	— 3.7	5.5	0.2	— 2.6	3.9
1980	5.8	— 0.4	—10.2	4.1	4.7	2.7
1981	— 4.6	1.3	3.6	— 2.3	— 0.2	— 1.0
1982	— 1.8	— 6.1	— 1.0	4.0	— 3.9	— 2.0
1983	3.3	1.9	3.3	7.5	— 1.2	3.5
1984	— 0.9	— 3.9	1.3	0.5	— 5.9	1.7
1985	7.4	0.9	— 0.3	— 0.5	5.4	1.2
1986	0.2	7.1	5.3	— 1.4	5.0	1.4
1987	13.2	3.7	2.6	— 1.1	0.6	4.8
1988	4.0	4.2	— 3.3	0.9	0.3	4.3
1989	7.1	— 2.9	2.1	5.0	3.5	— 0.8
1990	— 6.9	0.9	2.4	— 2.7	9.2	— 0.9
1991	4.2	6.7	2.2	0.03	3.9	— 4.8
1992	— 2.0	1.0	— 2.2	2.8	0.1	— 1.7
1993	0.7	1.0	1.9	— 2.5	2.3	0.1
1994	3.3	— 3.0	— 4.6	1.2	1.2	— 2.7
1995	2.4	3.6	2.7	2.8	3.6	2.1
1996	3.3	0.7	0.8	1.3	2.3	0.2
1997	6.1	0.6	— 4.3	5.8	5.9	4.3
1998	1.0	7.0	5.0	0.9	— 1.9	3.9
1999	4.1	— 3.2	3.9	3.8	— 2.5	5.4
2000	— 5.1	— 2.0	9.7	— 3.1	— 2.2	2.4
2001	3.5	— 9.2	— 6.4	7.7	0.5	— 2.5
2002	— 1.6	— 2.1	3.7	— 6.1	— 0.9	— 7.2
2003	— 2.7	— 1.7	1.0	8.0	5.1	1.1

STANDARD & POOR'S 500
MONTHLY PERCENT CHANGES

JUL	AUG	SEP	OCT	NOV	DEC		Year's Change
0.8%	3.3%	5.6%	0.4%	— 0.1%	4.6%	**1950**	21.8%
6.9	3.9	— 0.1	— 1.4	— 0.3	3.9	**1951**	16.5
1.8	— 1.5	— 2.0	— 0.1	4.6	3.5	**1952**	11.8
2.5	— 5.8	0.1	5.1	0.9	0.2	**1953**	— 6.6
5.7	— 3.4	8.3	— 1.9	8.1	5.1	**1954**	45.0
6.1	— 0.8	1.1	— 3.0	7.5	— 0.1	**1955**	26.4
5.2	— 3.8	— 4.5	0.5	— 1.1	3.5	**1956**	2.6
1.1	— 5.6	— 6.2	— 3.2	1.6	— 4.1	**1957**	— 14.3
4.3	1.2	4.8	2.5	2.2	5.2	**1958**	38.1
3.5	— 1.5	— 4.6	1.1	1.3	2.8	**1959**	8.5
— 2.5	2.6	— 6.0	— 0.2	4.0	4.6	**1960**	— 3.0
3.3	2.0	— 2.0	2.8	3.9	0.3	**1961**	23.1
6.4	1.5	— 4.8	0.4	10.2	1.3	**1962**	— 11.8
— 0.3	4.9	— 1.1	3.2	— 1.1	2.4	**1963**	18.9
1.8	— 1.6	2.9	0.8	— 0.5	0.4	**1964**	13.0
1.3	2.3	3.2	2.7	— 0.9	0.9	**1965**	9.1
— 1.3	— 7.8	— 0.7	4.8	0.3	— 0.1	**1966**	— 13.1
4.5	— 1.2	3.3	— 2.9	0.1	2.6	**1967**	20.1
— 1.8	1.1	3.9	0.7	4.8	— 4.2	**1968**	7.7
— 6.0	4.0	— 2.5	4.4	— 3.5	— 1.9	**1969**	— 11.4
7.3	4.4	3.3	— 1.1	4.7	5.7	**1970**	0.1
— 4.1	3.6	— 0.7	— 4.2	— 0.3	8.6	**1971**	10.8
0.2	3.4	— 0.5	0.9	4.6	1.2	**1972**	15.6
3.8	— 3.7	4.0	— 0.1	—11.4	1.7	**1973**	— 17.4
— 7.8	— 9.0	—11.9	16.3	— 5.3	— 2.0	**1974**	— 29.7
— 6.8	— 2.1	— 3.5	6.2	2.5	— 1.2	**1975**	31.5
— 0.8	— 0.5	2.3	— 2.2	— 0.8	5.2	**1976**	19.1
— 1.6	— 2.1	— 0.2	— 4.3	2.7	0.3	**1977**	— 11.5
5.4	2.6	— 0.7	— 9.2	1.7	1.5	**1978**	1.1
0.9	5.3	NC	— 6.9	4.3	1.7	**1979**	12.3
6.5	0.6	2.5	1.6	10.2	— 3.4	**1980**	25.8
— 0.2	— 6.2	— 5.4	4.9	3.7	— 3.0	**1981**	9.7
— 2.3	11.6	0.8	11.0	3.6	1.5	**1982**	14.8
— 3.3	1.1	1.0	— 1.5	1.7	— 0.9	**1983**	17.3
— 1.6	10.6	— 0.3	— 0.01	— 1.5	2.2	**1984**	1.4
— 0.5	— 1.2	— 3.5	4.3	6.5	4.5	**1985**	26.3
— 5.9	7.1	— 8.5	5.5	2.1	— 2.8	**1986**	14.6
4.8	3.5	— 2.4	—21.8	— 8.5	7.3	**1987**	2.0
— 0.5	— 3.9	4.0	2.6	— 1.9	1.5	**1988**	12.4
8.8	1.6	— 0.7	— 2.5	1.7	2.1	**1989**	27.3
— 0.5	— 9.4	— 5.1	— 0.7	6.0	2.5	**1990**	— 6.6
4.5	2.0	— 1.9	1.2	— 4.4	11.2	**1991**	26.3
3.9	— 2.4	0.9	0.2	3.0	1.0	**1992**	4.5
— 0.5	3.4	— 1.0	1.9	— 1.3	1.0	**1993**	7.1
3.1	3.8	— 2.7	2.1	— 4.0	1.2	**1994**	— 1.5
3.2	— 0.03	4.0	— 0.5	4.1	1.7	**1995**	34.1
— 4.6	1.9	5.4	2.6	7.3	— 2.2	**1996**	20.3
7.8	— 5.7	5.3	— 3.4	4.5	1.6	**1997**	31.0
— 1.2	—14.6	6.2	8.0	5.9	5.6	**1998**	26.7
— 3.2	— 0.6	— 2.9	6.3	1.9	5.8	**1999**	19.5
— 1.6	6.1	— 5.3	— 0.5	— 8.0	0.4	**2000**	— 10.1
— 1.1	— 6.4	— 8.2	1.8	7.5	0.8	**2001**	— 13.0
— 7.9	0.5	—11.0	8.6	5.7	— 6.0	**2002**	— 23.4
						2003	

STANDARD & POOR'S 500
MONTHLY CLOSING PRICES

	JAN	FEB	MAR	APR	MAY	JUN
1950	17.05	17.22	17.29	18.07	18.78	17.69
1951	21.66	21.80	21.40	22.43	21.52	20.96
1952	24.14	23.26	24.37	23.32	23.86	24.96
1953	26.38	25.90	25.29	24.62	24.54	24.14
1954	26.08	26.15	26.94	28.26	29.19	29.21
1955	36.63	36.76	36.58	37.96	37.91	41.03
1956	43.82	45.34	48.48	48.38	45.20	46.97
1957	44.72	43.26	44.11	45.74	47.43	47.37
1958	41.70	40.84	42.10	43.44	44.09	45.24
1959	55.42	55.41	55.44	57.59	58.68	58.47
1960	55.61	56.12	55.34	54.37	55.83	56.92
1961	61.78	63.44	65.06	65.31	66.56	64.64
1962	68.84	69.96	69.55	65.24	59.63	54.75
1963	66.20	64.29	66.57	69.80	70.80	69.37
1964	77.04	77.80	78.98	79.46	80.37	81.69
1965	87.56	87.43	86.16	89.11	88.42	84.12
1966	92.88	91.22	89.23	91.06	86.13	84.74
1967	86.61	86.78	90.20	94.01	89.08	90.64
1968	92.24	89.36	90.20	97.59	98.68	99.58
1969	103.01	98.13	101.51	103.69	103.46	97.71
1970	85.02	89.50	89.63	81.52	76.55	72.72
1971	95.88	96.75	100.31	103.95	99.63	99.70
1972	103.94	106.57	107.20	107.67	109.53	107.14
1973	116.03	111.68	111.52	106.97	104.95	104.26
1974	96.57	96.22	93.98	90.31	87.28	86.00
1975	76.98	81.59	83.36	87.30	91.15	95.19
1976	100.86	99.71	102.77	101.64	100.18	104.28
1977	102.03	99.82	98.42	98.44	96.12	100.48
1978	89.25	87.04	89.21	96.83	97.24	95.53
1979	99.93	96.28	101.59	101.76	99.08	102.91
1980	114.16	113.66	102.09	106.29	111.24	114.24
1981	129.55	131.27	136.00	132.81	132.59	131.21
1982	120.40	113.11	111.96	116.44	111.88	109.61
1983	145.30	148.06	152.96	164.42	162.39	168.11
1984	163.41	157.06	159.18	160.05	150.55	153.18
1985	179.63	181.18	180.66	179.83	189.55	191.85
1986	211.78	226.92	238.90	235.52	247.35	250.84
1987	274.08	284.20	291.70	288.36	290.10	304.00
1988	257.07	267.82	258.89	261.33	262.16	273.50
1989	297.47	288.86	294.87	309.64	320.52	317.98
1990	329.08	331.89	339.94	330.80	361.23	358.02
1991	343.93	367.07	375.22	375.35	389.83	371.16
1992	408.79	412.70	403.69	414.95	415.35	408.14
1993	438.78	443.38	451.67	440.19	450.19	450.53
1994	481.61	467.14	445.77	450.91	456.50	444.27
1995	470.42	487.39	500.71	514.71	533.40	544.75
1996	636.02	640.43	645.50	654.17	669.12	670.63
1997	786.16	790.82	757.12	801.34	848.28	885.14
1998	980.28	1049.34	1101.75	1111.75	1090.82	1133.84
1999	1279.64	1238.33	1286.37	1335.18	1301.84	1372.71
2000	1394.46	1366.42	1498.58	1452.43	1420.60	1454.60
2001	1366.01	1239.94	1160.33	1249.46	1255.82	1224.42
2002	1130.20	1106.73	1147.39	1076.92	1067.14	989.82
2003	855.70	841.15	849.18	916.92	963.59	974.50

STANDARD & POOR'S 500
MONTHLY CLOSING PRICES

JUL	AUG	SEP	OCT	NOV	DEC	
17.84	18.42	19.45	19.53	19.51	20.41	**1950**
22.40	23.28	23.26	22.94	22.88	23.77	**1951**
25.40	25.03	24.54	24.52	25.66	26.57	**1952**
24.75	23.32	23.35	24.54	24.76	24.81	**1953**
30.88	29.83	32.31	31.68	34.24	35.98	**1954**
43.52	43.18	43.67	42.34	45.51	45.48	**1955**
49.39	47.51	45.35	45.58	45.08	46.67	**1956**
47.91	45.22	42.42	41.06	41.72	39.99	**1957**
47.19	47.75	50.06	51.33	52.48	55.21	**1958**
60.51	59.60	56.88	57.52	58.28	59.89	**1959**
55.51	56.96	53.52	53.39	55.54	58.11	**1960**
66.76	68.07	66.73	68.62	71.32	71.55	**1961**
58.23	59.12	56.27	56.52	62.26	63.10	**1962**
69.13	72.50	71.70	74.01	73.23	75.02	**1963**
83.18	81.83	84.18	84.86	84.42	84.75	**1964**
85.25	87.17	89.96	92.42	91.61	92.43	**1965**
83.60	77.10	76.56	80.20	80.45	80.33	**1966**
94.75	93.64	96.71	93.90	94.00	96.47	**1967**
97.74	98.86	102.67	103.41	108.37	103.86	**1968**
91.83	95.51	93.12	97.24	93.81	92.06	**1969**
78.05	81.52	84.21	83.25	87.20	92.15	**1970**
95.58	99.03	98.34	94.23	93.99	102.09	**1971**
107.39	111.09	110.55	111.58	116.67	118.05	**1972**
108.22	104.25	108.43	108.29	95.96	97.55	**1973**
79.31	72.15	63.54	73.90	69.97	68.56	**1974**
88.75	86.88	83.87	89.04	91.24	90.19	**1975**
103.44	102.91	105.24	102.90	102.10	107.46	**1976**
98.85	96.77	96.53	92.34	94.83	95.10	**1977**
100.68	103.29	102.54	93.15	94.70	96.11	**1978**
103.81	109.32	109.32	101.82	106.16	107.94	**1979**
121.67	122.38	125.46	127.47	140.52	135.76	**1980**
130.92	122.79	116.18	121.89	126.35	122.55	**1981**
107.09	119.51	120.42	133.71	138.54	140.64	**1982**
162.56	164.40	166.07	163.55	166.40	164.93	**1983**
150.66	166.68	166.10	166.09	163.58	167.24	**1984**
190.92	188.63	182.08	189.82	202.17	211.28	**1985**
236.12	252.93	231.32	243.98	249.22	242.17	**1986**
318.66	329.80	321.83	251.79	230.30	247.08	**1987**
272.02	261.52	271.91	278.97	273.70	277.72	**1988**
346.08	351.45	349.15	340.36	345.99	353.40	**1989**
356.15	322.56	306.05	304.00	322.22	330.22	**1990**
387.81	395.43	387.86	392.46	375.22	417.09	**1991**
424.21	414.03	417.80	418.68	431.35	435.71	**1992**
448.13	463.56	458.93	467.83	461.79	466.45	**1993**
458.26	475.49	462.69	472.35	453.69	459.27	**1994**
562.06	561.88	584.41	581.50	605.37	615.93	**1995**
639.95	651.99	687.31	705.27	757.02	740.74	**1996**
954.29	899.47	947.28	914.62	955.40	970.43	**1997**
1120.67	957.28	1017.01	1098.67	1163.63	1229.23	**1998**
1328.72	1320.41	1282.71	1362.93	1388.91	1469.25	**1999**
1430.83	1517.68	1436.51	1429.40	1314.95	1320.28	**2000**
1211.23	1133.58	1040.94	1059.78	1139.45	1148.08	**2001**
911.62	916.07	815.28	885.76	936.31	879.82	**2002**
						2003

DOW JONES INDUSTRIALS
MONTHLY PERCENT CHANGES

	JAN	FEB	MAR	APR	MAY	JUN
1950	0.8%	0.8%	1.3%	4.0%	4.2%	— 6.4%
1951	5.7	1.3	— 1.6	4.5	— 3.7	— 2.8
1952	0.5	— 3.9	3.6	— 4.4	2.1	4.3
1953	— 0.7	— 1.9	— 1.5	— 1.8	— 0.9	— 1.5
1954	4.1	0.7	3.0	5.2	2.6	1.8
1955	1.1	0.7	— 0.5	3.9	— 0.2	6.2
1956	— 3.6	2.7	5.8	0.8	— 7.4	3.1
1957	— 4.1	— 3.0	2.2	4.1	2.1	— 0.3
1958	3.3	— 2.2	1.6	2.0	1.5	3.3
1959	1.8	1.6	— 0.3	3.7	3.2	0.03
1960	— 8.4	1.2	— 2.1	— 2.4	4.0	2.4
1961	5.2	2.1	2.2	0.3	2.7	— 1.8
1962	— 4.3	1.1	— 0.2	— 5.9	— 7.8	— 8.5
1963	4.7	— 2.9	3.0	5.2	1.3	— 2.8
1964	2.9	1.9	1.6	— 0.3	1.2	1.3
1965	3.3	0.1	— 1.6	3.7	— 0.5	— 5.4
1966	1.5	— 3.2	— 2.8	1.0	— 5.3	— 1.6
1967	8.2	— 1.2	3.2	3.6	— 5.0	0.9
1968	— 5.5	— 1.7	0.02	8.5	— 1.4	— 0.1
1969	0.2	— 4.3	3.3	1.6	— 1.3	— 6.9
1970	— 7.0	4.5	1.0	— 6.3	— 4.8	— 2.4
1971	3.5	1.2	2.9	4.1	— 3.6	— 1.8
1972	1.3	2.9	1.4	1.4	0.7	— 3.3
1973	— 2.1	— 4.4	— 0.4	— 3.1	— 2.2	— 1.1
1974	0.6	0.6	— 1.6	— 1.2	— 4.1	0.03
1975	14.2	5.0	3.9	6.9	1.3	5.6
1976	14.4	— 0.3	2.8	— 0.3	— 2.2	2.8
1977	— 5.0	— 1.9	— 1.8	0.8	— 3.0	2.0
1978	— 7.4	— 3.6	2.1	10.6	0.4	— 2.6
1979	4.2	— 3.6	6.6	— 0.8	— 3.8	2.4
1980	4.4	— 1.5	— 9.0	4.0	4.1	2.0
1981	— 1.7	2.9	3.0	— 0.6	— 0.6	— 1.5
1982	— 0.4	— 5.4	— 0.2	3.1	— 3.4	— 0.9
1983	2.8	3.4	1.6	8.5	— 2.1	1.8
1984	— 3.0	— 5.4	0.9	0.5	— 5.6	2.5
1985	6.2	— 0.2	— 1.3	— 0.7	4.6	1.5
1986	1.6	8.8	6.4	— 1.9	5.2	0.9
1987	13.8	3.1	3.6	— 0.8	0.2	5.5
1988	1.0	5.8	— 4.0	2.2	— 0.1	5.4
1989	8.0	— 3.6	1.6	5.5	2.5	— 1.6
1990	— 5.9	1.4	3.0	— 1.9	8.3	0.1
1991	3.9	5.3	1.1	— 0.9	4.8	— 4.0
1992	1.7	1.4	— 1.0	3.8	1.1	— 2.3
1993	0.3	1.8	1.9	— 0.2	2.9	— 0.3
1994	6.0	— 3.7	— 5.1	1.3	2.1	— 3.5
1995	0.2	4.3	3.7	3.9	3.3	2.0
1996	5.4	1.7	1.9	— 0.3	1.3	0.2
1997	5.7	0.9	— 4.3	6.5	4.6	4.7
1998	— 0.02	8.1	3.0	3.0	— 1.8	0.6
1999	1.9	— 0.6	5.2	10.2	— 2.1	3.9
2000	— 4.8	— 7.4	7.8	— 1.7	— 2.0	— 0.7
2001	0.9	— 3.6	— 5.9	8.7	1.6	— 3.8
2002	— 1.0	1.9	2.9	— 4.4	— 0.2	— 6.9
2003	— 3.5	— 2.0	1.3	6.1	4.4	1.5

DOW JONES INDUSTRIALS
MONTHLY PERCENT CHANGES

JUL	AUG	SEP	OCT	NOV	DEC		Year's Change
0.1%	3.6%	4.4%	− 0.6%	1.2%	3.4%	**1950**	17.6%
6.3	4.8	0.3	− 3.2	− 0.4	3.0	**1951**	14.4
1.9	− 1.6	− 1.6	− 0.5	5.4	2.9	**1952**	8.4
2.7	− 5.1	1.1	4.5	2.0	− 0.2	**1953**	− 3.8
4.3	− 3.5	7.3	− 2.3	9.8	4.6	**1954**	44.0
3.2	0.5	− 0.3	− 2.5	6.2	1.1	**1955**	20.8
5.1	− 3.0	− 5.3	1.0	− 1.5	5.6	**1956**	2.3
1.0	− 4.8	− 5.8	− 3.3	2.0	− 3.2	**1957**	−12.8
5.2	1.1	4.6	2.1	2.6	4.7	**1958**	34.0
4.9	− 1.6	− 4.9	2.4	1.9	3.1	**1959**	16.4
− 3.7	1.5	− 7.3	0.04	2.9	3.1	**1960**	− 9.3
3.1	2.1	− 2.6	0.4	2.5	1.3	**1961**	18.7
6.5	1.9	− 5.0	1.9	10.1	0.4	**1962**	−10.8
− 1.6	4.9	0.5	3.1	− 0.6	1.7	**1963**	17.0
1.2	− 0.3	4.4	− 0.3	0.3	− 0.1	**1964**	14.6
1.6	1.3	4.2	3.2	− 1.5	2.4	**1965**	10.9
− 2.6	− 7.0	− 1.8	4.2	− 1.9	− 0.7	**1966**	−18.9
5.1	− 0.3	2.8	− 5.1	− 0.4	3.3	**1967**	15.2
− 1.6	1.5	4.4	1.8	3.4	− 4.2	**1968**	4.3
− 6.6	2.6	− 2.8	5.3	− 5.1	− 1.5	**1969**	−15.2
7.4	4.1	− 0.5	− 0.7	5.1	5.6	**1970**	4.8
− 3.7	4.6	− 1.2	− 5.4	− 0.9	7.1	**1971**	6.1
− 0.5	4.2	− 1.1	0.2	6.6	0.2	**1972**	14.6
3.9	− 4.2	6.7	1.0	−14.0	3.5	**1973**	−16.6
− 5.6	−10.4	−10.4	9.5	− 7.0	− 0.4	**1974**	−27.6
− 5.4	0.5	− 5.0	5.3	2.9	− 1.0	**1975**	38.3
− 1.8	− 1.1	1.7	− 2.6	− 1.8	6.1	**1976**	17.9
− 2.9	− 3.2	− 1.7	− 3.4	1.4	0.2	**1977**	−17.3
5.3	1.7	− 1.3	− 8.5	0.8	0.7	**1978**	− 3.1
0.5	4.9	− 1.0	− 7.2	0.8	2.0	**1979**	4.2
7.8	− 0.3	0.02	− 0.9	7.4	− 3.0	**1980**	14.9
− 2.5	− 7.4	− 3.6	0.3	4.3	− 1.6	**1981**	− 9.2
− 0.4	11.5	− 0.6	10.7	4.8	0.7	**1982**	19.6
− 1.9	1.4	1.4	− 0.6	4.1	− 1.4	**1983**	20.3
− 1.5	9.8	− 1.4	0.1	− 1.5	1.9	**1984**	− 3.7
0.9	− 1.0	− 0.4	3.4	7.1	5.1	**1985**	27.7
− 6.2	6.9	− 6.9	6.2	1.9	− 1.0	**1986**	22.6
6.3	3.5	− 2.5	−23.2	− 8.0	5.7	**1987**	2.3
− 0.6	− 4.6	4.0	1.7	− 1.6	2.6	**1988**	11.8
9.0	2.9	− 1.6	− 1.8	2.3	1.7	**1989**	27.0
0.9	−10.0	− 6.2	− 0.4	4.8	2.9	**1990**	− 4.3
4.1	0.6	− 0.9	1.7	− 5.7	9.5	**1991**	20.3
2.3	− 4.0	0.4	− 1.4	2.4	− 0.1	**1992**	4.2
0.7	3.2	− 2.6	3.5	0.1	1.9	**1993**	13.7
3.8	4.0	− 1.8	1.7	− 4.3	2.5	**1994**	2.1
3.3	− 2.1	3.9	− 0.7	6.7	0.8	**1995**	33.5
− 2.2	1.6	4.7	2.5	8.2	− 1.1	**1996**	26.0
7.2	− 7.3	4.2	− 6.3	5.1	1.1	**1997**	22.6
− 0.8	−15.1	4.0	9.6	6.1	0.7	**1998**	16.1
− 2.9	1.6	− 4.5	3.8	1.4	5.7	**1999**	25.2
0.7	6.6	− 5.0	3.0	− 5.1	3.6	**2000**	− 6.2
0.2	− 5.4	−11.1	2.6	8.6	1.7	**2001**	− 7.1
− 5.5	− 0.8	−12.4	10.6	5.9	− 6.2	**2002**	−16.8
						2003	

DOW JONES INDUSTRIALS MONTHLY POINT CHANGES

	JAN	FEB	MAR	APR	MAY	JUN
1950	1.66	1.65	2.61	8.28	9.09	− 14.31
1951	13.42	3.22	− 4.11	11.19	− 9.48	− 7.01
1952	1.46	− 10.61	9.38	− 11.83	5.31	11.32
1953	− 2.13	− 5.50	− 4.40	− 5.12	− 2.47	− 4.02
1954	11.49	2.15	8.97	15.82	8.16	6.04
1955	4.44	3.04	− 2.17	15.95	− 0.79	26.52
1956	− 17.66	12.91	28.14	4.33	− 38.07	14.73
1957	− 20.31	− 14.54	10.19	19.55	10.57	− 1.64
1958	14.33	− 10.10	6.84	9.10	6.84	15.48
1959	10.31	9.54	− 1.79	22.04	20.04	− 0.19
1960	− 56.74	7.50	− 13.53	− 14.89	23.80	15.12
1961	32.31	13.88	14.55	2.08	18.01	− 12.76
1962	− 31.14	8.05	− 1.10	− 41.62	− 51.97	− 52.08
1963	30.75	− 19.91	19.58	35.18	9.26	− 20.08
1964	22.39	14.80	13.15	− 2.52	9.79	10.94
1965	28.73	0.62	− 14.43	33.26	− 4.27	− 50.01
1966	14.25	− 31.62	− 27.12	8.91	− 49.61	− 13.97
1967	64.20	− 10.52	26.61	31.07	− 44.49	7.70
1968	− 49.64	− 14.97	0.17	71.55	− 13.22	− 1.20
1969	2.30	− 40.84	30.27	14.70	− 12.62	− 64.37
1970	− 56.30	33.53	7.98	− 49.50	− 35.63	− 16.91
1971	29.58	10.33	25.54	37.38	− 33.94	− 16.67
1972	11.97	25.96	12.57	13.47	6.55	− 31.69
1973	− 21.00	− 43.95	− 4.06	− 29.58	− 20.02	− 9.70
1974	4.69	4.98	− 13.85	− 9.93	− 34.58	0.24
1975	87.45	35.36	29.10	53.19	10.95	46.70
1976	122.87	− 2.67	26.84	− 2.60	− 21.62	27.55
1977	− 50.28	− 17.95	− 17.29	7.77	− 28.24	17.64
1978	− 61.25	− 27.80	15.24	79.96	3.29	− 21.66
1979	34.21	− 30.40	53.36	− 7.28	− 32.57	19.65
1980	37.11	− 12.71	− 77.39	31.31	33.79	17.07
1981	− 16.72	27.31	29.29	− 6.12	− 6.00	− 14.87
1982	− 3.90	− 46.71	− 1.62	25.59	− 28.82	− 7.61
1983	29.16	36.92	17.41	96.17	− 26.22	21.98
1984	− 38.06	− 65.95	10.26	5.86	− 65.90	27.55
1985	75.20	− 2.76	− 17.23	− 8.72	57.35	20.05
1986	24.32	138.07	109.55	− 34.63	92.73	16.01
1987	262.09	65.95	80.70	− 18.33	5.21	126.96
1988	19.39	113.40	− 83.56	44.27	− 1.21	110.59
1989	173.75	− 83.93	35.23	125.18	61.35	− 40.09
1990	−162.66	36.71	79.96	− 50.45	219.90	4.03
1991	102.73	145.79	31.68	− 25.99	139.63	−120.75
1992	54.56	44.28	− 32.20	123.65	37.76	− 78.36
1993	8.92	60.78	64.30	− 7.56	99.88	− 11.35
1994	224.27	−146.34	−196.06	45.73	76.68	−133.41
1995	9.42	167.19	146.64	163.58	143.87	90.96
1996	278.18	90.32	101.52	− 18.06	74.10	11.45
1997	364.82	64.65	−294.26	425.51	322.05	341.75
1998	− 1.75	639.22	254.09	263.56	−163.42	52.07
1999	177.40	− 52.25	479.58	1002.88	−229.30	411.06
2000	−556.59	−812.22	793.61	−188.01	−211.58	− 74.44
2001	100.51	−392.08	−616.50	856.19	176.97	−409.54
2002	−101.50	186.13	297.81	−457.72	− 20.97	−681.99
2003	−287.82	−162.73	101.05	487.96	370.17	135.18
TOTALS	949.19	−54.82	1551.10	3201.76	866.09	−304.34
# Up	36	30	35	34	28	27
# Down	18	24	19	20	26	27

DOW JONES INDUSTRIALS MONTHLY POINT CHANGES

JUL	AUG	SEP	OCT	NOV	DEC	Year's Close	
0.29	7.47	9.49	— 1.35	2.59	7.81	235.41	1950
15.22	12.39	0.91	— 8.81	— 1.08	7.96	269.23	1951
5.30	— 4.52	— 4.43	— 1.38	14.43	8.24	291.90	1952
7.12	— 14.16	2.82	11.77	5.56	— 0.47	280.90	1953
14.39	— 12.12	24.66	— 8.32	34.63	17.62	404.39	1954
14.47	2.33	— 1.56	— 11.75	28.39	5.14	488.40	1955
25.03	— 15.77	— 26.79	4.60	— 7.07	26.69	499.47	1956
5.23	— 24.17	— 28.05	— 15.26	8.83	— 14.18	435.69	1957
24.81	5.64	23.46	11.13	14.24	26.19	583.65	1958
31.28	— 10.47	— 32.73	14.92	12.58	20.18	679.36	1959
— 23.89	9.26	— 45.85	0.22	16.86	18.67	615.89	1960
21.41	14.57	— 18.73	2.71	17.68	9.54	731.14	1961
36.65	11.25	— 30.20	10.79	59.53	2.80	652.10	1962
— 11.45	33.89	3.47	22.44	— 4.71	12.43	762.95	1963
9.60	2.62	36.89	— 2.29	2.35	— 1.30	874.13	1964
13.71	11.36	37.48	30.24	— 14.11	22.55	969.26	1965
— 22.72	— 58.97	— 14.19	32.85	— 15.48	— 5.90	785.69	1966
43.98	— 2.95	25.37	— 46.92	— 3.93	29.30	905.11	1967
— 14.80	13.01	39.78	16.60	32.69	— 41.33	943.75	1968
— 57.72	21.25	— 23.63	42.90	— 43.69	— 11.94	800.36	1969
50.59	30.46	— 3.90	— 5.07	38.48	44.83	838.92	1970
— 32.71	39.64	— 10.88	— 48.19	— 7.66	58.86	890.20	1971
— 4.29	38.99	— 10.46	2.25	62.69	1.81	1020.02	1972
34.69	— 38.83	59.53	9.48	—134.33	28.61	850.86	1973
— 44.98	— 78.85	— 70.71	57.65	— 46.86	— 2.42	616.24	1974
— 47.48	3.83	— 41.46	42.16	24.63	— 8.26	852.41	1975
— 18.14	— 10.90	16.45	— 25.26	— 17.71	57.43	1004.65	1976
— 26.23	— 28.58	— 14.38	— 28.76	11.35	1.47	831.17	1977
43.32	14.55	— 11.00	— 73.37	6.58	5.98	805.01	1978
4.44	41.21	— 9.05	— 62.88	6.65	16.39	838.74	1979
67.40	— 2.73	— 0.17	— 7.93	68.85	— 29.35	963.99	1980
— 24.54	— 70.87	— 31.49	2.57	36.43	— 13.98	875.00	1981
— 3.33	92.71	— 5.06	95.47	47.56	7.26	1046.54	1982
— 22.74	16.94	16.97	— 7.93	50.82	— 17.38	1258.64	1983
— 17.12	109.10	— 17.67	0.67	— 18.44	22.63	1211.57	1984
11.99	— 13.44	— 5.38	45.68	97.82	74.54	1546.67	1985
—117.41	123.03	—130.76	110.23	36.42	— 18.28	1895.95	1986
153.54	90.88	— 66.67	—602.75	—159.98	105.28	1938.83	1987
— 12.98	— 97.08	81.26	35.74	— 34.14	54.06	2168.57	1988
220.60	76.61	— 44.45	— 47.74	61.19	46.93	2753.20	1989
24.51	— 290.84	—161.88	— 10.15	117.32	74.01	2633.66	1990
118.07	18.78	— 26.83	52.33	—174.42	274.15	3168.83	1991
75.26	— 136.43	14.31	— 45.38	78.88	— 4.05	3301.11	1992
23.39	111.78	— 96.13	125.47	3.36	70.14	3754.09	1993
139.54	148.92	— 70.23	64.93	—168.89	95.21	3834.44	1994
152.37	— 97.91	178.52	— 33.60	319.01	42.63	5117.12	1995
—125.72	87.30	265.96	147.21	492.32	— 73.43	6448.27	1996
549.82	— 600.19	322.84	—503.18	381.05	85.12	7908.25	1997
— 68.73	—1344.22	303.55	749.48	524.45	64.88	9181.43	1998
—315.65	174.13	—492.33	392.91	147.95	619.31	11497.12	1999
74.09	693.12	—564.18	320.22	—556.65	372.36	10786.85	2000
20.41	— 573.06	—1102.19	227.58	776.42	169.94	10021.50	2001
—506.67	—73.09	—1071.57	805.10	499.06	—554.46	8341.63	2002
							2003
513.22	**—1548.37**	**—2821.27**	**1890.03**	**2730.50**	**1812.22**		
32	29	19	31	36	38		
21	24	34	22	17	15		

DOW JONES INDUSTRIALS MONTHLY CLOSING PRICES

	JAN	FEB	MAR	APR	MAY	JUN
1950	201.79	203.44	206.05	214.33	223.42	209.11
1951	248.83	252.05	247.94	259.13	249.65	242.64
1952	270.69	260.08	269.46	257.63	262.94	274.26
1953	289.77	284.27	279.87	274.75	272.28	268.26
1954	292.39	294.54	303.51	319.33	327.49	333.53
1955	408.83	411.87	409.70	425.65	424.86	451.38
1956	470.74	483.65	511.79	516.12	478.05	492.78
1957	479.16	464.62	474.81	494.36	504.93	503.29
1958	450.02	439.92	446.76	455.86	462.70	478.18
1959	593.96	603.50	601.71	623.75	643.79	643.60
1960	622.62	630.12	616.59	601.70	625.50	640.62
1961	648.20	662.08	676.63	678.71	696.72	683.96
1962	700.00	708.05	706.95	665.33	613.36	561.28
1963	682.85	662.94	682.52	717.70	726.96	706.88
1964	785.34	800.14	813.29	810.77	820.56	831.50
1965	902.86	903.48	889.05	922.31	918.04	868.03
1966	983.51	951.89	924.77	933.68	884.07	870.10
1967	849.89	839.37	865.98	897.05	852.56	860.26
1968	855.47	840.50	840.67	912.22	899.00	897.80
1969	946.05	905.21	935.48	950.18	937.56	873.19
1970	744.06	777.59	785.57	736.07	700.44	683.53
1971	868.50	878.83	904.37	941.75	907.81	891.14
1972	902.17	928.13	940.70	954.17	960.72	929.03
1973	999.02	955.07	951.01	921.43	901.41	891.71
1974	855.55	860.53	846.68	836.75	802.17	802.41
1975	703.69	739.05	768.15	821.34	832.29	878.99
1976	975.28	972.61	999.45	996.85	975.23	1002.78
1977	954.37	936.42	919.13	926.90	898.66	916.30
1978	769.92	742.12	757.36	837.32	840.61	818.95
1979	839.22	808.82	862.18	854.90	822.33	841.98
1980	875.85	863.14	785.75	817.06	850.85	867.92
1981	947.27	974.58	1003.87	997.75	991.75	976.88
1982	871.10	824.39	822.77	848.36	819.54	811.93
1983	1075.70	1112.62	1130.03	1226.20	1199.98	1221.96
1984	1220.58	1154.63	1164.89	1170.75	1104.85	1132.40
1985	1286.77	1284.01	1266.78	1258.06	1315.41	1335.46
1986	1570.99	1709.06	1818.61	1783.98	1876.71	1892.72
1987	2158.04	2223.99	2304.69	2286.36	2291.57	2418.53
1988	1958.22	2071.62	1988.06	2032.33	2031.12	2141.71
1989	2342.32	2258.39	2293.62	2418.80	2480.15	2440.06
1990	2590.54	2627.25	2707.21	2656.76	2876.66	2880.69
1991	2736.39	2882.18	2913.86	2887.87	3027.50	2906.75
1992	3223.39	3267.67	3235.47	3359.12	3396.88	3318.52
1993	3310.03	3370.81	3435.11	3427.55	3527.43	3516.08
1994	3978.36	3832.02	3635.96	3681.69	3758.37	3624.96
1995	3843.86	4011.05	4157.69	4321.27	4465.14	4556.10
1996	5395.30	5485.62	5587.14	5569.08	5643.18	5654.63
1997	6813.09	6877.74	6583.48	7008.99	7331.04	7672.79
1998	7906.50	8545.72	8799.81	9063.37	8899.95	8952.02
1999	9358.83	9306.58	9786.16	10789.04	10559.74	10970.80
2000	10940.53	10128.31	10921.92	10733.91	10522.33	10447.89
2001	10887.36	10495.28	9878.78	10734.97	10911.94	10502.40
2002	9920.00	10106.13	10403.94	9946.22	9925.25	9243.26
2003	8053.81	7891.08	7992.13	8480.09	8850.26	8985.44

DOW JONES INDUSTRIALS MONTHLY CLOSING PRICES

JUL	AUG	SEP	OCT	NOV	DEC	
209.40	216.87	226.36	225.01	227.60	235.41	**1950**
257.86	270.25	271.16	262.35	261.27	269.23	**1951**
279.56	275.04	270.61	269.23	283.66	291.90	**1952**
275.38	261.22	264.04	275.81	281.37	280.90	**1953**
347.92	335.80	360.46	352.14	386.77	404.39	**1954**
465.85	468.18	466.62	454.87	483.26	488.40	**1955**
517.81	502.04	475.25	479.85	472.78	499.47	**1956**
508.52	484.35	456.30	441.04	449.87	435.69	**1957**
502.99	508.63	532.09	543.22	557.46	583.65	**1958**
674.88	664.41	631.68	646.60	659.18	679.36	**1959**
616.73	625.99	580.14	580.36	597.22	615.89	**1960**
705.37	719.94	701.21	703.92	721.60	731.14	**1961**
597.93	609.18	578.98	589.77	649.30	652.10	**1962**
695.43	729.32	732.79	755.23	750.52	762.95	**1963**
841.10	838.48	875.37	873.08	875.43	874.13	**1964**
881.74	893.10	930.58	960.82	946.71	969.26	**1965**
847.38	788.41	774.22	807.07	791.59	785.69	**1966**
904.24	901.29	926.66	879.74	875.81	905.11	**1967**
883.00	896.01	935.79	952.39	985.08	943.75	**1968**
815.47	836.72	813.09	855.99	812.30	800.36	**1969**
734.12	764.58	760.68	755.61	794.09	838.92	**1970**
858.43	898.07	887.19	839.00	831.34	890.20	**1971**
924.74	963.73	953.27	955.52	1018.21	1020.02	**1972**
926.40	887.57	947.10	956.58	822.25	850.86	**1973**
757.43	678.58	607.87	665.52	618.66	616.24	**1974**
831.51	835.34	793.88	836.04	860.67	852.41	**1975**
984.64	973.74	990.19	964.93	947.22	1004.65	**1976**
890.07	861.49	847.11	818.35	829.70	831.17	**1977**
862.27	876.82	865.82	792.45	799.03	805.01	**1978**
846.42	887.63	878.58	815.70	822.35	838.74	**1979**
935.32	932.59	932.42	924.49	993.34	963.99	**1980**
952.34	881.47	849.98	852.55	888.98	875.00	**1981**
808.60	901.31	896.25	991.72	1039.28	1046.54	**1982**
1199.22	1216.16	1233.13	1225.20	1276.02	1258.64	**1983**
1115.28	1224.38	1206.71	1207.38	1188.94	1211.57	**1984**
1347.45	1334.01	1328.63	1374.31	1472.13	1546.67	**1985**
1775.31	1898.34	1767.58	1877.81	1914.23	1895.95	**1986**
2572.07	2662.95	2596.28	1993.53	1833.55	1938.83	**1987**
2128.73	2031.65	2112.91	2148.65	2114.51	2168.57	**1988**
2660.66	2737.27	2692.82	2645.08	2706.27	2753.20	**1989**
2905.20	2614.36	2452.48	2442.33	2559.65	2633.66	**1990**
3024.82	3043.60	3016.77	3069.10	2894.68	3168.83	**1991**
3393.78	3257.35	3271.66	3226.28	3305.16	3301.11	**1992**
3539.47	3651.25	3555.12	3680.59	3683.95	3754.09	**1993**
3764.50	3913.42	3843.19	3908.12	3739.23	3834.44	**1994**
4708.47	4610.56	4789.08	4755.48	5074.49	5117.12	**1995**
5528.91	5616.21	5882.17	6029.38	6521.70	6448.27	**1996**
8222.61	7622.42	7945.26	7442.08	7823.13	7908.25	**1997**
8883.29	7539.07	7842.62	8592.62	9116.55	9181.43	**1998**
10655.15	10829.28	10336.95	10729.86	10877.81	11497.12	**1999**
10521.98	11215.10	10650.92	10971.14	10414.49	10786.85	**2000**
10522.81	9949.75	8847.56	9075.14	9851.56	10021.50	**2001**
8736.59	8663.50	7591.93	8397.03	8896.09	8341.63	**2002**
						2003

NASDAQ COMPOSITE
MONTHLY PERCENT CHANGES

	JAN	FEB	MAR	APR	MAY	JUN
1971	10.2%	2.6%	4.6%	6.0%	— 3.6%	— 0.4%
1972	4.2	5.5	2.2	2.5	0.9	— 1.8
1973	— 4.0	— 6.2	— 2.4	— 8.2	— 4.8	— 1.6
1974	3.0	— 0.6	— 2.2	— 5.9	— 7.7	— 5.3
1975	16.6	4.6	3.6	3.8	5.8	4.7
1976	12.1	3.7	0.4	— 0.6	— 2.3	2.6
1977	— 2.4	— 1.0	— 0.5	1.4	0.1	4.3
1978	— 4.0	0.6	4.7	8.5	4.4	0.05
1979	6.6	— 2.6	7.5	1.6	— 1.8	5.1
1980	7.0	— 2.3	— 17.1	6.9	7.5	4.9
1981	— 2.2	0.1	6.1	3.1	3.1	— 3.5
1982	— 3.8	— 4.8	— 2.1	5.2	— 3.3	— 4.1
1983	6.9	5.0	3.9	8.2	5.3	3.2
1984	— 3.7	— 5.9	— 0.7	— 1.3	— 5.9	2.9
1985	12.7	2.0	— 1.7	0.5	3.6	1.9
1986	3.3	7.1	4.2	2.3	4.4	1.3
1987	12.2	8.4	1.2	— 2.8	— 0.3	2.0
1988	4.3	6.5	2.1	1.2	— 2.3	6.6
1989	5.2	— 0.4	1.8	5.1	4.4	— 2.4
1990	— 8.6	2.4	2.3	— 3.6	9.3	0.7
1991	10.8	9.4	6.5	0.5	4.4	— 6.0
1992	5.8	2.1	— 4.7	— 4.2	1.1	— 3.7
1993	2.9	— 3.7	2.9	— 4.2	5.9	0.5
1994	3.0	— 1.0	— 6.2	— 1.3	0.2	— 4.0
1995	0.4	5.1	3.0	3.3	2.4	8.0
1996	0.7	3.8	0.1	8.1	4.4	— 4.7
1997	6.9	— 5.1	— 6.7	3.2	11.1	3.0
1998	3.1	9.3	3.7	1.8	— 4.8	6.5
1999	14.3	— 8.7	7.6	3.3	— 2.8	8.7
2000	— 3.2	19.2	— 2.6	— 15.6	— 11.9	16.6
2001	12.2	—22.4	— 14.5	15.0	— 0.3	2.4
2002	— 0.8	—10.5	6.6	— 8.5	— 4.3	— 9.4
2003	— 1.1	1.3	0.3	9.2	9.0	1.7

Based on NASDAQ composite, prior to February 5, 1971, based on National Quotation Bureau indices

NASDAQ COMPOSITE
MONTHLY PERCENT CHANGES

JUL	AUG	SEP	OCT	NOV	DEC		Year's Change
— 2.3%	3.0%	0.6%	— 3.6%	— 1.1%	9.8%	1971	27.4%
— 1.8	1.7	— 0.3	0.5	2.1	0.6	1972	17.2
7.6	— 3.5	6.0	— 0.9	— 15.1	— 1.4	1973	— 31.1
— 7.9	— 10.9	— 10.7	17.2	— 3.5	— 5.0	1974	— 35.1
— 4.4	— 5.0	— 5.9	3.6	2.4	— 1.5	1975	29.8
1.1	— 1.7	1.7	— 1.0	0.9	7.4	1976	26.1
0.9	— 0.5	0.7	— 3.3	5.8	1.8	1977	7.3
5.0	6.9	— 1.6	— 16.4	3.2	2.9	1978	12.3
2.3	6.4	— 0.3	— 9.6	6.4	4.8	1979	28.1
8.9	5.7	3.4	2.7	8.0	— 2.8	1980	33.9
— 1.9	— 7.5	— 8.0	8.4	3.1	— 2.7	1981	— 3.2
— 2.3	6.2	5.6	13.3	9.3	0.04	1982	18.7
— 4.6	— 3.8	1.4	— 7.4	4.1	— 2.5	1983	19.9
— 4.2	10.9	— 1.8	— 1.2	— 1.8	2.0	1984	— 11.2
1.7	— 1.2	— 5.8	4.4	7.3	3.5	1985	31.4
— 8.4	3.1	— 8.4	2.9	— 0.3	— 2.8	1986	7.5
2.4	4.6	— 2.3	— 27.2	— 5.6	8.3	1987	— 5.4
— 1.9	— 2.8	3.0	— 1.4	— 2.9	2.7	1988	15.4
4.3	3.4	0.8	— 3.7	0.1	— 0.3	1989	19.3
— 5.2	— 13.0	— 9.6	— 4.3	8.9	4.1	1990	— 17.8
5.5	4.7	0.2	3.1	— 3.5	11.9	1991	56.8
3.1	— 3.0	3.6	3.8	7.9	3.7	1992	15.5
0.1	5.4	2.7	2.2	— 3.2	3.0	1993	14.7
2.3	6.0	— 0.2	1.7	— 3.5	0.2	1994	— 3.2
7.3	1.9	2.3	— 0.7	2.2	— 0.7	1995	39.9
— 8.8	5.6	7.5	— 0.4	5.8	— 0.1	1996	22.7
10.5	— 0.4	6.2	— 5.5	0.4	— 1.9	1997	21.6
— 1.2	— 19.9	13.0	4.6	10.1	12.5	1998	39.6
— 1.8	3.8	0.2	8.0	12.5	22.0	1999	85.6
— 5.0	11.7	— 12.7	— 8.3	— 22.9	— 4.9	2000	— 39.3
— 6.2	— 10.9	— 17.0	12.8	14.2	1.0	2001	— 21.1
— 9.2	— 1.0	— 10.9	13.5	11.2	— 9.7	2002	— 31.5
						2003	

NASDAQ COMPOSITE
MONTHLY CLOSING PRICES

	JAN	FEB	MAR	APR	MAY	JUN
1971	98.77	101.34	105.97	112.30	108.25	107.80
1972	118.87	125.38	128.14	131.33	132.53	130.08
1973	128.40	120.41	117.46	107.85	102.64	100.98
1974	94.93	94.35	92.27	86.86	80.20	75.96
1975	69.78	73.00	75.66	78.54	83.10	87.02
1976	87.05	90.26	90.62	90.08	88.04	90.32
1977	95.54	94.57	94.13	95.48	95.59	99.73
1978	100.84	101.47	106.20	115.18	120.24	120.30
1979	125.82	122.56	131.76	133.82	131.42	138.13
1980	161.75	158.03	131.00	139.99	150.45	157.78
1981	197.81	198.01	210.18	216.74	223.47	215.75
1982	188.39	179.43	175.65	184.70	178.54	171.30
1983	248.35	260.67	270.80	293.06	308.73	318.70
1984	268.43	252.57	250.78	247.44	232.82	239.65
1985	278.70	284.17	279.20	280.56	290.80	296.20
1986	335.77	359.53	374.72	383.24	400.16	405.51
1987	392.06	424.97	430.05	417.81	416.54	424.67
1988	344.66	366.95	374.64	379.23	370.34	394.66
1989	401.30	399.71	406.73	427.55	446.17	435.29
1990	415.81	425.83	435.54	420.07	458.97	462.29
1991	414.20	453.05	482.30	484.72	506.11	475.92
1992	620.21	633.47	603.77	578.68	585.31	563.60
1993	696.34	670.77	690.13	661.42	700.53	703.95
1994	800.47	792.50	743.46	733.84	735.19	705.96
1995	755.20	793.73	817.21	843.98	864.58	933.45
1996	1059.79	1100.05	1101.40	1190.52	1243.43	1185.02
1997	1379.85	1309.00	1221.70	1260.76	1400.32	1442.07
1998	1619.36	1770.51	1835.68	1868.41	1778.87	1894.74
1999	2505.89	2288.03	2461.40	2542.85	2470.52	2686.12
2000	3940.35	4696.69	4572.83	3860.66	3400.91	3966.11
2001	2772.73	2151.83	1840.26	2116.24	2110.49	2160.54
2002	1934.03	1731.49	1845.35	1688.23	1615.73	1463.21
2003	1320.91	1337.52	1341.17	1464.31	1595.91	1622.80

Based on NASDAQ composite, prior to February 5, 1971, based on National Quotation Bureau indices

NASDAQ COMPOSITE
MONTHLY CLOSING PRICES

JUL	AUG	SEP	OCT	NOV	DEC	
105.27	108.42	109.03	105.10	103.97	114.12	**1971**
127.75	129.95	129.61	130.24	132.96	133.73	**1972**
108.64	104.87	111.20	110.17	93.51	92.19	**1973**
69.99	62.37	55.67	65.23	62.95	59.82	**1974**
83.19	79.01	74.33	76.99	78.80	77.62	**1975**
91.29	89.70	91.26	90.35	91.12	97.88	**1976**
100.65	100.10	100.85	97.52	103.15	105.05	**1977**
126.32	135.01	132.89	111.12	114.69	117.98	**1978**
141.33	150.44	149.98	135.53	144.26	151.14	**1979**
171.81	181.52	187.76	192.78	208.15	202.34	**1980**
211.63	195.75	180.03	195.24	201.37	195.84	**1981**
167.35	177.71	187.65	212.63	232.31	232.41	**1982**
303.96	292.42	296.65	274.55	285.67	278.60	**1983**
229.70	254.64	249.94	247.03	242.53	247.35	**1984**
301.29	297.71	280.33	292.54	313.95	324.93	**1985**
371.37	382.86	350.67	360.77	359.57	349.33	**1986**
434.93	454.97	444.29	323.30	305.16	330.47	**1987**
387.33	376.55	387.71	382.46	371.45	381.38	**1988**
453.84	469.33	472.92	455.63	456.09	454.82	**1989**
438.24	381.21	344.51	329.84	359.06	373.84	**1990**
502.04	525.68	526.88	542.98	523.90	586.34	**1991**
580.83	563.12	583.27	605.17	652.73	676.95	**1992**
704.70	742.84	762.78	779.26	754.39	776.80	**1993**
722.16	765.62	764.29	777.49	750.32	751.96	**1994**
1001.21	1020.11	1043.54	1036.06	1059.20	1052.13	**1995**
1080.59	1141.50	1226.92	1221.51	1292.61	1291.03	**1996**
1593.81	1587.32	1685.69	1593.61	1600.55	1570.35	**1997**
1872.39	1499.25	1693.84	1771.39	1949.54	2192.69	**1998**
2638.49	2739.35	2746.16	2966.43	3336.16	4069.31	**1999**
3766.99	4206.35	3672.82	3369.63	2597.93	2470.52	**2000**
2027.13	1805.43	1498.80	1690.20	1930.58	1950.40	**2001**
1328.26	1314.85	1172.06	1329.75	1478.78	1335.51	**2002**
						2003

BEST & WORST <u>DOW</u> DAYS SINCE 1901 BY POINTS AND PERCENT

BEST TWENTY DAYS SINCE 1901 BY POINTS

Day	DJIA Close	Points Change	% Change
3/16/2000	10630.60	499.19	4.9
7/24/2002	8191.29	488.95	6.3
7/29/2002	8711.88	447.49	5.4
4/5/2001	9918.05	402.63	4.2
4/18/2001	10615.83	399.10	3.9
9/8/1998	8020.78	380.53	5.0
10/15/2002	8255.68	378.28	4.8
9/24/2001	8603.86	368.05	4.5
10/1/2002	7938.79	346.86	4.6
5/16/2001	11215.92	342.95	3.2
12/5/2000	10898.72	338.62	3.2
10/28/1997	7498.32	337.17	4.7
10/15/1998	8299.36	330.58	4.1
7/5/2002	9379.50	324.53	3.6
3/15/2000	10131.41	320.17	3.3
10/11/2002	7850.29	316.34	4.2
5/8/2002	10141.83	305.28	3.1
4/3/2000	11221.93	300.01	2.7
1/3/2001	10945.75	299.60	2.8
9/1/1998	7827.43	288.36	3.8

WORST TWENTY DAYS SINCE 1901 BY POINTS

Day	DJIA Close	Points Change	% Change
9/17/2001	8920.70	− 684.81	− 7.1
4/14/2000	10305.77	− 617.78	− 5.7
10/27/1997	7161.15	− 554.26	− 7.2
8/31/1998	7539.07	− 512.61	− 6.4
10/19/1987	1738.74	− 508.00	− 22.6
3/12/2001	10208.25	− 436.37	− 4.1
7/19/2002	8019.26	− 390.23	− 4.6
9/20/2001	8376.21	− 382.92	− 4.4
10/12/2000	10034.58	− 379.21	− 3.6
3/7/2000	9796.03	− 374.47	− 3.7
1/4/2000	10997.93	− 359.58	− 3.2
8/27/1998	8165.99	− 357.36	− 4.2
9/3/2002	8308.05	− 355.45	− 4.1
3/14/2001	9973.46	− 317.34	− 3.1
3/24/2003	8214.68	− 307.29	− 3.6
8/4/1998	8487.31	− 299.43	− 3.4
9/27/2002	7701.45	− 295.67	− 3.7
2/18/2000	10219.52	− 295.05	− 2.8
4/3/2001	9485.71	− 292.22	− 3.0
1/28/2000	10738.87	− 289.15	− 2.6

BEST TWENTY DAYS SINCE 1950 BY %

Day	DJIA Close	Points Change	% Change
10/21/1987	2027.85	186.84	10.1
7/24/2002	8191.29	488.95	6.3
10/20/1987	1841.01	102.27	5.9
7/29/2002	8711.88	447.49	5.4
5/27/1970	663.20	32.04	5.1
9/8/1998	8020.78	380.53	5.0
10/29/1987	1938.33	91.51	5.0
3/16/2000	10630.60	499.19	4.9
8/17/1982	831.24	38.81	4.9
10/15/2002	8255.68	378.28	4.8
10/9/1974	631.02	28.39	4.7
10/28/1997	7498.32	337.17	4.7
5/29/1962	603.96	27.03	4.7
10/1/2002	7938.79	346.86	4.6
1/17/1991	2623.51	114.60	4.6
11/26/1963	743.52	32.03	4.5
9/24/2001	8603.86	368.05	4.5
11/1/1978	827.79	35.34	4.5
11/3/1982	1065.49	43.41	4.2
4/5/2001	9918.05	402.63	4.2

WORST TWENTY DAYS SINCE 1950 BY %

Day	DJIA Close	Points Change	% Change
10/19/1987	1738.74	− 508.00	− 22.6
10/26/1987	1793.93	− 156.83	− 8.0
10/27/1997	7161.15	− 554.26	− 7.2
9/17/2001	8920.70	− 684.81	− 7.1
10/13/1989	2569.26	− 190.58	− 6.9
1/8/1988	1911.31	− 140.58	− 6.9
9/26/1955	455.56	− 31.89	− 6.5
8/31/1998	7539.07	− 512.61	− 6.4
5/28/1962	576.93	− 34.95	− 5.7
4/14/2000	10305.77	− 617.78	− 5.7
4/14/1988	2005.64	− 101.46	− 4.8
6/26/1950	213.91	− 10.44	− 4.7
7/19/2002	8019.26	− 390.23	− 4.6
9/11/1986	1792.89	− 86.61	− 4.6
10/16/1987	2246.74	− 108.35	− 4.6
9/20/2001	8376.21	− 382.92	− 4.4
8/27/1998	8165.99	− 357.36	− 4.2
9/3/2002	8308.05	− 355.45	− 4.1
3/12/2001	10208.25	− 436.37	− 4.1
11/30/1987	1833.55	− 76.93	− 4.0

BEST FIFTEEN DAYS 1901-1949 BY %

Day	DJIA Close	Points Change	% Change
3/15/1933	62.10	8.26	15.3
10/6/1931	99.34	12.86	14.9
10/30/1929	258.47	28.40	12.3
9/21/1932	75.16	7.67	11.4
8/3/1932	58.22	5.06	9.5
2/11/1932	78.60	6.80	9.5
11/14/1929	217.28	18.59	9.4
12/18/1931	80.69	6.90	9.4
2/13/1932	85.82	7.22	9.2
5/6/1932	59.01	4.91	9.1
4/19/1933	68.31	5.66	9.0
10/8/1931	105.79	8.47	8.7
6/10/1932	48.94	3.62	8.0
9/5/1939	148.12	10.03	7.3
6/3/1931	130.37	8.67	7.1

WORST FIFTEEN DAYS 1901-1949 BY %

Day	DJIA Close	Points Change	% Change
10/28/1929	260.64	− 38.33	− 12.8
10/29/1929	230.07	− 30.57	− 11.7
11/6/1929	232.13	− 25.55	− 9.9
8/12/1932	63.11	− 5.79	− 8.4
3/14/1907	55.84	− 5.05	− 8.3
7/21/1933	88.71	− 7.55	− 7.8
10/18/1937	125.73	− 10.57	− 7.8
2/1/1917	88.52	− 6.91	− 7.2
10/5/1932	66.07	− 5.09	− 7.2
9/24/1931	107.79	− 8.20	− 7.1
7/20/1933	96.26	− 7.32	− 7.1
7/30/1914	52.32	− 3.88	− 6.9
11/11/1929	220.39	− 16.14	− 6.8
5/14/1940	128.27	− 9.36	− 6.8
10/5/1931	86.48	− 6.29	− 6.8

BEST & WORST <u>NASDAQ</u> DAYS
SINCE 1971 BY POINTS AND PERCENT

BEST TWENTY DAYS
SINCE 1971 BY POINTS

Day	NASDAQ Close	Points Change	% Change
1/3/2001	2616.69	324.83	14.2
12/5/2000	2889.80	274.05	10.5
4/18/2000	3793.57	254.41	7.2
5/30/2000	3459.48	254.37	7.9
10/19/2000	3418.60	247.04	7.8
10/13/2000	3316.77	242.09	7.9
6/2/2000	3813.38	230.88	6.4
4/25/2000	3711.23	228.75	6.6
4/17/2000	3539.16	217.87	6.6
6/1/2000	3582.50	181.59	5.3
4/7/2000	4446.45	178.89	4.2
10/31/2000	3369.63	178.23	5.6
12/22/2000	2517.02	176.90	7.6
11/14/2000	3138.27	171.55	5.8
2/23/2000	4550.33	168.21	3.8
1/10/2000	4049.67	167.05	4.3
12/8/2000	2917.43	164.77	6.0
3/3/2000	4914.79	160.28	3.4
4/18/2001	2079.44	156.22	8.1
1/7/2000	3882.62	155.49	4.2

WORST TWENTY DAYS
SINCE 1971 BY POINTS

Day	NASDAQ Close	Points Change	% Change
4/14/2000	3321.29	− 355.49	− 9.7
4/3/2000	4223.68	− 349.15	− 7.6
4/12/2000	3769.63	− 286.27	− 7.1
4/10/2000	4188.20	− 258.25	− 5.8
1/4/2000	3901.69	− 229.46	− 5.6
3/14/2000	4706.63	− 200.61	− 4.1
5/10/2000	3384.73	− 200.28	− 5.6
5/23/2000	3164.55	− 199.66	− 5.9
10/25/2000	3229.57	− 190.22	− 5.6
3/29/2000	4644.67	− 189.22	− 3.9
3/20/2000	4610.00	− 188.13	− 3.9
3/30/2000	4457.89	− 186.78	− 4.0
11/8/2000	3231.70	− 184.09	− 5.4
7/28/2000	3663.00	− 179.23	− 4.7
12/20/2000	2332.78	− 178.93	− 7.1
1/2/2001	2291.86	− 178.66	− 7.2
5/2/2000	3785.45	− 172.63	− 4.4
11/10/2000	3028.99	− 171.36	− 5.4
4/24/2000	3482.48	− 161.40	− 4.4
1/5/2001	2407.65	− 159.18	− 6.2

BEST TWENTY DAYS
SINCE 1971 BY %

Day	NASDAQ Close	Points Change	% Change
1/3/2001	2616.69	324.83	14.2
12/5/2000	2889.80	274.05	10.5
4/5/2001	1785.00	146.20	8.9
4/18/2001	2079.44	156.22	8.1
5/30/2000	3459.48	254.37	7.9
10/13/2000	3316.77	242.09	7.9
10/19/2000	3418.60	247.04	7.8
5/8/2002	1696.29	122.47	7.8
12/22/2000	2517.02	176.90	7.6
10/21/1987	351.86	24.07	7.3
4/18/2000	3793.57	254.41	7.2
4/25/2000	3711.23	228.75	6.6
4/17/2000	3539.16	217.87	6.6
6/2/2000	3813.38	230.88	6.4
4/10/2001	1852.03	106.32	6.1
9/8/1998	1660.86	94.34	6.0
12/8/2000	2917.43	164.77	6.0
10/3/2001	1580.81	88.48	5.9
7/29/2002	1335.25	73.13	5.8
11/14/2000	3138.27	171.55	5.8

WORST TWENTY DAYS
SINCE 1971 BY %

Day	NASDAQ Close	Points Change	% Change
10/19/1987	360.21	− 46.12	−11.4
4/14/2000	3321.29	− 355.49	− 9.7
10/20/1987	327.79	− 32.42	− 9.0
10/26/1987	298.90	− 29.55	− 9.0
8/31/1998	1499.25	− 140.43	− 8.6
4/3/2000	4223.68	− 349.15	− 7.6
1/2/2001	2291.86	− 178.66	− 7.2
12/20/2000	2332.78	− 178.93	− 7.1
4/12/2000	3769.63	− 286.27	− 7.1
10/27/1997	1535.09	− 115.83	− 7.0
9/17/2001	1579.55	− 115.83	− 6.8
3/12/2001	1923.38	− 129.40	− 6.3
1/5/2001	2407.65	− 159.18	− 6.2
4/3/2001	1673.00	− 109.97	− 6.2
3/27/1980	124.09	− 8.13	− 6.1
3/28/2001	1854.13	− 118.13	− 6.0
5/23/2000	3164.55	− 199.66	− 5.9
4/10/2000	4188.20	− 258.25	− 5.8
5/10/2000	3384.73	− 200.28	− 5.6
4/19/1999	2345.61	− 138.43	− 5.6

Based on NASDAQ composite, prior to February 5, 1971, based on National Quotation Bureau indices

BEST & WORST DOW WEEKS
SINCE 1901 BY POINTS AND PERCENT

BEST TWENTY WEEKS SINCE 1901 BY POINTS

Week Ending	DJIA Close	Points Change	% Change
3/17/2000	10595.23	666.41	6.7
3/21/2003	8521.97	662.26	8.4
9/28/2001	8847.56	611.75	7.4
7/2/1999	11139.24	586.68	5.6
4/20/2000	10844.05	538.28	5.2
3/24/2000	11112.72	517.49	4.9
10/16/1998	8416.76	517.24	6.5
3/3/2000	10367.20	505.08	5.1
6/2/2000	10794.76	495.52	4.8
5/18/2001	11301.74	480.43	4.4
10/18/2002	8322.40	472.11	6.0
1/8/1999	9643.32	461.89	5.0
4/20/2001	10579.85	452.91	4.5
10/22/1999	10470.25	450.54	4.5
8/9/2002	8745.45	432.32	5.2
3/5/1999	9736.08	429.50	4.6
5/17/2002	10353.08	413.16	4.2
3/1/2002	10368.86	400.71	4.0
11/6/1998	8975.46	383.36	4.5
10/8/1999	10649.76	376.76	3.7

WORST TWENTY WEEKS SINCE 1901 BY POINTS

Week Ending	DJIA Close	Points Change	% Change
9/21/2001	8235.81	−1369.70	− 14.3
3/16/2001	9823.41	− 821.21	− 7.7
4/14/2000	10305.77	− 805.71	− 7.3
7/12/2002	8684.53	− 694.97	− 7.4
7/19/2002	8019.26	− 665.27	− 7.7
10/15/1999	10019.71	− 630.05	− 5.9
2/11/2000	10425.21	− 538.59	− 4.9
9/24/1999	10279.33	− 524.30	− 4.9
1/28/2000	10738.87	− 512.84	− 4.6
8/28/1998	8051.68	− 481.97	− 5.6
8/31/2001	9949.75	− 473.42	− 4.5
1/21/2000	11251.71	− 471.27	− 4.0
1/24/2003	8131.01	− 455.73	− 5.3
3/10/2000	9928.82	− 438.38	− 4.2
9/4/1998	7640.25	− 411.43	− 5.1
10/13/2000	10192.18	− 404.36	− 3.8
7/24/1998	8937.36	− 400.61	− 4.3
1/9/1998	7580.42	− 384.62	− 4.8
3/28/2003	8145.77	− 376.20	− 4.4
2/23/2001	10441.90	− 357.92	− 3.3

BEST TWENTY WEEKS SINCE 1950 BY %

Week Ending	DJIA Close	Points Change	% Change
10/11/1974	658.17	73.61	12.6
8/20/1982	869.29	81.24	10.3
10/8/1982	986.85	79.11	8.7
3/21/2003	8521.97	662.26	8.4
8/3/1984	1202.08	87.46	7.8
9/28/2001	8847.56	611.75	7.4
9/20/1974	670.76	43.57	6.9
3/17/2000	10595.23	666.41	6.7
10/16/1998	8416.76	517.24	6.5
6/7/1974	853.72	51.55	6.4
11/2/1962	604.58	35.56	6.2
1/9/1976	911.13	52.42	6.1
11/5/1982	1051.78	60.06	6.1
10/18/2002	8322.40	472.11	6.0
6/3/1988	2071.30	114.86	5.9
1/18/1991	2646.78	145.29	5.8
12/18/1987	1975.30	108.26	5.8
11/14/1980	986.35	53.93	5.8
5/29/1970	700.44	38.27	5.8
12/11/1987	1867.04	100.30	5.7

WORST TWENTY WEEKS SINCE 1950 BY %

Week Ending	DJIA Close	Points Change	% Change
9/21/2001	8235.81	−1369.70	− 14.3
10/23/1987	1950.76	− 295.98	− 13.2
10/16/1987	2246.74	− 235.47	− 9.5
10/13/1989	2569.26	− 216.26	− 7.8
3/16/2001	9823.41	− 821.21	− 7.7
7/19/2002	8019.26	− 665.27	− 7.7
12/4/1987	1766.74	− 143.74	− 7.5
9/13/1974	627.19	− 50.69	− 7.5
9/12/1986	1758.72	− 141.03	− 7.4
7/12/2002	8684.53	− 694.97	− 7.4
9/27/1974	621.95	− 48.81	− 7.3
4/14/2000	10305.77	− 805.71	− 7.3
6/30/1950	209.11	− 15.24	− 6.8
6/22/1962	539.19	− 38.99	− 6.7
12/6/1974	577.60	− 41.06	− 6.6
10/20/1978	838.01	− 59.08	− 6.6
10/12/1979	838.99	− 58.62	− 6.5
8/23/1974	686.80	− 44.74	− 6.1
10/9/1987	2482.21	− 158.78	− 6.0
10/4/1974	584.56	− 37.39	− 6.0

BEST TEN WEEKS 1901-1949 BY %

Week Ending	DJIA Close	Points Change	% Change
8/6/1932	66.56	12.30	22.7
6/25/1938	131.94	18.71	16.5
4/22/1933	72.24	9.36	14.9
10/10/1931	105.61	12.84	13.8
7/30/1932	54.26	6.42	13.4
6/27/1931	156.93	17.97	12.9
9/24/1932	74.83	8.39	12.6
8/27/1932	75.61	8.43	12.5
3/18/1933	60.56	6.72	12.5
8/15/1903	38.80	4.09	11.8

WORST TEN WEEKS 1901-1949 BY %

Week Ending	DJIA Close	Points Change	% Change
7/22/1933	88.42	− 17.68	− 16.7
5/18/1940	122.43	− 22.42	− 15.5
10/8/1932	61.17	− 10.92	− 15.1
10/3/1931	92.77	− 14.59	− 13.6
9/17/1932	66.44	− 10.10	− 13.2
10/21/1933	83.64	− 11.95	− 12.5
12/12/1931	78.93	− 11.21	− 12.4
5/8/1915	62.77	− 8.74	− 12.2
6/21/1930	215.30	− 28.95	− 11.9
12/8/1928	257.33	− 33.47	− 11.5

BEST & WORST NASDAQ WEEKS
SINCE 1971 BY POINTS AND PERCENT

BEST TWENTY WEEKS SINCE 1971 BY POINTS

Week Ending	NASDAQ Close	Points Change	% Change
6/2/2000	3813.38	608.27	19.0
2/4/2000	4244.14	357.07	9.2
3/3/2000	4914.79	324.29	7.1
4/20/2000	3643.88	322.59	9.7
12/8/2000	2917.43	272.14	10.3
4/12/2001	1961.43	241.07	14.0
7/14/2000	4246.18	222.98	5.5
1/12/2001	2626.50	218.85	9.1
4/28/2000	3860.66	216.78	5.9
12/23/1999	3969.44	216.38	5.8
4/20/2001	2163.41	201.98	10.3
9/1/2000	4234.33	191.65	4.7
7/2/1999	2741.02	188.37	7.4
1/14/2000	4064.27	181.65	4.7
2/25/2000	4590.50	178.76	4.1
11/3/2000	3451.58	173.22	5.3
1/21/2000	4235.40	171.13	4.2
1/29/1999	2505.89	167.01	7.1
10/20/2000	3483.14	166.37	5.0
3/24/2000	4963.03	164.90	3.4

WORST TWENTY WEEKS SINCE 1971 BY POINTS

Week Ending	NASDAQ Close	Points Change	% Change
4/14/2000	3321.29	−1125.16	− 25.3
7/28/2000	3663.00	− 431.45	− 10.5
11/10/2000	3028.99	− 422.59	− 12.2
3/31/2000	4572.83	− 390.20	− 7.9
1/28/2000	3887.07	− 348.33	− 8.2
10/6/2000	3361.01	− 311.81	− 8.5
5/12/2000	3529.06	− 287.76	− 7.5
9/21/2001	1423.19	− 272.19	− 16.1
11/22/2000	2755.34	− 271.85	− 9.0
12/15/2000	2653.27	− 264.16	− 9.1
12/1/2000	2645.29	− 259.09	− 8.9
9/8/2000	3978.41	− 255.92	− 6.0
3/17/2000	4798.13	− 250.49	− 5.0
10/27/2000	3278.36	− 204.78	− 5.9
2/9/2001	2470.97	− 189.53	− 7.1
1/7/2000	3882.62	− 186.69	− 4.6
6/15/2001	2028.43	− 186.67	− 8.4
5/26/2000	3205.11	− 185.29	− 5.5
7/23/1999	2692.40	− 172.08	− 6.0
2/23/2001	2262.51	− 162.87	− 6.7

BEST TWENTY WEEKS SINCE 1971 BY %

Week Ending	NASDAQ Close	Points Change	% Change
6/2/2000	3813.38	608.27	19.0
4/12/2001	1961.43	241.07	14.0
4/20/2001	2163.41	201.98	10.3
12/8/2000	2917.43	272.14	10.3
4/20/2000	3643.88	322.59	9.7
10/11/1974	60.42	5.26	9.5
2/4/2000	4244.14	357.07	9.2
1/12/2001	2626.50	218.85	9.1
5/17/2002	1741.39	140.54	8.8
10/16/1998	1620.95	128.46	8.6
12/18/1987	326.91	24.34	8.0
5/2/1997	1305.33	96.04	7.9
1/9/1987	380.65	27.39	7.8
8/3/1984	246.24	16.94	7.4
7/2/1999	2741.02	188.37	7.4
1/29/1999	2505.89	167.01	7.1
10/5/2001	1605.30	106.50	7.1
3/3/2000	4914.79	324.29	7.1
3/8/2002	1929.67	126.93	7.0
1/8/1999	2344.41	151.72	6.9

WORST TWENTY WEEKS SINCE 1971 BY %

Week Ending	NASDAQ Close	Points Change	% Change
4/14/2000	3321.29	−1125.16	−25.3
10/23/1987	328.45	− 77.88	−19.2
9/21/2001	1423.19	− 272.19	−16.1
11/10/2000	3028.99	− 422.59	−12.2
7/28/2000	3663.00	− 431.45	−10.5
12/15/2000	2653.27	− 264.16	− 9.1
11/22/2000	2755.34	− 271.85	− 9.0
12/1/2000	2645.29	− 259.09	− 8.9
8/28/1998	1639.68	− 157.93	− 8.8
10/20/1978	123.82	− 11.76	− 8.7
10/6/2000	3361.01	− 311.81	− 8.5
6/15/2001	2028.43	− 186.67	− 8.4
9/12/1986	346.78	− 31.58	− 8.3
1/28/2000	3887.07	− 348.33	− 8.2
3/16/2001	1890.91	− 161.87	− 7.9
3/31/2000	4572.83	− 390.20	− 7.9
10/12/1979	140.71	− 11.58	− 7.6
10/9/1998	1492.49	− 122.49	− 7.6
5/12/2000	3529.06	− 287.76	− 7.5
12/6/1974	58.21	− 4.74	− 7.5

Based on NASDAQ composite, prior to February 5, 1971, based on National Quotation Bureau indices

BEST & WORST <u>DOW</u> MONTHS
SINCE 1901 BY POINTS AND PERCENT

BEST TWENTY MONTHS SINCE 1901 BY POINTS

Month	DJIA Close	Points Change	% Change
Apr-1999	10789.04	1002.88	10.2
Apr-2001	10734.97	856.19	8.7
Oct-2002	8397.03	805.10	10.6
Mar-2000	10921.92	793.61	7.8
Nov-2001	9851.56	776.42	8.6
Oct-1998	8592.10	749.48	9.6
Aug-2000	11215.10	693.12	6.6
Feb-1998	8545.72	639.22	8.1
Dec-1999	11497.12	619.31	5.7
Jul-1997	8222.61	549.82	7.2
Nov-1998	9116.55	524.45	6.1
Nov-2002	8896.09	499.06	5.9
Nov-1996	6521.70	492.32	8.2
Apr-2003	8480.09	487.96	6.1
Mar-1999	9786.16	479.58	5.2
Apr-1997	7008.99	425.51	6.5
Jun-1999	10970.80	411.06	3.9
Oct-1999	10729.86	392.91	3.8
Nov-1997	7823.13	381.05	5.1
Dec-2000	10786.85	372.36	3.6

WORST TWENTY MONTHS SINCE 1901 BY POINTS

Month	DJIA Close	Points Change	% Change
Aug-1998	7539.07	−1344.22	− 15.1
Sep-2001	8847.56	−1102.19	− 11.1
Sep-2002	7591.93	−1071.57	− 12.4
Feb-2000	10128.31	− 812.22	− 7.4
Jun-2002	9243.26	− 681.99	− 6.9
Mar-2001	9878.78	− 616.50	− 5.9
Oct-1987	1993.53	− 602.75	− 23.2
Aug-1997	7622.42	− 600.19	− 7.3
Aug-2001	9949.75	− 573.06	− 5.4
Sep-2000	10650.92	− 564.18	− 5.0
Nov-2000	10414.49	− 556.65	− 5.1
Jan-2000	10940.53	− 556.59	− 4.8
Dec-2002	8341.63	− 554.46	− 6.2
Jul-2002	8736.59	− 506.67	− 5.5
Oct-1997	7442.08	− 503.18	− 6.3
Sep-1999	10336.95	− 492.33	− 4.5
Apr-2002	9946.22	− 457.72	− 4.4
Jun-2001	10502.40	− 409.54	− 3.8
Feb-2001	10495.28	− 392.08	− 3.6
Jul-1999	10655.15	− 315.65	− 2.9

BEST TWENTY MONTHS SINCE 1950 BY %

Month	DJIA Close	Points Change	% Change
Jan-1976	975.28	122.87	14.4
Jan-1975	703.69	87.45	14.2
Jan-1987	2158.04	262.09	13.8
Aug-1982	901.31	92.71	11.5
Oct-1982	991.72	95.47	10.7
Oct-2002	8397.03	805.10	10.6
Apr-1978	837.32	79.96	10.6
Apr-1999	10789.04	1002.88	10.2
Nov-1962	649.30	59.53	10.1
Nov-1954	386.77	34.63	9.8
Aug-1984	1224.38	109.10	9.8
Oct-1998	8592.10	749.48	9.6
Oct-1974	665.52	57.65	9.5
Dec-1991	3168.83	274.15	9.5
Jul-1989	2660.66	220.60	9.0
Feb-1986	1709.06	138.07	8.8
Apr-2001	10734.97	856.19	8.7
Nov-2001	9851.56	776.42	8.6
Apr-1968	912.22	71.55	8.5
Apr-1983	1226.20	96.17	8.5

WORST TWENTY MONTHS SINCE 1950 BY %

Month	DJIA Close	Points Change	% Change
Oct-1987	1993.53	− 602.75	− 23.2
Aug-1998	7539.07	−1344.22	− 15.1
Nov-1973	822.25	− 134.33	− 14.0
Sep-2002	7591.93	−1071.57	− 12.4
Sep-2001	8847.56	−1102.19	− 11.1
Sep-1974	607.87	− 70.71	− 10.4
Aug-1974	678.58	− 78.85	− 10.4
Aug-1990	2614.36	− 290.84	− 10.0
Mar-1980	785.75	− 77.39	− 9.0
Jun-1962	561.28	− 52.08	− 8.5
Oct-1978	792.45	− 73.37	− 8.5
Jan-1960	622.62	− 56.74	− 8.4
Nov-1987	1833.55	− 159.98	− 8.0
May-1962	613.36	− 51.97	− 7.8
Aug-1981	881.47	− 70.87	− 7.4
Feb-2000	10128.31	− 812.22	− 7.4
May-1956	478.05	− 38.07	− 7.4
Jan-1978	769.92	− 61.25	− 7.4
Sep-1960	580.14	− 45.85	− 7.3
Aug-1997	7622.42	− 600.19	− 7.3

BEST TEN MONTHS 1901-1949 BY %

Month	DJIA Close	Points Change	% Change
Apr-1933	77.66	22.26	40.2
Aug-1932	73.16	18.90	34.8
Jul-1932	54.26	11.42	26.7
Jun-1938	133.88	26.14	24.3
Apr-1915	71.78	10.95	18.0
Jun-1931	150.18	21.72	16.9
Nov-1928	293.38	41.22	16.3
Nov-1904	52.76	6.59	14.3
May-1919	105.50	12.62	13.6
Sep-1939	152.54	18.13	13.5

WORST TEN MONTHS 1901-1949 BY %

Month	DJIA Close	Points Change	% Change
Sep-1931	96.61	− 42.80	− 30.7
Mar-1938	98.95	− 30.69	− 23.7
Apr-1932	56.11	− 17.17	− 23.4
May-1940	116.22	− 32.21	− 21.7
Oct-1929	273.51	− 69.94	− 20.4
May-1932	44.74	− 11.37	− 20.3
Jun-1930	226.34	− 48.73	− 17.7
Dec-1931	77.90	− 15.97	− 17.0
Feb-1933	51.39	− 9.51	− 15.6
May-1931	128.46	− 22.73	− 15.0

BEST & WORST <u>NASDAQ</u> MONTHS
SINCE 1971 BY POINTS AND PERCENT

BEST TWENTY MONTHS SINCE 1971 BY POINTS

Month	NASDAQ Close	Points Change	% Change
Feb-2000	4696.69	756.34	19.2
Dec-1999	4069.31	733.15	22.0
Jun-2000	3966.11	565.20	16.6
Aug-2000	4206.35	439.36	11.7
Nov-1999	3336.16	369.73	12.5
Jan-1999	2505.89	313.20	14.3
Jan-2001	2772.73	302.21	12.2
Apr-2001	2116.24	275.98	15.0
Dec-1998	2192.69	243.15	12.5
Nov-2001	1930.58	240.38	14.2
Oct-1999	2966.43	220.27	8.0
Jun-1999	2686.12	215.60	8.7
Sep-1998	1693.84	194.59	13.0
Oct-2001	1690.20	191.40	12.8
Nov-1998	1949.54	178.15	10.1
Mar-1999	2461.40	173.37	7.6
Oct-2002	1329.75	157.69	13.5
Jul-1997	1593.81	151.74	10.5
Feb-1998	1770.51	151.15	9.3
Nov-2002	1478.78	149.03	11.2

WORST TWENTY MONTHS SINCE 1971 BY POINTS

Month	NASDAQ Close	Points Change	% Change
Nov-2000	2597.93	− 771.70	− 22.9
Apr-2000	3860.66	− 712.17	− 15.6
Feb-2001	2151.83	− 620.90	− 22.4
Sep-2000	3672.82	− 533.53	− 12.7
May-2000	3400.91	− 459.75	− 11.9
Aug-1998	1499.25	− 373.14	− 19.9
Mar-2001	1840.26	− 311.57	− 14.5
Sep-2001	1498.80	− 306.63	− 17.0
Oct-2000	3369.63	− 303.19	− 8.3
Aug-2001	1805.43	− 221.70	− 10.9
Feb-1999	2288.03	− 217.86	− 8.7
Feb-2002	1731.49	− 202.54	− 10.5
Jul-2000	3766.99	− 199.12	− 5.0
Apr-2002	1688.23	− 157.12	− 8.5
Jun-2002	1463.21	− 152.52	− 9.4
Dec-2002	1335.51	− 143.27	− 9.7
Sep-2002	1172.06	− 142.79	− 10.9
Jul-2002	1328.26	− 134.95	− 9.2
Jul-2001	2027.13	− 133.41	− 6.2
Jan-2000	3940.35	− 128.96	− 3.2

BEST TWENTY MONTHS SINCE 1971 BY %

Month	NASDAQ Close	Points Change	% Change
Dec-1999	4069.31	733.15	22.0
Feb-2000	4696.69	756.34	19.2
Oct-1974	65.23	9.56	17.2
Jan-1975	69.78	9.96	16.6
Jun-2000	3966.11	565.20	16.6
Apr-2001	2116.24	275.98	15.0
Jan-1999	2505.89	313.20	14.3
Nov-2001	1930.58	240.38	14.2
Oct-2002	1329.75	157.69	13.5
Oct-1982	212.63	24.98	13.3
Sep-1998	1693.84	194.59	13.0
Oct-2001	1690.20	191.40	12.8
Jan-1985	278.70	31.35	12.7
Dec-1998	2192.69	243.15	12.5
Nov-1999	3336.16	369.73	12.5
Jan-2001	2772.73	302.21	12.2
Jan-1987	392.06	42.73	12.2
Jan-1976	87.05	9.43	12.1
Dec-1991	586.34	62.44	11.9
Aug-2000	4206.35	439.36	11.7

WORST TWENTY MONTHS SINCE 1971 BY %

Month	NASDAQ Close	Points Change	% Change
Oct-1987	323.30	− 120.99	− 27.2
Nov-2000	2597.93	− 771.70	− 22.9
Feb-2001	2151.83	− 620.90	− 22.4
Aug-1998	1499.25	− 373.14	− 19.9
Mar-1980	131.00	− 27.03	− 17.1
Sep-2001	1498.80	− 306.63	− 17.0
Oct-1978	111.12	− 21.77	− 16.4
Apr-2000	3860.66	− 712.17	− 15.6
Nov-1973	93.51	− 16.66	− 15.1
Mar-2001	1840.26	− 311.57	− 14.5
Aug-1990	381.21	− 57.03	− 13.0
Sep-2000	3672.82	− 533.53	− 12.7
May-2000	3400.91	− 459.75	− 11.9
Aug-2001	1805.43	− 221.70	− 10.9
Aug-1974	62.37	− 7.62	− 10.9
Sep-2002	1172.06	− 142.79	− 10.9
Sep-1974	55.67	− 6.70	− 10.7
Feb-2002	1731.49	− 202.54	− 10.5
Dec-2002	1335.51	− 143.27	− 9.7
Oct-1979	135.53	− 14.45	− 9.6

Based on NASDAQ composite, prior to February 5, 1971, based on National Quotation Bureau indices

BEST & WORST <u>DOW</u> AND <u>NASDAQ</u> YEARS

<u>DOW</u> SINCE 1901 BY POINTS AND PERCENT

BEST FIFTEEN YEARS SINCE 1901 BY POINTS

Year	DJIA Close	Points Change	% Change
1999	11497.12	2315.69	25.2
1997	7908.25	1459.98	22.6
1996	6448.27	1331.15	26.0
1995	5117.12	1282.68	33.5
1998	9181.43	1273.18	16.1
1989	2753.20	584.63	27.0
1991	3168.83	535.17	20.3
2003	8850.26	508.63	6.1
1993	3754.09	452.98	13.7
1986	1895.95	349.28	22.6
1985	1546.67	335.10	27.7
1975	852.41	236.17	38.3
1988	2168.57	229.74	11.8
1983	1258.64	212.10	20.3
1982	1046.54	171.54	19.6

WORST FIFTEEN YEARS SINCE 1901 BY POINTS

Year	DJIA Close	Points Change	% Change
2002	8341.63	−1679.87	− 16.8
2001	10021.50	− 765.35	− 7.1
2000	10786.85	− 710.27	− 6.2
1974	616.24	− 234.62	− 27.6
1966	785.69	− 183.57	− 18.9
1977	831.17	− 173.48	− 17.3
1973	850.86	− 169.16	− 16.6
1969	800.36	− 143.39	− 15.2
1990	2633.66	− 119.54	− 4.3
1981	875.00	− 88.99	− 9.2
1931	77.90	− 86.68	− 52.7
1930	164.58	− 83.90	− 33.8
1962	652.10	− 79.04	− 10.8
1957	435.69	− 63.78	− 12.8
1960	615.89	− 63.47	− 9.3

BEST FIFTEEN YEARS SINCE 1901 BY %

Year	DJIA Close	Points Change	% Change
1915	99.15	44.57	81.7
1933	99.90	39.97	66.7
1928	300.00	97.60	48.2
1908	63.11	20.07	46.6
1954	404.39	123.49	44.0
1904	50.99	15.01	41.7
1935	144.13	40.09	38.5
1975	852.41	236.17	38.3
1905	70.47	19.48	38.2
1958	583.65	147.96	34.0
1995	5117.12	1282.68	33.5
1919	107.23	25.03	30.5
1925	156.66	36.15	30.0
1927	202.40	45.20	28.8
1938	154.76	33.91	28.1

WORST FIFTEEN YEARS SINCE 1901 BY %

Year	DJIA Close	Points Change	% Change
1931	77.90	− 86.68	− 52.7
1907	43.04	− 26.08	− 37.7
1930	164.58	− 83.90	− 33.8
1920	71.95	− 35.28	− 32.9
1937	120.85	− 59.05	− 32.8
1974	616.24	− 234.62	− 27.6
1903	35.98	− 11.12	− 23.6
1932	59.93	− 17.97	− 23.1
1917	74.38	− 20.62	− 21.7
1966	785.69	− 183.57	− 18.9
1910	59.60	− 12.96	− 17.9
1977	831.17	− 173.48	− 17.3
1929	248.48	− 51.52	− 17.2
2002	8341.63	−1679.87	− 16.8
1973	850.86	− 169.16	− 16.6

<u>NASDAQ</u> SINCE 1971 BY POINTS AND PERCENT

BEST TEN YEARS SINCE 1971 BY POINTS

Year	NASDAQ Close	Points Change	% Change
1999	4069.31	1876.62	85.6
1998	2192.69	622.34	39.6
1995	1052.13	300.17	39.9
1997	1570.35	279.32	21.6
1996	1291.03	238.90	22.7
1991	586.34	212.50	56.8
1993	776.80	99.85	14.7
1992	676.95	90.61	15.5
1985	324.93	77.58	31.4
1989	454.82	73.44	19.3

WORST TEN YEARS SINCE 1971 BY POINTS

Year	NASDAQ Close	Points Change	% Change
2000	2470.52	−1598.79	− 39.3
2002	1335.51	− 614.89	− 31.5
2001	1950.40	− 520.12	− 21.1
1990	373.84	− 80.98	− 17.8
1973	92.19	− 41.54	− 31.1
1974	59.82	− 32.37	− 35.1
1984	247.35	− 31.25	− 11.2
1994	751.96	− 24.84	− 3.2
1987	330.47	− 18.86	− 5.4
1981	195.84	− 6.50	− 3.2

BEST TEN YEARS SINCE 1971 BY %

Year	NASDAQ Close	Points Change	% Change
1999	4069.31	1876.62	85.6
1991	586.34	212.50	56.8
1995	1052.13	300.17	39.9
1998	2192.69	622.34	39.6
1980	202.34	51.20	33.9
1985	324.93	77.58	31.4
1975	77.62	17.80	29.8
1979	151.14	33.16	28.1
1971	114.12	24.51	27.4
1976	97.88	20.26	26.1

WORST TEN YEARS SINCE 1971 BY %

Year	NASDAQ Close	Points Change	% Change
2000	2470.52	−1598.79	− 39.3
1974	59.82	− 32.37	− 35.1
2002	1335.51	− 614.89	− 31.5
1973	92.19	− 41.54	− 31.1
2001	1950.40	− 520.12	− 21.1
1990	373.84	− 80.98	− 17.8
1984	247.35	− 31.25	− 11.2
1987	330.47	− 18.86	− 5.4
1981	195.84	− 6.50	− 3.2
1994	751.96	− 24.84	− 3.2

Based on NASDAQ composite, prior to February 5, 1971, based on National Quotation Bureau indices

STRATEGY PLANNING & RECORD SECTION

CONTENTS

PORTFOLIO AT START OF 2004

DATE ACQUIRED	NO. OF SHARES	SECURITY	PRICE	TOTAL COST	PAPER PROFITS	PAPER LOSSES

PORTFOLIO AT START OF 2004

DATE ACQUIRED	NO. OF SHARES	SECURITY	PRICE	TOTAL COST	PAPER PROFITS	PAPER LOSSES

ADDITIONAL PURCHASES

DATE ACQUIRED	NO. OF SHARES	SECURITY	PRICE	TOTAL COST	REASON FOR PURCHASE PRIME OBJECTIVE, ETC.

ADDITIONAL PURCHASES

DATE ACQUIRED	NO. OF SHARES	SECURITY	PRICE	TOTAL COST	REASON FOR PURCHASE PRIME OBJECTIVE, ETC.

ADDITIONAL PURCHASES

DATE ACQUIRED	NO. OF SHARES	SECURITY	PRICE	TOTAL COST	REASON FOR PURCHASE PRIME OBJECTIVE, ETC.

SHORT–TERM TRANSACTIONS

Pages 167–176 can accompany next year's income tax return (Schedule D). Enter transactions as completed to avoid last minute pressures.

NO. OF SHARES	SECURITY	DATE ACQUIRED	DATE SOLD	SALE PRICE	COST	LOSS	GAIN

TOTALS: Carry over to next page

167

SHORT–TERM TRANSACTIONS *(continued)*

NO. OF SHARES	SECURITY	DATE ACQUIRED	DATE SOLD	SALE PRICE	COST	LOSS	GAIN

TOTALS:

Carry over to next page

SHORT–TERM TRANSACTIONS *(continued)*

NO. OF SHARES	SECURITY	DATE ACQUIRED	DATE SOLD	SALE PRICE	COST	LOSS	GAIN

TOTALS:

Carry over to next page

SHORT–TERM TRANSACTIONS *(continued)*

NO. OF SHARES	SECURITY	DATE ACQUIRED	DATE SOLD	SALE PRICE	COST	LOSS	GAIN

TOTALS:

Carry over to next page

SHORT–TERM TRANSACTIONS *(continued)*

NO. OF SHARES	SECURITY	DATE ACQUIRED	DATE SOLD	SALE PRICE	COST	LOSS	GAIN

TOTALS:
Carry over to next page

SHORT–TERM TRANSACTIONS *(continued)*

NO. OF SHARES	SECURITY	DATE ACQUIRED	DATE SOLD	SALE PRICE	COST	LOSS	GAIN
					TOTALS:		

LONG–TERM TRANSACTIONS

Pages 167–176 can accompany next year's income tax return (Schedule D). Enter transactions as completed to avoid last minute pressures.

NO. OF SHARES	SECURITY	DATE ACQUIRED	DATE SOLD	SALE PRICE	COST	LOSS	GAIN

TOTALS: Carry over to next page

LONG-TERM TRANSACTIONS *(continued)*

NO. OF SHARES	SECURITY	DATE ACQUIRED	DATE SOLD	SALE PRICE	COST	LOSS	GAIN

TOTALS:

Carry over to next page

LONG–TERM TRANSACTIONS *(continued)*

NO. OF SHARES	SECURITY	DATE ACQUIRED	DATE SOLD	SALE PRICE	COST	LOSS	GAIN
					TOTALS:		

Carry over to next page

175

LONG–TERM TRANSACTIONS *(continued)*

NO. OF SHARES	SECURITY	DATE ACQUIRED	DATE SOLD	SALE PRICE	COST	LOSS	GAIN
						TOTALS:	

INTEREST/DIVIDENDS RECEIVED DURING 2004

SHARES	STOCK/BOND	FIRST QUARTER		SECOND QUARTER		THIRD QUARTER		FOURTH QUARTER	
		$		$		$		$	

BROKERAGE ACCOUNT DATA 2004

	MARGIN INTEREST	TRANSFER TAXES	CAPITAL ADDED	CAPITAL WITHDRAWN
JAN				
FEB				
MAR				
APR				
MAY				
JUN				
JUL				
AUG				
SEP				
OCT				
NOV				
DEC				

PORTFOLIO AT END OF 2004

DATE ACQUIRED	NO. OF SHARES	SECURITY	PRICE	TOTAL COST	PAPER PROFITS	PAPER LOSSES

PORTFOLIO AT END OF 2004

DATE ACQUIRED	NO. OF SHARES	SECURITY	PRICE	TOTAL COST	PAPER PROFITS	PAPER LOSSES

PORTFOLIO PRICE RECORD 2004 (FIRST HALF)

Place purchase price above stock name and weekly closes below

STOCKS Week Ending	1	2	3	4	5	6	7	8	9	10
JANUARY 2										
9										
16										
23										
30										
FEBRUARY 6										
13										
20										
27										
MARCH 5										
12										
19										
26										
APRIL 2										
9										
16										
23										
30										
MAY 7										
14										
21										
28										
JUNE 4										
11										
18										
25										

PORTFOLIO PRICE RECORD 2004 (FIRST HALF)

Place purchase price above stock name and weekly closes below

STOCKS / Week Ending	11	12	13	14	15	16	17	18	Dow Jones Industrial Average	Net Change For Week
JANUARY 2										
9										
16										
23										
30										
FEBRUARY 6										
13										
20										
27										
MARCH 5										
12										
19										
26										
APRIL 2										
9										
16										
23										
30										
MAY 7										
14										
21										
28										
JUNE 4										
11										
18										
25										

PORTFOLIO PRICE RECORD 2004 (SECOND HALF)

Place purchase price above stock name and weekly closes below

	STOCKS									
Week Ending	**1**	**2**	**3**	**4**	**5**	**6**	**7**	**8**	**9**	**10**
JULY 2										
9										
16										
23										
30										
AUGUST 6										
13										
20										
27										
SEPTEMBER 3										
10										
17										
24										
OCTOBER 1										
8										
15										
22										
29										
NOVEMBER 5										
12										
19										
26										
DECEMBER 3										
10										
17										
24										
31										

PORTFOLIO PRICE RECORD 2004 (SECOND HALF)

Place purchase price above stock name and weekly closes below

STOCKS Week Ending	11	12	13	14	15	16	17	18	Dow Jones Industrial Average	Net Change For Week
JULY										
2										
9										
16										
23										
30										
AUGUST										
6										
13										
20										
27										
SEPTEMBER										
3										
10										
17										
24										
OCTOBER										
1										
8										
15										
22										
29										
NOVEMBER										
5										
12										
19										
26										
DECEMBER										
3										
10										
17										
24										
31										

WEEKLY INDICATOR DATA 2004 (FIRST HALF)

	Week Ending	Dow Jones Industrial Average	Net Change For Week	Net Change On Friday	Net Change Next Monday	S&P Or NASDAQ	NYSE Ad-vances	NYSE De-clines	New Highs	New Lows	CBOE Put/Call Ratio	90-Day Treas. Rate	Moody's AAA Rate
JANUARY	2												
	9												
	16												
	23												
	30												
FEBRUARY	6												
	13												
	20												
	27												
MARCH	5												
	12												
	19												
	26												
APRIL	2												
	9												
	16												
	23												
	30												
MAY	7												
	14												
	21												
	28												
JUNE	4												
	11												
	18												
	25												

WEEKLY INDICATOR DATA 2004 (SECOND HALF)

Week Ending	Dow Jones Industrial Average	Net Change For Week	Net Change On Friday	Net Change Next Monday	S&P Or NASDAQ	NYSE Ad-vances	NYSE De-clines	New Highs	New Lows	CBOE Put/Call Ratio	90-Day Treas. Rate	Moody's AAA Rate
JULY												
2												
9												
16												
23												
30												
AUGUST												
6												
13												
20												
27												
SEPTEMBER												
3												
10												
17												
24												
OCTOBER												
1												
8												
15												
22												
29												
NOVEMBER												
5												
12												
19												
26												
DECEMBER												
3												
10												
17												
24												
31												

MONTHLY INDICATOR DATA 2004

	DJIA 4th from Last Day Prev. Mo.	DJIA 2nd Trading Day	Point Change These 5 Days	Point Change Rest Of Mo.	% Change Whole Period	% Change Your Stocks	Prime Rate	Trade Deficit $ Billion	CPI % Change	% Unem- ployment Rate
JAN										
FEB										
MAR										
APR										
MAY										
JUN										
JUL										
AUG										
SEP										
OCT										
NOV										
DEC										

INSTRUCTIONS:

Weekly Indicator Data (pages 184-185). Keeping data on several indicators may give you a better feel of the market. In addition to the closing DJIA and its net change for the week, post the net change for Friday's Dow and also the following Monday's. A series of "down Fridays" followed by "down Mondays" often precedes a downswing. Tracking either the S&P or NASDAQ composite, and advances and declines, will help prevent the Dow from misleading you. New highs and lows and put/call ratios (www.cboe.com) are also useful indicators. All these weekly figures appear in weekend papers or *Barron's*. Data for 90-day Treasury Rate and Moody's AAA Bond Rate are quite important to track short- and long-term interest rates. These figures are available from:

Weekly U.S. Financial Data
Federal Reserve Bank of St. Louis
P.O. Box 442
St. Louis MO 63166
http://research.stlouisfed.org

Monthly Indicator Data. The purpose of the first four columns is to enable you to track the market's bullish bias near the end, beginning and middle of the month, which has been shifting lately (see pages 136, 137). Prime Rate, Trade Deficit, Consumer Price Index, and Unemployment Rate are worthwhile indicators to follow. Or, readers may wish to use those columns for other data.

IF YOU DON'T PROFIT FROM YOUR INVESTMENT MISTAKES, SOMEONE ELSE WILL

No matter how much we may deny it, almost every successful person in Wall Street pays a great deal of attention to trading suggestions—especially when they come from "the right sources."

One of the hardest things to learn is to distinguish between good tips and bad ones. Usually the best tips have a logical reason in back of them, which accompanies the tip. Poor tips usually have no reason to support them.

The important thing to remember is that the market discounts. It does not review, it does not reflect. The Street's real interest in "tips," inside information, buying and selling suggestions, and everything else of this kind emanates from a desire to find out just what the market has on hand to discount. The process of finding out involves separating the wheat from the chaff—and there is plenty of chaff.

HOW TO MAKE USE OF STOCK "TIPS"

- The source should be **reliable**. (By listing all "tips" and suggestions on a Performance Record of Recommendations, such as below, and then periodically evaluating the outcomes, you will soon know the "batting average" of your sources.)

- The story should make sense. Would the merger violate anti-trust laws? Are there too many computers on the market already? How many years will it take to become profitable?

- The stock should not have had a recent sharp run-up. Otherwise, the story may already be discounted and confirmation or denial in the press would most likely be accompanied by a sell-off in the stock.

PERFORMANCE RECORD OF RECOMMENDATIONS

STOCK RECOMMENDED	BY WHOM	DATE	PRICE	REASON FOR RECOMMENDATION	SUBSEQUENT ACTION OF STOCK

INDIVIDUAL RETIREMENT ACCOUNTS: MOST AWESOME INVESTMENT INCENTIVE EVER DEVISED

IRA INVESTMENTS OF $2,000 A YEAR COMPOUNDING AT VARIOUS RATES OF RETURN FOR DIFFERENT PERIODS

Annual Rate	5 Yrs	10 Yrs	15 Yrs	20 Yrs	25 Yrs	30 Yrs	35 Yrs	40 Yrs	45 Yrs	50 Yrs
1%	$10,304	$21,134	$32,516	$44,478	$57,050	$70,265	$84,154	$98,750	$114,092	$130,216
2%	10,616	22,337	35,279	49,567	65,342	82,759	101,989	123,220	146,661	172,542
3%	10,937	23,616	38,314	55,353	75,106	98,005	124,552	155,327	191,003	232,362
4%	11,266	24,973	41,649	61,938	86,623	116,657	153,197	197,653	251,741	317,548
5%	11,604	26,414	45,315	69,439	100,227	139,522	189,673	253,680	335,370	439,631
6%	11,951	27,943	49,345	77,985	116,313	167,603	236,242	328,095	451,016	615,512
7%	12,307	29,567	53,776	87,730	135,353	202,146	295,827	427,219	611,504	869,972
8%	12,672	31,291	58,649	98,846	157,909	244,692	372,204	559,562	834,852	1,239,344
9%	13,047	33,121	64,007	111,529	184,648	297,150	470,249	736,584	1,146,372	1,776,882
10%	13,431	35,062	69,899	126,005	216,364	361,887	596,254	973,704	1,581,591	2,560,599
11%	13,826	37,123	76,380	142,530	253,998	441,826	758,329	1,291,654	2,190,338	3,704,672
12%	14,230	39,309	83,507	161,397	298,668	540,585	966,926	1,718,285	3,042,435	5,376,041
13%	14,645	41,629	91,343	182,940	351,700	662,630	1,235,499	2,290,972	4,235,612	7,818,486
14%	15,071	44,089	99,961	207,537	414,665	813,474	1,581,346	3,059,817	5,906,488	11,387,509
15%	15,508	46,699	109,435	235,620	489,424	999,914	2,026,691	4,091,908	8,245,795	16,600,747
16%	15,955	49,466	119,850	267,681	578,177	1,230,323	2,600,054	5,476,957	11,519,435	24,210,705
17%	16,414	52,400	131,298	304,277	683,525	1,515,008	3,337,989	7,334,781	16,097,540	35,309,434
18%	16,884	55,510	143,878	346,042	808,544	1,866,637	4,287,298	9,825,183	22,494,522	51,478,901
19%	17,366	58,807	157,700	393,695	956,861	2,300,775	5,507,829	13,160,993	31,424,150	75,006,500
20%	17,860	62,301	172,884	448,051	1,132,755	2,836,516	7,076,019	17,625,259	43,875,144	109,193,258

OPTION TRADING CODES

Option trading codes contain the stock ticker symbol, the expiration month code, and the striking price code.

For NASDAQ stocks with more than three letters in the stock code, the option ticker symbol is shortened to three letters, usually ending in Q. For example, Microsoft's stock symbol is MSFT, so its option ticker symbol is MSQ.

Each expiration month has a separate code for calls and puts. Also, each striking price has a separate code, which is identical for calls and puts. In an option listing, the ticker symbol is first, followed by the expiration month code, and then the striking price code. For example, the Microsoft January 90 call would have the code MSQAR, and the Microsoft January 90 put would have the code MSQMR.

Expiration Month Codes

	Call Code
January	A
February	B
March	C
April	D
May	E
June	F
July	G
August	H
September	I
October	J
November	K
December	L

	Put Code
January	M
February	N
March	O
April	P
May	Q
June	R
July	S
August	T
September	U
October	V
November	W
December	X

Striking Price Codes

Code	Striking Prices	
A	5	105
B	10	110
C	15	115
D	20	120
E	25	125
F	30	130
G	35	135
H	40	140
I	45	145
J	50	150
K	55	155
L	60	160
M	65	165
N	70	170
O	75	175
P	80	180
Q	85	185
R	90	190
S	95	195
T	100	200
U	7½	37½
V	12½	42½
W	17½	47½
X	22½	52½
Y	27½	57½
Z	32½	62½

Option Information Courtesy of Bernie Shaeffer, *The Option Advisor* (John Wiley & Sons)

TOP NINETY-SIX EXCHANGE TRADED FUNDS
(Traded on the American Stock Exchange. See page 118 for Sector Seasonalities.)

Ticker	Exchange Traded Fund
DIA	DIAMONDS Series Trust I (30 Dow Stocks)
QQQ	Nasdaq-100 Index
MDY	MidCap SPDRS
SPY	SPDRS S&P 500
XLY	Select Sector SPDR-Consumer
XLP	Select Sector SPDR-Consumer Staples
XLE	Select Sector SPDR-Energy
XLF	Select Sector SPDR-Financial
XLV	Select Sector SPDR-Health Care
XLI	Select Sector SPDR-Industrial
XLB	Select Sector SPDR-Materials
XLK	Select Sector SPDR-Technology
XLU	Select Sector SPDR-Utilities
MII	streetTRACKS Morgan Stanley Internet
MTK	streetTRACKS Morgan Stanley Technology
RWR	streetTRACKS Wilshire REIT
FFF	FORTUNE 500 Index
FEF	FORTUNE e-50 Index
ICF	iShares Cohen & Steers Realty Majors
IYM	iShares Dow Jones US Basic Materials
IYC	iShares Dow Jones US Consumer Cyclical
IYE	iShares Dow Jones US Energy
IYF	iShares Dow Jones US Financial Sector
IYG	iShares Dow Jones US Financial Services
IYH	iShares Dow Jones US Healthcare
IYJ	iShares Dow Jones US Industrial
IYK	iShares Dow Jones US Non-Consumer Cyc
IYR	iShares Dow Jones US Real Estate
IYW	iShares Dow Jones US Technology
IYZ	iShares Dow Jones US Telecom
IYY	iShares Dow Jones US Total Market
IDU	iShares Dow Jones US Utilities
IGE	iShares Goldman Sachs Natural Resources
IGN	iShares Goldman Sachs Networking
IGW	iShares Goldman Sachs Semiconductor
IGV	iShares Goldman Sachs Software
IGM	iShares Goldman Sachs Technology
EWA	iShares MSCI - Australia
EWO	iShares MSCI - Austria
EWK	iShares MSCI - Belgium
EWZ	iShares MSCI - Brazil
EWC	iShares MSCI - Canada
EFA	iShares MSCI - EAFE
EZU	iShares MSCI - EMU (European Union)
EWQ	iShares MSCI - France
EWG	iShares MSCI - Germany
EWH	iShares MSCI - Hong Kong
EWI	iShares MSCI - Italy

Ticker	Exchange Traded Fund
BHH	B2B Internet HOLDRS
BBH	Biotech HOLDRS
BDH	Broadband HOLDRS
IAH	Internet Architecture HOLDRS
HHH	Internet HOLDRS
IIH	Internet Infrastructure HOLDRS
MKH	Market 2000+ HOLDRS (50 Big Caps)
OIH	Oil Service HOLDRS
PPH	Pharmaceutical HOLDRS
RKH	Regional Bank HOLDRS
RTH	Retail HOLDRS
SMH	Semiconductor HOLDRS
SWH	Software HOLDRS
TBH	Telebras HOLDRS (Foreign Telecoms)
TTH	Telecom HOLDRS
UTH	Utilities HOLDRS
WMH	Wireless HOLDRS
VXF	Vanguard Extended Market VIPERs
VTI	Vanguard Total Stock Market VIPERs
EWJ	iShares MSCI - Japan
EWM	iShares MSCI - Malaysia (Free)
EWW	iShares MSCI - Mexico (Free)
EWN	iShares MSCI - Netherlands
EWS	iShares MSCI - Singapore (Free)
EWY	iShares MSCI - South Korea
EWP	iShares MSCI - Spain
EWD	iShares MSCI - Sweden
EWL	iShares MSCI - Switzerland
EWT	iShares MSCI - Taiwan
EWU	iShares MSCI - United Kingdom
EPP	iShares MSCI Pacific Ex-Japan
IBB	iShares Nasdaq Biotechnology
IWB	iShares Russell 1000
IWM	iShares Russell 2000
IWV	iShares Russell 3000
IWR	iShares Russell Midcap
IVV	iShares S&P 500
IEV	iShares S&P Europe 350
IOO	iShares S&P Global 100
IXC	iShares S&P Global Energy
IXG	iShares S&P Global Financial
IXJ	iShares S&P Global Healthcare
IXN	iShares S&P Global Info Technology
IXP	iShares S&P Global Telecommunications
ILF	iShares S&P Latin America 40
IJH	iShares S&P MidCap 400
IJR	iShares S&P SmallCap 600
ITF	iShares S&P TOPIX 150 (Tokyo)

G.M. LOEB'S "BATTLE PLAN" FOR INVESTMENT SURVIVAL

LIFE IS CHANGE: Nothing can ever be the same a minute from now as it was a minute ago. Everything you own is changing in price and value. You can find that last price of an active security on the stock ticker, but you cannot find the next price anywhere. The value of your money is changing. Even the value of your home is changing, though no one walks in front of it with a sandwich board consistently posting the changes.

RECOGNIZE CHANGE: Your basic objective should be to profit from change. The art of investing is being able to recognize change and to adjust investment goals accordingly.

WRITE THINGS DOWN: You will score more investment success and avoid more investment failures if you write things down. Very few investors have the drive and inclination to do this.

KEEP A CHECKLIST: If you aim to improve your investment results, get into the habit of keeping a checklist on every issue you consider buying. Before making a commitment, it will pay you to write down the answers to at least some of the basic questions—How much am I investing in this company? How much do I think I can make? How much do I have to risk? How long do I expect to take to reach my goal?

HAVE A SINGLE RULING REASON: Above all, writing things down is the best way to find "the ruling reason." When all is said and done, there is invariably a single reason that stands out above all others why a particular security transaction can be expected to show a profit. All too often many relatively unimportant statistics are allowed to obscure this single important point.

Any one of a dozen factors may be the point of a particular purchase or sale. It could be a technical reason—an increase in earnings or dividend not yet discounted in the market price—a change of management—a promising new product—an expected improvement in the market's valuation of earnings—or many others. But, in any given case, one of these factors will almost certainly be more important than all the rest put together.

CLOSING OUT A COMMITMENT: If you have a loss, the solution is automatic, provided you decide what to do at the time you buy. Otherwise, the question divides itself into two parts. Are we in a bull or bear market? Few of us really know until it is too late. For the sake of the record, if you think it is a bear market, just put that consideration first and sell as much as your conviction suggests and your nature allows.

If you think it is a bull market, or at least a market where some stocks move up, some mark time and only a few decline, do not sell unless:

✓ You see a bear market ahead.

✓ You see trouble for a particular company in which you own shares.

✓ Time and circumstances have turned up a new and seemingly far better buy than the issue you like least in your list.

✓ Your shares stop going up and start going down.

A subsidiary question is, which stock to sell first? Two further observations may help:

✓ Do not sell solely because you think a stock is "overvalued."

✓ If you want to sell some of your stocks and not all, in most cases it is better to go against your emotional inclinations and sell first the issues with losses, small profits or none at all, the weakest, the most disappointing, etc.

Mr. Loeb is the author of *The Battle for Investment Survival*, John Wiley & Sons.

G.M. LOEB'S INVESTMENT SURVIVAL CHECKLIST

OBJECTIVES AND RISKS

Security		Price	Shares	Date

"Ruling reason" for commitment	Amount of commitment
	$ _____
	% of my investment capital
	_____%

Price objective	Est. time to achieve it	I will risk	Which would be
		_____ points	$ _____

TECHNICAL POSITION

Price action of stock:		Dow Jones Industrial Average
☐ hitting new highs	☐ in a trading range	
☐ pausing in an uptrend	☐ moving up from low ground	Trend of Market
☐ acting stronger than market	☐ _____	

SELECTED YARDSTICKS

	Price Range		Earnings Per Share Actual or Projected	Price/Earnings Ratio Actual or Projected
	High	Low		
Current Year				
Previous Year				
Merger Possibilities				Years for earnings to double in past
Comment on Future				Years for market price to double in past

PERIODIC RE-CHECKS

Date	Stock Price	D.J.I.A.	Comment	Action taken, if any

COMPLETED TRANSACTIONS

Date Closed	Period of time held	Profit or loss

Reason for profit or loss

IMPORTANT CONTACTS

NAME	TELEPHONE		E-MAIL